WOMEN WORLD LEADERS

presents

TEARS TO TRIUMPH

Releasing pain to receive God's restoration

May God bless your life Exceedingly Abundantly Beyond...

Kimberly A Hobbs

VISIONARY AUTHOR

KIMBERLY ANN HOBBS

Ephesians 3:20

For information regarding special discounts for bulk purchases, please contact the publisher: LaBoo Publishing Enterprise, LLC
staff@laboopublishing.com
www.laboopublishing.com

Scripture quotations marked (NIV) are taken from the Holy Bible, New International Version®, NIV®. Copyright © 1973, 1978, 1984, 2011 by Biblica, Inc.™ Used by permission of Zondervan. All rights reserved worldwide. www.zondervan.com

Scripture quotations marked ESV are from the Holy Bible, English Standard Version, copyright © 2001 by Crossway Bibles, a publishing ministry of Good News Publishers. Used by permission. All rights reserved.

Scripture quotations marked TPT are from The Passion Translation®. Copyright © 2017, 2018 by Passion & Fire Ministries, Inc. Used by permission. All rights reserved. ThePassionTranslation.com.

Scripture taken from the New King James Version®. Copyright © 1982 by Thomas Nelson. Used by permission. All rights reserved.

The Holy Bible, King James Version. Cambridge Edition: 1769; *King James Bible Online,* 2019. www.kingjamesbibleonline.org.

Scripture quotations marked (NLT) are taken from the Holy Bible, New Living Translation, copyright ©1996, 2004, 2015 by Tyndale House Foundation. Used by permission of Tyndale House Publishers, Inc., Carol Stream, Illinois 60188. All rights reserved.

The Christian Standard Bible. Copyright © 2017 by Holman Bible Publishers. Used by permission. Christian Standard Bible®, and CSB® are federally registered trademarks of Holman Bible Publishers, all rights reserved.

THE LIVING BIBLE (TLB): Scripture taken from THE **LIVING BIBLE** copyright© 1971. Used by permission **of Tyndale House Publishers,** Inc.

Zondervan Publishing House. *The Amplified Bible* (1965). Thirtieth printing, March 1985. Library of Congress Catalog Card Number 65-19500.

Table of Contents

Introduction

As a visionary for *Tears to Triumph*, I was inspired to do this project because of the passion I have for encouraging others into the loving arms of our Savior and King, Jesus Christ. God led me to this portion of scripture to share with you: "And I pray that He would unveil within you the unlimited riches of His glory and favor until supernatural strength floods your innermost being with His divine might and explosive power."

By consistently using your faith, the life of Christ will be released deep inside you, and the resting place of His love will become the very source and root of your life. Then you will be empowered to discover what every holy one experiences – the enormous magnitude of the astonishing love of Christ in all its dimensions. How deeply intimate and far-reaching is His love! How enduring and inclusive it is! Endless love beyond measurement that transcends our understanding. This extravagant love pours into you until you are filled to overflowing with the fullness of God!

Never doubt God's mighty power to work in you and accomplish all this. He will achieve infinitely more than your greatest request, your most unbelievable dream, and exceed your wildest imagination! He will outdo them all, for His miraculous power always energizes you.

May we all realize that no matter what struggles we may be going through, or what tears we may shed, Christ's love is far-reaching for all of us. It's an endless love beyond your understanding, and He wants to fill you with it until you are overflowing with the fullness of God." *(Ephesians 3:16-20, TPT)*

As a founder of Women World Leaders, God has given me the privilege to meet many transformed women who have been filled with God's love through their adversities within their life stories. These women are moving beyond the past circumstances that had them bound for some time. They are now moving into the realm of influence; which God has called them to do by sharing their stories of triumph. They are learning to rely on God's POWER each day as they move forward, glorifying Him in each step they take.

These women realize their tears were not shed for an empty reason, but through them, they have become stronger and now desire to use their stories for a beautiful purpose, which is to glorify God. They wish to bring hope and healing to others through sharing the triumphs and victories that God has given them beyond their despair.

As you read each chapter, may you relate to some of the circumstances these authors have endured and possibly share in compassion while finding the priceless truths that God has scattered throughout these pages. When we surrender our past to God, He can do the unimaginable. May you see through these stories that your joy comes from the Lord; He is the one who moves mountains, calms the raging seas, heals the sick, and who wants to take your burdens away.

God has given us promises that we can cling to, despite the tears we have shed or are still shedding. We can believe these promises are true, and may we know them well enough to keep them deeply etched in our souls. No matter how the enemy tries to steal these promises from us, we can clench them even tighter because we know they are permanently engraved within.

As you read on, we hope that you can see the wholeness of God shine through the brokenness. The excruciating pain doesn't have to remain beyond the tragedy. You will see God can do exceedingly, abundantly beyond what could be asked for or imagined, and we hope you can see it for your own life, as well.

On behalf of each of the authors who so graciously desire to glorify God within their stories, we pray this prayer over you as you begin reading *Tears to Triumph*.

Dear Lord,

You said in Your Word that "whoever believes in You will have rivers of living water flowing from their heart." (John 7:38) We thank You for each author that has claimed their faith in You. They may have cried liquid words to You for many reasons and throughout many seasons, and You have said You've heard them all! Thank you, God, for rescuing them in their pain.

We pray for each reader who calls out to You in their weaknesses. We pray that You will comfort them, speak to them, and fill them afresh.

Your Word says that the Spirit also helps us in our weaknesses. "For we do not know what we should pray for as we ought, but the Spirit Himself makes intercession for us with groanings, which cannot be uttered." (Romans 8:26)

Thank you, God, for Your Word and Your Words that are alive within the pages of Tears to Triumph. From the first chapter of this book to the very last page, may the lives of others be impacted by Your truth and Your love, and may You be revealed with glory through the stories.

May this book bring hope, healing, forgiveness, strength, love, and promise to each reader from You. May the triumphant joy, which can only be found by knowing your Son Jesus as their Lord and Savior, personally be upon each person as they read this book. God, please bless this book in its entirety as it reaches throughout the world for your glory. We pray a protective covering over each author who has shared such intimate secrets of her heart, and may Your enduring love wrap around them as they dedicate their stories to You. All glory belongs to You, our King, for the furthering of Your Kingdom in Jesus' name. Amen.

Kimberly Hobbs is an International Bestselling Author, her most recent book "Fuel for Life" is a 90-day spiritual coaching guide into abundant living.

She is a Speaker, Teacher, Leader and Life Coach.

She has been a guest speaker on Moody Bible radio's God at work, as well as other television appearances encouraging others. She is Co-Founder of Women World Leaders, a worldwide ministry that empowers women to find their purpose which God has designed for them.

Kimberly is an established artist with much of her work reaching around the country and across the world. Through Kerus Global in South Africa, she helps raise support for her mission passion projects and over 100 orphaned children whom she loves. Kimberly sits on the advisory board for Kerus Global Education.

Kimberly is married and lives in South Florida with her husband Ken, they have children and grandchildren. Together they own and operate a successful financial coaching business.

Exceedingly Abundantly Beyond

Kimberly Ann Hobbs

"Now on to him who is able to do exceedingly abundantly above all we can ask or imagine according to the power that's at work within us." (Ephesians 3:20)

The POWER is the amazing power of God who works within each of our lives if we allow Him. God's ways are not our ways, and His thoughts are far better than our thoughts. Some of us may take a lifetime to learn these truths; I am one of them. Through the raging storms of my life and shedding enough tears that could fill an ocean, God gave me a tremendous story. It wasn't until I began the journey of writing my story that God brought complete triumph to me, along with hope, healing, and restoration to my conflicted life. Also, I experienced a deep sense of unconditional love from my Savior. These breakthroughs were the triumphs God showed me and the extreme value that He placed on my life even before creating me. Through writing, I have been able to learn that I am God's vessel – a masterpiece – set apart and chosen. I have a beautiful purpose in God's Kingdom here on Earth and through-out eternity.

Before asking God for wisdom living, I lived numb on the inside. It was a state of being for me for many years. To others who viewed my external life, it seemed that I loved God and loved my life. I desired a normal life, and I convinced myself and others that I loved God above all else. Underneath, though, I possessed a penetrating, self-destructing fear that God didn't love me in return unless I was "good." My thoughts continuously spoke loudly and sealed that lie within me. *You're not good; your life will never be good enough to be a vessel, a certain someone chosen by God.* Understanding now that those thoughts were lies, I can see God has a beautiful purpose for me, along with others.

Back in my beginnings, how could I wrap my fingers around a purpose I never felt worthy of or wasn't sure belonged to me? I buried the wounds of stinging disappointments many times over without resolve. Those hurts fell into a place that I locked up tightly inside of me. Even though I tried to grow closer to God, each time I made a mistake, I would beat myself up mentally and allow guilt to overtake me. The enemy capitalized on my mistakes and used them against me, tearing me down with comparisons to other people and their lifestyles. It wore me down emotionally. The lies from hell held me back and prevented me from having hopes, dreams, and being "someone" for Jesus, my ultimate purpose in life.

My dream in my late teens was to have a "Little House on the Prairie" lifestyle. I would have a husband, a family, live in the country, have a lot of animals, love Jesus, and live happily ever after. I quickly set out to achieve those goals, and within a couple of years (my late teenage years), I married a man who I loved very much. Innocence was our life back then, and we walked closely with God.

I gave birth to two beautiful girls while working hard at home and living a harmonious life with my husband. At a very young age, we purchased our first home, were very involved in our church, and lived a simple life with our growing girls. Eventually, we were able to build our dream home – a log cabin in the country on five beautiful acres. We built a charming barn and had several horses and many animals surrounding us inside and outside of our cabin. My dream was coming true.

I loved my new life. I was a stay-at-home mom, and I loved taking care of my home, my husband, and our children. I was Suzie Homemaker to the outside world looking in. We all loved God, and our family and simplicity were what we thrived on. No one outside of our family entered our life. My life, even though simple, had all the beauty, elegance, and appeal one could want. Our home life was wonderful, and our church life was involved. We consistently read our Bibles and taught our girls to love Jesus. Life couldn't get much better for me because I thought I had it all. People who knew me felt the same way. However, this was only a chapter in my life.

It all fell apart when we took a break from God.

As active as we were in a small church, we carried much of the serving load and got burned out. So, we removed ourselves from everything having to do with church and God, but we felt it would be a temporary withdrawal. The enemy had other plans. We thought we needed a "rest period" from church duties and commitments. We wanted to focus on our new home, some worldly friends we'd met, and a new lifestyle living out in the country. Church life became a chore, and eventually, we stopped it altogether. We slowly lost all connection to God. We allowed the enemy's plan to take hold of us.

What had been our focus of life – God, family, and church – soon turned to the absence of God in our home and became our new way of living. We were having fun while living carefree from any accountability we once had when we had a church family. It soon became a very dark, ugly, and painful time of living. The temptations we allowed into our home from "outside influences" became more and more challenging to overcome. Our shame haunted us, and without the presence of God in our lives, sin grew out of control.

My husband and I were enticed and tempted in sexual ways from outside influences that we consensually allowed to enter our home. The invitations that we accepted involved watching pornography films with our friends. This drew us into a lustful fantasy world filled with forbidden desires. Something we had kept ourselves protected from our entire married life was now directly in front of us. Our once Godly marriage quickly grew into an evil bed, consisting of twisted marital pleasures and unusual behavior all while stricken with aggressive desire. The door was wide open to sexual entanglement involving another married couple, and our marriage became a playground with this couple whose friendship from the past began creeping closer. We were deceived into believing our consent to playing "harmless sexual games" wouldn't lead to anything else but arousal between each other. The enemy had other plans. What seemed fun at first lured us deeper into an entangled mess that our once pure marriage could not sustain. Our sanctified marriage bed became defiled. We tried to hide, but to God, we were already exposed.

It is then that the haunting memory that I still fight 'til this day took root. The pain of regret and consequence slithered its way in and wreaked havoc; the sad thing is that I allowed its entrance. As I stated, we had no armor for battle because we let go of God's presence in our lives. A battlefield we never saw coming emerged, and thus began the battle of the spirits – good versus evil.

> *"For all of our fault and flaws are in full view to you. Everything we want to hide, you search out and expose by the radiance of your face." (Psalm 4:8, TPT)*

More than our weakened marriage could endure, the enemy's foothold stomped out any signs of spiritual harmony or God within our lives. My life grew into a monster of lies, deceit, and wickedness. I couldn't give up the sexual addiction that had developed. Therefore, our twenty-year marriage began to crumble, and I woke up inside another chapter in my life.

Through the challenges I faced while losing the perfect life I had dreamed of having, I cried out to God, "How could this be happening? We were so close to each other and to you, God." But, it seemed He didn't hear my cries. Tears filled up buckets, and the addiction to the sin that weighed me down took over my life. I even asked God to eliminate all desires for sex so that I could be free from the addiction. I just wanted my healthy, happy, stable life with my innocent family back intact, but that did not happen. That part of my life was ending, almost over.

My life continued void of happiness or joy. I went back and forth like a ping-pong ball between wanting my husband back and wanting the fix of satisfying the flesh. I was led into a life that would have a strong hold over me, a sexual addiction that dug its hooks into me so deeply I needed something powerful to pry them out. I wallowed in a pit of unforeseen misery. I tried hard to find glimpses of my past life. I wanted it back untainted and whole just as God had given it. At times, the painful grieving of what I was losing became so intense that I wanted to die. All the years of building a marriage and the joys of innocence within it were disappearing before my eyes. I found myself seeking temporary satisfaction of sexual gratification to ease my broken heart but only for a fleeting moment. Then, it was gone! I continued to battle lust and sex at a deeper level now within the arms of a forbidden relationship. A lustful, loveless union cultivated during those so-called "innocent" marriage games, but it involved an outside party – someone who had been lurking, prowling, and waiting to pounce on what had already become disgusting.

Broken, I cried tears of despair. I cried hard until there were no tears left to cry anymore. It was not what I wanted, but sin had its grasp on me and made it appear as if this was exactly what I wanted. I couldn't let go, but deep inside of me, I did not want what was happening. The tears from this secretive behavior – along with the hurt of loss – were stifled until stuffed as deep as I could push them inside my gut. I felt this helped me eliminate the pain.

How do I escape this misery? I tried to go to church here and there, and I prayed sometimes. But, I still felt an absence from God's presence.

One day, feeling like my prayers might have worked, I met a man who took my mind off all my worries. He was a charming, wise, interesting man and extremely wealthy. Was he the tool sent by God to rescue me from all my sadness? He wanted to be my knight in shining armor. He led me to believe he was, and in my torturous, tangled mind, I thought he might be but in a different sort of way. I soon found myself confiding in him.

Once again, I was lured into another lifestyle. This one was intense enough that it distracted me from the chains of sexual addiction that had me shackled. I found myself burying any thoughts of resurrecting my simple "House on the Prairie" life, so I began to let it go. The broken life I was currently living – the one filled with illicit sex, shame, and rejection – instantly halted!

I was now mesmerized by what was happening to me. I was about to enter a completely new life – a vast, unseen world filled with a different type of stimulation. My eyes were tantalized at every moment, and my attention lured to its money and power. So much so that I could never have imagined it, not even in my wildest dreams.

Some of the people who I would soon meet and the places I would travel to were experienced only on television or in the movies, and I was about to enter that door. Here starts another chapter of my life.

A relationship developed with this man, and I moved into another level of life. As time progressed, I found myself being fed quantities of earthly abundance. I soon became attached to the man who had shown me an entirely new way to live. Although I never asked for a thing, I had everything a woman could want as far as earthly pleasures. In what seemed like the blink of an eye, I was showered with brand-new luxury vehicles, such as Maseratis, Ferraris, and Bentleys. They were given to me one by one, and I drove them all. I could barely get used to driving one exotic car before another would arrive in the garage with a big white bow on it. Whatever I mentioned I liked would show up with my name on it in one of the garages.

I was gifted jewels of all kinds, diamonds, and even a seven-carat engagement ring. Rolexes, Chopard, and designer clothes became a part of my regular attire. I owned over one hundred designer handbags and a collection of shoes like Louis Vuitton, Chanel, Prada, Louboutin, and more. My clothes closet was the size of a large master bedroom and still couldn't contain it all.

I met movie stars, politicians, and had breakfast and dinner with some of our United States presidents. I attended galas, political functions, fundraisers, and numerous other affairs across the nation.

I rode and owned magnificent show horses, even owned several regular and miniature horses. I was given a life-size outdoor doll-house, which I had painted pink. It housed my miniature horses and was placed inside the enclosed tennis courts on the grounds where I resided then. I didn't play tennis, but I loved looking outside at the tennis courts to see my miniature horses playing around in the enclosure. With such an extravagant love for horses, whenever I saw one that caught my eye, it was purchased for me. I had Friesian show horses from Holland and many other varieties, eventually giving me a herd of horses.

I lived in multiple homes in various locations with live-in house-keepers who took care of my every need. I slept on ironed sheets every night and never made a bed. I was prevented from using a stove unless I practically begged to cook something that I would crave from my past life as Suzie Homemaker. Now, I dined at 5-star restaurants, usually having at least two engagements for dinner in a day. We had friends and acquaintances with us at every meal. We never dined alone with just the two of us. To keep me content, he brought in my family and friends to occasionally dine or travel with us. I traveled the world with the new people who I met, and I sometimes felt I lived more in the air inside planes than I did having my feet on the ground.

The more I was given, the more I began to give away. Why not? I had more than I could ever want. I was even given a bi-weekly paycheck to use as fun money since I gave up a business that I had recently started to be with him. I didn't spend the money on myself, though. I gave it to church, family members, my girls, and other friends who were in need. It made me feel good to be able to do so. However, in hindsight, I was trying to relieve the guilt of being absent from so many lives while present in someone else's. Although my loved ones were still around me at times, the emptiness inside me grew – an indescribable void. I felt like I was slowly losing my life, my identity. Comparing this life to what I had given up was brutal to me. I was haunted by the happy memories of my twenty-year marriage, which I missed. I was miserable! Though I appeared happy and content to everyone who knew me during this timeframe, I was dying a slow, disconnected death in reality.

The more I was given, the emptier I watched my life become. I compromised everything, and eventually lost my voice, the ability to speak up for what I wanted. I grew silent in a world of opulence and festivity. My dreams and desires now belonged to someone else, their lifestyle, their friends, and their religion. Of course, they all loved me, and I loved them. But, I was still empty, void of my true identity.

Until...

Through a miracle, my life changed yet again. I was able to walk away from all of it: my fiancé of seven years and a lifestyle of luxury, furs, cars, money, and famous people. How did I do this? This question is still asked and has now become my testimony of how much God loves me. It's my miracle. I had grown to love a man who gave me the world, but what did it profit me if I gained the whole world and lost my soul? That was the question I began to ask myself. I loved him, but I knew I loved God more. So, what could I do about it?

My answer came during a trip to Israel with my fiancé. I requested that we take my oldest daughter, my future son-in-law, and accompany a small church group of about thirty people who were scheduled to leave the next month. Since money was not an issue, it all came to be, and we went. We were in the garden tomb on the last night of the trip, when God spoke to me in the silence.

"Do you love me? Do you trust me? If you do, then walk away from this lifestyle and repent of it all. Confess your entire past right now. I want your heart back, but I want all of it," God said.

I heard His voice clearly. What seemed like an eternity sitting in silence in that garden was only several minutes. I was trembling with fear because I knew what I heard and from whom I heard it! I was faced with a choice.

Could I surrender everything to Jesus? Could I turn completely from this life of luxury to newness in Christ and dependence on Him? Could I let go and never look back? How could I do it? How would I do it?

Simply put, I surrendered all to Jesus. I prayed with all my heart, asking Jesus to forgive me and give me the strength needed to walk into a life of serving Him without looking back. Right there in the garden tomb in Israel, I fully surrendered, and my life changed forever. My burden was lifted, and the shame of my life was removed. I was now on the road to abundant life, and it was only the beginning.

It most definitely was not an easy road for me. I had to hurt someone very deeply by exiting a relationship where I was treated like a princess. Since we were not married, I had to do what I knew to be right in God's eyes and move out. Knowing I couldn't take anything with me, the fear began to escalate quickly. Where would I go? What about money? This man had paid for EVERYTHING, and what money I was gifted, I had given away. If I left, it would all stop.

With God's help, I began to pray fervently, continuously asking Him to direct my thoughts, my steps, and help me not to be afraid. I asked Him to help me get my life back on the proper pathway. Focusing now on God and His Kingdom, I decided to serve Him with a purpose and a plan. I had to forgive myself and understand that God had a certain plan for my life. I began moving in obedience to what God was calling me to do. *Jeremiah 29:11: "For I know the plans I have for you," says the Lord, "plans to prosper you and not to harm you, plans to give you hope and a future."*

That evening in Israel, I did a complete halt and turned my life toward God. It wasn't me or anything I could physically do. It was God working inside me, the POWER of God. There is no explanation for what I walked away from and walked toward other than it took supernatural power to do so! I left everything behind. I took myself, my clothes, and some things that were given to me and went to stay at my mother's house for a few weeks. I knew God would take care of me, and He did.

God put the idea in me to write. I was not an author, nor did I have any experience at that time, but I heard His voice through listening. God was calling me to start over again with my life but in South Florida rather than Ohio. I had to leave my current situation to be able to focus on what God was calling me to do. It had to be somewhere far away without any distractions. Within three weeks, I found myself driving to South Florida. I left extended family and forty-five years of life in Ohio to start another chapter of my life once again.

I needed to detox from the residue of fruitful abundance, and God led me to an old, grungy, dilapidated one-bedroom condo from the 1950s located on a golf course community in Pompano, Florida. I was not thrilled, but I put on my gloves and began to clean years of dirt and grime in that quiet place. With God's help, I was able to bring myself back to a humble way of living, and it was there that I allowed God to begin His work in me through writing.

Not knowing where to begin in my new writing journey, I prayed and asked God for a verse to launch my writings. I closed my eyes, opened the Bible, and pointed to a single verse. It was *Ephesians 3:20*. Having never read that verse before, I had to ask God what it meant. I read it over and over for hours and hours. The same verse! Is this how I start my writing? I couldn't figure it out at first, but God told me the answer was yes. It has now become my life verse, and I use it in everything I do. It's my lead and my lean.

"Now unto him who is able to do exceedingly abundantly above all we can ask or imagine, according to the power that is at work within us." (Ephesians 3:20)

It didn't make sense to me at first, but as I studied it, I realized what power God was talking about. It was the power I had from the Holy Spirit, who now resides inside me. I began to write and write and write...through lonely days and nights. As I cried out to God to ease my lonely heart, I wrote out my detailed story, and my life began to heal. God gave me scriptures daily, which I used throughout my book. Those scriptures, along with constant prayer, breathed life back into my soul. I secluded myself and wrote every day for hours upon hours for an entire year. True abundant living – though it took time – came alive to me. My life finally had meaning. God worked through me as I began leading people to Jesus through my story, and God got all the glory. I loved it! It felt right, and I felt loved. It was all about Jesus and giving all to Him. I shared my story with everyone whose path I crossed. Again, people looked at my outward appearance, but now they knew for sure who occupied my inward heart.

Although I loved what I was doing with writing a book, I desired companionship. I knew I needed to pray for a husband – a man who I could do life with while serving God. I knew he was somewhere on this planet, and that God was preparing him for me and me for him. I trusted God; I believed Him when He said in His Word, *"If you ask anything in my name, I will do it."*

The man I'd receive would be a man who would serve God above all else while protecting me and living a life of surrendered obedience. He would be a man who would love me and understand my past, not be jealous of it in any way. A man who would love my grown girls like they were his own. A man who would desire to do missions with me, ministry with me, and go wherever he felt God would call us. A man who would allow me to serve God in my calling as well as together with him.

I prayed daily that God would bring this man into my life. Sometimes I prayed more than once a day and often cried to God in my loneliness. I even tried to help God, but thankfully, I quickly realized I needed to trust Him fully. God had me wait for years. He had me waiting while He grew the woman that He wanted me to become. I wouldn't change any of that now. Surrendering my life back to God brought me the man of my prayers and the true love of my life.

Together, we now travel the world. We help care for many orphaned children in Soshanguve, South Africa, and we love them all. We work closely with the staff at Kerus Global, which assists these children and so much more. We get to live in the sunshiny state of Florida. God also blessed us with a huge home that we use to "give back" to Him for service. We started several ministry groups with Christian family members who live close by. The groups have grown and are touching countless lives.

One group, in particular, motivated me to write more over the past few years than I ever have before. God led me to write the book *Fuel for Life: Abundant Living through Daily Coaching*. My life's trials and victories through redemption have helped me to become a great encourager to others. I'm now speaking publicly at events, leading Women World Leaders, and writing books. God breathed *Tears to Triumph* into a reality for me.

God has planted a vision within me that has grown in an *Ephesians 3:20* type of way. He gave me a beautiful, dear friend who shared the same vision, and together, we started a purposeful ministry for women that is flourishing around the world. All the glory goes to God. Women World Leaders has become my way of giving back for all that has been forgiven in my life. God doesn't require me to give back to Him out of demand, but I choose to because it's how strongly I desire to serve Him for all that He has done for me.

God has given me the gift of empowering leaders exceedingly and abundantly. I am overwhelmed and overjoyed each day that I wake up to serve my King and Savior, Jesus Christ. I am forgiven; I am transformed into a new creation – one that I never imagined when facing my darkest days. I am a nobody, but to God, I am somebody. My tears turned to triumph as I was shown forgiveness and unspeakable love. I have a PURPOSE. God has always wanted to use me, but I had to travel this journey in life to realize it. God wants to use anyone willing to be designated and used for His purposes. We have a beautiful purpose to fulfill – one that God has planted deep inside each of us. You are a masterpiece.

> *"For we are God's masterpiece. He has created us anew in Christ Jesus, so we can do the good things he planned for us long ago." (Ephesians 2:10)*

If God can use me – an ordinary woman who didn't have any extreme goals – to do extraordinary things, He can use you, too. You're an extraordinary person, and if you seek out God with all your heart, you will do extraordinary things for Him. God says, *"If you seek me, you will find me."*

I'm grateful I found God. I know that despite my sin and brokenness, He forgave me completely and gave me another chance. Through my journey of pain and perseverance, I found my King, and now the triumphant glory of God is displayed throughout my repentance testimony. I humbly serve God with all my heart, mind, body, and soul, and through serving Him, He pours out abundant and generous gifts. As *Luke 6:38* describes, my blessings are overflowing measures; my cup is running over daily, and my joy is indescribable. I am a filled vessel – pressed down, shaken together, and making room for more. I've realized I am chosen with an incredible PURPOSE, which is to strengthen and encourage others during a time such as this. Thank You, my Savior, for forgiving me so I can live freely with joy overflowing to love and serve you!

"I praise you because I am fearfully and wonderfully made; your works are wonderful, I know that full well." (Psalm 139:14)

Repentance

Kimberly Ann Hobbs

Genuine repentance pleads with the Lord to forgive and deliver from the burden of sin and the fear of judgment and hell. True repentance is not only changing behavior by stopping what is wrong, but it's learning to do what's right. The Bible commands it, our wickedness demands it, justice requires it, Christ preached it, and God expects it.

> *"Repent, and turn yourselves from all your transgressions, so iniquity shall not be your ruin." (Ezekiel 18:30)*

Repentance involves a change of heart and purpose, which inevitably results in a change of behavior. Repentance is not voluntarily suffering for the punishment of sin, nor is it remorse. It's also not self-condemnation.

Repentance involves a change of one's view – a recognition of sin involving personal guilt, defilement, and helplessness. There is also the emotional part of repentance that consists of a change of feeling, manifesting itself in sorrow for sin committed against a holy God. In addition, repentance involves a change of purpose, an inward turning away from sin, and an attitude to seek pardon and cleansing. Repentance is a response of the total person, which is why it can be described as total surrender.

Being sorry for sin is not repentance. Judas felt remorse, but he didn't repent. *(Matthew 27:3, TPT)* When Judas, the betrayer, saw that Jesus had been sentenced to death, remorse filled his heart. He returned thirty pieces of silver to the chief priests and leaders saying, "I have sinned because I have betrayed an innocent man."

Repentance isn't just a resolve to do better. It's not a change of mind; it's a change of heart. It means turning from sin totally and going in the opposite direction. In the case of Christianity, one turns from sin to the Savior. It's an inward response, not an external activity.

> *"Then turn away from your sins, turn to God, and prove it by a changed life." (Luke 3:8, TPT)*

Repentance calls for total surrender and total commitment to the will of God. It allows for a whole new relationship with God within an obedient lifestyle. It awakens joyous devotions to serving God with a clean heart that has been forgiven. A repentant heart is one that God can use. Repentance and faith go hand-in-hand.

> *"And without faith living within us it would be impossible to please God. For we come to God in faith knowing that he is real and that he rewards the faith of those who passionately seek him." (Hebrews 11:6)*

I believe you cannot have "saving repentance" unless it's accompanied by "saving faith" in the Lord Jesus Christ. Your life can be changed, your sins can be forgiven, and you can live a new life.

Repentance frees us to live a new life in Jesus Christ. Every day you can live with a joyful gladness in your heart. It means your chains can be broken, and your life can be free to serve God with purpose and pleasure with nothing separating you and Him. What a desirable way to exist.

* *

but was unable to tell them what was happening back then, which is the reason I am writing this today. I wanted to speak but couldn't find the words. Instead, I lived in a constant state of fear.

This story is not about my abusive beginning, but it may have contributed to the trauma I experienced as a child from witnessing the abuse.

I never noticed there was anything wrong with me until I was in the first grade. All the children in my classroom were told that we would make a personal recording of poems for our mothers for Mother's Day. I can remember one poem titled "Only One Mother"; it will always have significant meaning to me.

When it was time to make our recordings, we were taken into a room with many gadgets inside it. I became extremely nervous and started to cry. After calming me down, the teacher instructed me to read the poem out loud. I tried again and again, but my voice wouldn't cooperate. She would ask me to start over, and I tried the best I could. Still, nothing came out. Finally, after several attempts, the teacher had captured enough recording and allowed me to stop. I was so happy to present it to my mother as a gift on Mother's Day. She loved it and kept it forever.

Reflecting now, the teacher must have told my mother what had happened that day in the recording room, because shortly after, my mother suggested we visit a doctor. However, despite many visits to different doctors and speech therapists, no one was able to identify a problem. After spending a lot of money and much frustration, we still had no definitive answers. So, we stopped the visits. As I look back, I know now that was the beginning of my "thorn in the flesh." Was I given this for a purpose? I don't know, but my life continued. I began to wonder why this was happening to me. I seemed to be the only one who had this type of condition. I lived a somewhat normal life otherwise, until I had another experience at school that emotionally ripped at my core.

I had to get up and read in front of a classroom of my peers. Everything seemed to get cloudy, and I could hardly breathe. I tried to use what I was taught in therapy, but it didn't work. No words would come out. Frustrated and embarrassed, I just broke down and cried, and the teacher dismissed me after seeing me struggle to speak.

In grade school, the teachers were very understanding because my mother informed them of my problem, but as I approached high school, things began to change. English class and presenting book reports required me to speak. I would pray hard that the teacher would not call my name because I was petrified. Whenever I had to stand in front of my teachers and classmates, my heart would beat so hard that I thought it would burst out of my clothes.

Many days, I would come up with excuses – such as being sick – not to go to school whenever I knew I might be required to speak in one of my classes. When lying about being sick didn't work, I would tell my teacher that I had a bad cold and couldn't speak in front of the class. But, of course, I couldn't use those excuses but for so long, and when the time came that I had to get up and speak, nothing would come out. It only drew more attention to what I had been trying to hide for so many years. The embarrass-ing abnormality of my voice, or lack of it, stifled me.

The unfathomable pain made my situations much worse, and I would cry so hard that they would send me home. Once at home, I would go to my safe place – my bedroom – and cry uncontrollably. My sweet mother, the only one who understood my agony, would try to comfort me. She would lay by my side and stroke my head until I fell asleep. During those moments, I would silently pray for God to let me die. At a young age, I believed in God, but I didn't feel His presence anywhere around me, which you can imagine is quite hurtful to a child.

In my teenage years, my father never allowed me to have boys over, but when he went away on business trips, my mother would let all my friends come over – even boys. Having my friends around helped somewhat because it kept me from staying secluded and made me feel happier.

My mother was my hero. She always tried to encourage me to move beyond my disability and do something good with my life. My mother ended up sending me to modeling school, which was also a business school. She thought it would bring me out of the self-conscious state I was in due to my fragmented voice.

I became a good model, a great model as long as people were only looking at me. However, when I had to stand in front of people who would ask me questions, I was unable to speak to answer them. Nothing would come out. I wished with all my heart that I could be a silent model, but almost every job required me to do interviews or answer questions about where I grew up, what I wanted out of modeling, and why I chose it as a career. I went as far as securing the Miss Cleveland contest, but once the interviews became extensive, I dropped out because my voice wouldn't work. I couldn't bear to face more embarrassing moments. My looks didn't hinder me; it was my voice. Today, I still dream about what it would be like if I would have made it. What a great representative

I would have been! Unfortunately, everything back then was not only based on looks but also on one's ability to speak inside the world of modeling.

As I grew older, I needed a job. Because of my modeling school and business credentials, I was well qualified for a job at a prominent company in Cleveland. I was good at what I did, and the job did not require speaking. My job duty only involved typing, and I had my own little space to do it in. I still believe I received the job because of my looks, which often helped me to compensate for the inadequacy of my voice. So, I was extremely thankful to God for giving me good looks.

My life started getting better. I met new people at my job, and one day, a beautiful girl sat next to me. We became friends, and as I got to know her, I found out she had the same disability I did. Her voice was just like mine! To know that there was someone else just like me gave me a sense of relief. She was married and had children. I had dreamed of the same for myself, but never thought it would happen. Her story gave me hope.

Our meeting was a blessing to me. God was showing me that I was not alone in my humility. I realized if someone could love her voice, then things could come to fruition for me, too. This girl was sent by God to be my friend, and that was the beginning of my triumph. God was leading me through it. By no means was I cured. But, I had hope now that God would send someone to love me – voice and all.

I met many different men in my life but soon realized that I was only "arm candy" for most of them. So how would I find the man who would love me for me and not for how I looked?

At this time, I was a stay-at-home mom; it was something I always wanted in my dreams and how wonderful that God answered my prayers from so long ago. While tending to the daily responsibilities of taking care of my family and home, I began listening to a radio program about the Bible. It was the first time I heard the term "being saved." It sparked my interest, and I began to wonder what it meant to be saved. God was making himself known in my life, and I began to listen.

About this time, my brother and wife were talking about God, too, and we all decided we should get together and have a Bible study. We met one evening and tried to read the Bible together at my brother's antique store, where there was adequate space to gather and be comfortable. A man came to the store that evening to purchase an anniversary gift for his wife. He just happened to be a pastor. (Coincidence? Not!) When my brother told him that we were having a Bible study session, the pastor asked if he could sit in on it. At the end of the study, he posed a question to us.

"If you were to leave here and get in an accident and possibly die, where would you go?" the pastor asked.

Surprisingly, I was able to speak up and answered, "I think I'd go to heaven."

"Do you want to know for certain?" he asked me, and I replied yes.

He proceeded to tell me that if you confess Jesus as Lord and believe he died for your sins and was raised from the dead, you'll be saved. So, I said, "I believe that."

On my way home that night, I kept thinking about what the pastor said, not knowing if I was saved or not. The question of where would I go when I die continued to nag at my brain. Once I was at home in my bedroom, I got down on my knees before God and cried like a baby with my arms stretched out wide. "Lord, please save me," I said and solidified my decision to accept Christ. It was that easy. That night, I cried with joy as I fell to sleep.

The next day when I woke up, I looked at life differently. I know the Holy Spirit came into my heart. As I started attending church, I began to learn God had a purpose for my life. Despite my voice, which was always a hindrance, I knew God had a plan for me. I had to go through some more terrible things in my life, but those are for a future story. This is about how He showed up for me.

More years passed, and I had a fourth child. This time, it was a wanted pregnancy, and I soon had a precious baby boy from it. While my children were very young, my loving husband Mike's life was cut short, but not before he accepted Jesus as his Savior and got baptized, which gave me tremendous peace after his passing. God also sent me a vision that I will never forget. It was a vision of Mike in heaven. I saw it very clearly. I know it was God telling me that my husband was okay with Him in heaven, and I could go on with my life.

Because of my extreme loneliness, God set everything in motion for me as I still had young children at home. I would soon meet someone else who would be very special in my life, significant, and God sent.

My childhood friend tried convincing me to go to a Parents Without Partners meeting with her. At first, I did not want to go, but then I gave in. I had no idea it would be the night I would meet the "God-designated man" who He created just for me. God picked the meeting place, the right time, and the perfect man. All I had to do was show up.

I still faced the same challenges with my voice that never completely disappeared from childhood. Why did I have to face this trauma again, Lord? I did not know the answer, but this time, it was different. God asked me to trust Him, and so I did. I trusted Him and relinquished my control.

Despite my voice, I went to the meeting and noticed a man from across the large room who caught my eye right away. I immediately walked over to him, and he'd be the man I married eight weeks later. I knew beyond a doubt that this handsome, blue-eyed man was the one for me. God had him waiting on the other side of the room just for that moment and just for me. He was interested in me, too! We fell in love quickly, and we've been married now for thirty-five years. I love him with all of my heart. I still have a difficult time with my "thorn in the flesh," but I give it to God. I don't dwell on it anymore. Instead, I trust Him.

God has indeed given me everything I wanted in my life and more. My two husbands, my children, my family, and my home – all of which I love. What truly resonates with me is my new voice, which has been given to me in various forms of writing. I now have ways I can interact with many different people. I can reach countless people through writing – a means that I could have never imagined without my Savior. I didn't see it back then, but He saw it all along.

God knew my testimony of faith would one day be shared, and it all has come together now in my later years. Pushing through years of emotions, building trust, and looking to God for help through the scary times, I owe my strength, courage, and persistence all to Jesus. Through building trust in Him, God showed me what my purpose is for my life. It's to encourage others as I write and pray for them through social media and a group called Women World Leaders, which connects me to other women. I can testify that through writing this chapter, it has been quite enlightening to even me. I stepped out on faith and began fulfilling my purpose.

You may be battling with your own "thorn in the flesh," but God will use you to fulfill the purpose He has for you...if you trust Him. If you're being held back by your crippling issues or can't be the person you want to be, look into the life of Moses and what he accomplished. He also had an affliction (maybe like mine), and God used him to save and preserve his people from extinction. Perhaps that's why I have a thorn in the flesh; it could be so I can share my story with others who may be struggling with their thorn in the flesh. It could be to show that God was there for me when I cried out to him, showing He can be there for you through anything, too.

God knows your every need. He's the one who gave you life. You are not here by chance. You are here to fulfill God's purpose for you – whatever it may be. If you need Him to help you, ask Him into your heart to show you the way.

"For God so loved the world that he gave his only begotten son that whosoever believes in him should not perish but have everlasting life." (John 3:16)

> *"If you confess your sins with your mouth that Jesus is Lord and believe in your heart that God raised him from the dead, you will be saved." (Romans 10:9)*

I believe if he did it for me, then He wants to do it for you, too... if you will only ask.

Victory

Kimberly Ann Hobbs

As humans, we face different battles and temptations. But, God has overcome the world, and we are promised victory through faith. We can find many places in the Bible where God gives his people victory over battles. Victory is a gift. We thank God for giving us the victory as conquerors through Jesus Christ, the anointed one. *(1 Cor. 15:57, TPT)*

We can all rise above our circumstances and be victorious when we have God on our side to fight our battles for us. We are conquerors in Christ *(Romans 8:37)* and can claim victory over any challenge that comes our way because greater is He that is in you than that which is in the world. *(1 John 4:4)*

If you're facing some of life's most challenging situations or possibly a "thorn in the flesh" so to speak, you can claim victory over your circumstances, as well, because it's not by your power or might. It's by the Spirit that will accomplish God's will. *(Zechariah 4:6)* Being victorious in a situation is not a matter of education, progress, or even a feeling. It's a matter of faith.

"For whatever is born of God overcomes the world. And this is the victory that has overcome the world – our faith." (John 5:4–5, NKJV)

Victory can be claimed by being an overcomer. Only God can deliver you from the battle you are fighting. Faith is the victory that overcomes the world.

In our weakness, God gives us strength. Through difficult, painful places in our life, we can find God's grace. He has already told us, *"My grace is sufficient for you, for My strength is made perfect in weakness." (2 Corinthians 12:9)*

You can live a victorious life through Jesus Christ, our Lord and Savior, and win any battle.

* *

Patti Blood is a wife, mother of three, and grandmother to seven grandsons.

Born and raised in California, she now lives with her husband, Dan, in the Orange County area.

When Patti isn't cycling or spending time on exciting adventures with her grandsons, she enjoys traveling, long walks on the beach, swimming, and her favorite, Zumba. Patti also has a passion for gardening and providing a haven for regular visits by squirrels, birds, and an occasional, neighborhood raccoon.

Working in the business community for many years, Patti's entrepreneurial spirit led to owning her own business in the fashion industry. Now she spends as much quality time with her grandsons as possible. She is a prayer warrior and considers it a joy to coordinate prayer movements for anyone in need. Everyone who knows her appreciates her fun-loving spirit and amazing sense of humor.

Patti's passion project is Kerus Global Education, founded by her dear friends Drs. Jennie Cerullo and Marcia Ball. Kerus serves orphans and vulnerable children in Africa and advances educational initiatives to prevent HIV/AIDS. Patti leverages her business experience, commitment to prayer and vibrant personality to actively raise funds and organize special events for Kerus.

God Heard Me Cry

Patti Blood

I thought I was embarking on a fun, carefree vacation in Mexico with my family, but the trip would change my life forever. I was seventeen and in high school when my parents, siblings, and I vacationed in the house that my parents bought in Mexico while my brother was fighting in the Vietnam War. They felt it was an excellent place to retreat to help numb the pain of missing him. For you to best understand my story, let me take you back to my childhood.

I grew up with parents who both worked. There were four kids in our family: my older brother, my big sister, my younger brother, and me. Our family lived in a small home in Pasadena, California. My mother, who was a strict Hispanic woman, had a strong work ethic. She was raised in Los Angeles in a big family. My father was large in stature and had a gruff demeanor. He wasn't a great conversationalist unless it was to scold us, bark out some orders, or communicate with his eyes for us to get out of his chair, which was like his throne. My father was a police officer and mostly worked the graveyard shift. So, my mother was usually in control of our home. My little Hispanic grandmother lived in the house behind us and was the person who raised us. She didn't speak English, so if you wanted to communicate with her, you better know how to say it in Spanish. I adored my grandmother and was always around her. Because of that, I learned Spanish at a very early age.

My siblings and I went to a Catholic school about a mile from our house. My brother, sister, and I would attend Sunday mass, only because if we didn't, we wouldn't get our twenty-five cents to go to the movie theater later that day. My parents didn't attend, though. They slept in while we went to church.

Memories of my school aren't pleasant ones, just more rules to follow. I always felt the nuns who taught at my school didn't seem happy. One of the rules was we had to attend daily mass each morning before class started. I never remembered learning about a loving God – only one who would punish you if you did anything wrong. I don't remember learning about a loving God. My understanding of love came from my abuela, or Mama Lela as I called her.

Years later, my parents, my sister – who is three years my senior, my younger brother – who is five years younger than me, and I all piled into our big Chevy and headed for the long drive to Baja, California. My parents had just purchased the beach house there. In retrospect, I believe this could have been the happiest time of my life. I would get up early each morning to surf, come back to the house, and read numb-minding novels while lying on the beach.

My mother, who seemed more relaxed, started letting us invite random surfers to come surf at our private beach. She was missing my brother and missed watching him surf. One day, my sister and I heard from one of the surfers about a surf contest close to our house. We begged our mother to let us go and watch. Since my brother was in Vietnam, I was driving his '57 Chevy, so we had our own transportation. I was grateful that he trusted me with his prized possessions – his car and his surfboard.

The first time I met my surfer was at this contest. I'll never forget seeing him for the first time, standing in a group of other surfers. He was tall, blonde, and tan, and when he spoke, he had the most irresistible Australian accent!

My sister and I would visit for the next few days to watch the guys surf in the contest. We were privileged to watch these amazing and talented athletes from all over the world. My surfer invited us back to the finals and for the party the night following the contest. We begged our mother to let us go, and I was shocked when she said that we could.

That night, I seemed to belong to him. He introduced me to his friends and some important people in the surfing world. He didn't seem to be embarrassed that I was much younger. I did lie when I told him I was eighteen years old, though. We were able to spend a few more days hanging out together before he had to go back to Australia. Our last night at the bonfire, I remember talking with him through the night, and he told me that he was falling in love with me. I knew I was in love because I had never felt like this before. But, the reality was that my surfer would be leaving the next morning.

As we were sitting by the bonfire holding hands, he stated that this was the beginning of our lives together. He promised me that he would write and call as soon as he got home and that it wouldn't be the end of our time together. Then he looked at me and asked me if I trusted him. I nodded, and he invited me into his beach cabin.

Months passed, and I was now back at school. I never received a letter or call from my surfer. Back then, there was no such thing as email, Google search, or Facebook. There was no way for me to contact him. I began gaining weight and became moodier by the day. My breasts grew larger, and my girlfriends started teasing me about the changes in my body. They might not have known why, but I was pretty sure I did! I tried hard to hide my stomach with big dresses and baggy clothes, but it was getting harder to conceal what was happening to my body.

Years before this, my family moved into another house a few miles from our grandmother's. I often stayed with my grandmother to keep her company. One day, my sister and I were waiting for our parents to pick us up from our grandmother's house, and she told me that she was going to tell our parents that she was pregnant. That's right! She was pregnant at the same time!

When my parents walked through the door, my sister immediately started crying. My father asked her why she was crying, and she broke the news to them. I remember the look of horror on my mother's face, and my father rolled his eyes in disgust. My father looked over at me as I cried, too. He told me not to worry and that it was going to be okay, but I continued to cry. That's when he came over to me and jokingly said, "You're not pregnant, too, are you?" To his surprise, I nodded my head. My mother moaned and said, "Oh, great!"

Both my parents just walked out the door, leaving my sister and me at my grandmother's house. My sister walked home that day. I stayed with my grandmother until my father came and picked me up later that night. I remember my grandmother hugging me and telling me it was going to be okay. She didn't scold me or give me any disgusted looks. Instead, she showed me unconditional love.

I waited for my parents to sit my sister and me down for a talk, but they never did. My mom stayed angry, barely talking to us. My sister told my parents that she was keeping her baby and would marry her boyfriend as soon as he came home from Vietnam. My father informed me that I was not going to keep my baby and that we weren't going to discuss it. I remember my sister arguing with my dad, pleading with him to let me keep my baby and volunteering to help me raise the child. "Absolutely not!" my father responded in a raised voice. "End of discussion!" When my father got heated like that, everyone knew to back off. His word was final!

How could I possibly know once the words "I'm pregnant" came out of my mouth, I would experience a chain of events too overwhelming for a child of seventeen years of age? Never could I have imagined the heart-wrenching circumstances I would encounter. I agonized over the thought of my parents not letting me keep my baby.

As days went on, my tummy swelled, and as I started to show more, my parents hid me from family and friends. How dare I embarrass and shame them! I found out how much more it meant to my parents to keep their pride intact than it was for them to take care of their child during this difficult time. They even made me hide in a closet when company came over. Oh, the shame I felt as I sat in the closet waiting for their company to leave. Could it get any worse? I soon learned that it could.

One night, my parents made me get in my dad's car and told me to put on a blindfold. They instructed me not to remove the blindfold until we arrived at our destination. It didn't take much of an imagination to know they were taking me to get an abortion. I just knew in my heart that is where we were headed.

As I sat in the backseat, I prayed to God to help me. I was so scared! We got out of the car after about an hour's drive and went inside a hotel. As my parents knocked on the door, a man answered and said nothing other than, "Come in." The man pointed to a room and told me to go in there and undress. I was terrified as I saw a makeshift doctor's table. I got on it. The man came in, examined me, and after completing the examination, he told me to put my clothes on. I was horrified, humiliated, and numb. My mind was swimming. After he walked out of the room, I could hear him telling my parents that I was too far along and it was too dangerous. I was relieved; my prayers had been answered.

The long drive home was in complete silence. I remember getting home and just walking into my room. I expected at least one of my parents to step inside my room and explain what just happened, but I got nothing.

I remember thanking God that the doctor was unable to perform the abortion. At that time, I didn't have a real relationship with God. I did believe in God, though, and prayed to Him, especially when I needed something. I eventually learned that God was with me all that time, that He loved me. Ultimately, I would learn how much.

Would I ever know what God was doing for me on that day or what plan for my life would unfold? God did have a plan – a marvelous plan.

After I was spared the traumatic experience of an abortion, my parents took me to an adoption agency, which would place my baby with a good family once my baby arrived. I remember the day I walked into the big building. I was nervous and didn't know what to expect. A lady ushered my parents and me into her office and explained the details of the adoption. My mother seemed so nervous, but perhaps more embarrassed than nervous, while my father showed no signs of emotion at all. My parents didn't ask many questions; they just listened to the lady as she explained what we should expect. I didn't dare say a word until she asked me if this is what I wanted.

Is this what I want? Is she serious? I thought. Didn't she know how much I wanted to keep my baby? I would do anything to keep my baby. I looked over at my mother, her head down. My father gave me an all-too-familiar look. It was like his eyes were speaking to me and saying, "Don't embarrass us. Do what we decided." So, I nodded.

When we completed all the paperwork, we said our goodbyes and got back into my dad's car. Again, silence all the way home. I couldn't understand why my parents wouldn't tell me how sorry they were that I had to give up my baby, or why they wouldn't comfort me with a hug. Was there something wrong with me? Didn't they love me enough to talk to me about what was going on, or even inquire how I was feeling? Tears welled up in my eyes, and I could barely breathe. I wanted to scream, but I didn't dare. I was resigned to the fact that this was how my family dealt with things.

The day finally arrived when my water broke. I was with a friend, and she drove me to the hospital. I was quickly placed in the delivery room alone. She called my parents to let them know I was at the hospital and in labor. Scared and alone, I was hoping they would come right away, but it wasn't until the evening after my delivery that my parents showed up.

One of the strict rules of the adoption agency was that I wasn't allowed to hold my baby. The day the nurses were delivering the precious swaddled babies to the other mothers in my room, a nurse was headed my direction to hand my baby to me, but the head nurse stopped her, abruptly saying, "Not her!" It was so cold the way she said it. Embarrassment flooded over me as the other mothers looked at me.

My parents weren't home when I was released from the hospital. I had to arrange a ride home because my parents had gone to Mexico. Couldn't they have had enough compassion and concern to be at home when I got there? Didn't they understand the agony I felt? Didn't they care that my heart was broken into pieces?

The day I had to go to the adoption agency to finalize the documents for my baby to be adopted, I thought it would be burned in my mind and heart forever. Now eighteen, I had to go alone, as they no longer required my parents to be there. The receptionist walked me into a room and told me to wait. Minutes later, a door opened and in walked the director of the adoption agency...with my baby! She was wrapped in a soft pink blanket, and the director handed her to me. She told me that this would be the only time I would hold my precious baby. As I held her, I felt someone watching me through the two-way mirror directly across the room from me. I knew if I looked too long at my baby that I would break down into tears. It took everything I could do to keep my composure; I was ready to explode.

She was beautiful and so pink, just like a baby girl should be! I often imagined what she looked like. She had the scent of baby powder and was warm and cozy wrapped in her blanket. After just a few minutes, the director came back in and took my baby girl away. I felt like I couldn't breathe. The door opened once more, and the director returned – this time with a man and woman who began asking me personal things about myself, such as what I liked to do and my hobbies. I assumed this was the couple adopting my little girl. They seemed kind enough, dressed nicely, and were friendly enough, but would they ever know how loved she was and how my heart ached for my sweet baby?

After escorting the couple out of the room, the director called me back into her office. As I sat down, she told me that I needed to sign the last document of adoption. She made it clear that I would never see my baby again unless she came looking for me one day. I was shaking, trying hard to steady my hand. I signed on the dotted line and walked out, unable to even swallow. Once outside, I got in my car and drove away. I don't remember that long drive home; I only remember feeling all alone and like my heart was going to explode. No one was there for me, with me, or even seemed to care what I was going through. *What kind of parents do this? God, how can this be? Doesn't anyone care about me?* I felt so desperately alone.

Many years passed, and I was now married to an amazing man who was the perfect father to our two precious sons. I can't begin to tell you how my life turned around.

I was introduced to my husband's best friend and wife and found myself in awe of what a beautiful and godly couple they were. It seemed to me that they were always happy and full of joy, and I wanted the same for our lives.

One night, my friend and I had a long conversation about God. She knew that I grew up Catholic but didn't know much else about my past because I didn't share it with anyone. She invited me to church a few times, but I always declined. One day, I agreed to go. I remember hearing on that day that God loves me, He forgives me of all my sins, and how Jesus died for me because He loves me so much and doesn't care what I have done in my life. Those were words I never heard growing up, and it made me want to know more about Him.

The night when I was invited to a church event with my best friend's family, I heard a powerful message about forgiveness. The pastor called people forward who had never given their lives to Christ publicly. As I sat in my chair, I felt like my seat was on fire! I thought, *what is this?* I remember going forward that night and accepting Christ in my life. I knew I wanted to raise my children in a home like the one that my friend had and to be the kind of mother that she had.

I shared God with my husband, and after he received Christ, we were both baptized. We learned to read our Bibles, we went to church together, and we prayed as a family. We learned how powerful praying together would become in our lives.

One day, my phone rang. It was my cousin informing me that she just received an email from a girl who thought I might be her mother! My cousin told me that she gave the girl her phone number after speaking for a while and discovered that she certainly could be my daughter! Previously, my cousin had taken a "23 and Me" DNA test. Much later, my daughter also took a "23 and Me" DNA test, which showed a family match. My cousin divulged that she knew I had a baby, but no one in the family talked about it. My cousin said she sounded like a lovely person and wanted me to call her. She would be waiting.

I remember that day like it was yesterday. I headed to the beach with my beach chair in hand, my phone, and her phone number. I was a nervous wreck as I walked down to the edge of the water. I parked my chair in the sand, unaware of anyone around me. I then got out the number to call her. After I dialed, it rang a quick ring, and she answered – as if expecting my call. The voice on the line was soft and sweet. She told me that she had some questions and was hoping she had found her mother. Her first question was, "Why?"

Why? I gulped. I didn't expect that right off the bat. I explained to her that it wasn't because I didn't want her, but my father would not let me raise her. I was eighteen, in high school, and living at home – a very dysfunctional home. She asked a few more questions on her list, and then she asked if her father was a surfer from Australia. I thought, *Bingo! This is my daughter.* My daughter's name is Katie, and she was then forty-five years old.

When my daughter was born, she was adopted by a couple who lived in the same city where I lived. Her adopted mother, Patti, with the same name as me, and her father, Charlie, who had the same name as my father, brought her home. When she was two, her adopted mother died. Her adopted dad did not remarry until she was five years old. He married a lovely woman named Dorothy, who had two children.

When I asked Katie why she waited so long to look for me, she told me that she didn't know she was adopted until she was about eighteen! One night, her brother was angry with her and blurted it out. Once Katie found out she was adopted, she told her parents that she wanted to find her birth mother. She said they made every effort to find me, but the records were sealed tight. She said they gave up after a while, and it wasn't until the DNA testing that everything came together. A coincidence? I think not. God orchestrated it!

Katie and I had a long, pleasant conversation that day. She said she was enjoying a beautiful life. That day on the beach, I remember thanking God for the gift of this precious daughter. I thanked Him for protecting me from the ravages of abortion and for giving me the strength to withstand all my heartache while maintaining my sanity!

I told Katie about my husband, her two adult brothers and their families, and what they were like. I had the opportunity to meet Katie's family first. Her parents are loving, kind, and never judged me for putting her up for adoption. They told me that Katie was married to an amazing man and had three adorable sons. I have three more grandsons!

I remember the day Katie and her family flew to California to meet me and her family for the first time. We agreed to have a family reunion at a park by the beach. Gosh, my heart and mind were soaring that day!

We had agreed to meet at Katie's sister's house on the beach that afternoon. When I arrived, Katie's sister told me that Katie was with her boys on the beach and that I should go down there. As I started walking towards the beach, a tall, beautiful blonde appeared to be walking towards me. I headed in her direction, and her brother and sister stepped aside. As Katie and I reached out for each other and embraced for the first time, God was there! A love for her poured over me as we held each other and cried. I remember Katie sobbing years of tears away. What the enemy meant to rob from us, God returned in the form of a big beautiful family! This was my daughter!

We walked down to the water so I could meet my grandsons and son-in-law. Wow! This amazing family belonged to me! How great is our God to give me such an amazing and overwhelming gift so unexpected? My grandsons ran over to me and hugged me with big water-drenched hugs. I sure didn't care that they were all wet. We laughed and hugged and cried. My son-in-law came over and put his arms around me. I can still feel that strong embrace. This was my family!

As Katie met her brothers (my two sons) for the first time, I had to marvel at how much they looked alike. It was uncanny the similarities. They were siblings indeed. My heart was full beyond anything I could ever imagine containing. God did this!

One day, I was talking to Katie on the phone, and she told me that she was taking an online Bible study class and was in a group with some fantastic people. When Katie and I first spoke, I explained to her how important my faith was to me. I asked Katie if anyone in the group prayed the "prayer of salvation" with her. When Katie told me that she wasn't aware of that prayer, I asked her if she would like me to pray it with her. Katie told me she would love that! I asked her if she believed in God, if she believed He was the only way to heaven, and if she would want to accept Jesus into her heart. She agreed. Can you imagine the joy this mother felt having the privilege of leading my daughter to Christ? God continues to bless me repeatedly with beautiful opportunities with my daughter. What a gift giver God is! He did this!

Right before Christmas, Katie told me that she wanted to meet my mother. I was extremely nervous about that meeting. My mother wasn't an affectionate person. So, I wasn't sure what to expect the day they met. As we walked up the pathway to my mother's house, she was waiting for us. Katie walked right up to my mother and gave her the biggest hug! It was such a God thing. I was taken aback when I saw my mother embrace her. I knew it was my mother's way of saying she was sorry and asking for forgiveness without words. Then, I heard her tell Katie that she loved her! What a miracle of healing. What a tremendous example of the power of prayer and forgiveness and healing! I remember when Katie looked over at me. We both had tears in our eyes, along with a look of complete amazement and joy.

The healing that took place that day was nothing more than miraculous. It was the best Christmas present I could have ever received. I felt years of confusion, uncertainty, bitterness, and anger wash off my heart. Only God could do this. I found my mother that day – the one I had always wished I had. God did that!

> *"Behold, I was brought forth in iniquity, and in sin did my mother conceive me." (Psalm 51:5)*

> *"Have I not commanded you? Be strong and courageous. Do not be afraid; do not be discouraged, for the Lord your God will be with you wherever you go." (Joshua 1:9)*

> *"Even if we may not always understand why God allows certain things to happen to us, we can know He is able to bring good out of evil and triumph out of suffering." ~ Billy Graham*

TRIUMPH
Kimberly Ann Hobbs

Looking around the world today, we see so much evil, but in God's Word, we see God has ultimate triumph over evil. Have you been through hard times in your life? You might be in the middle of hard times right now, and things are not looking good at the moment. Remember, at the time of His greatest triumph, things did not look that great for Jesus either.

The supreme example of triumph was coming out of what seemed to be a catastrophe on the cross. What appeared to the blinded world to be the ultimate defeat was, in fact, the ultimate triumph. He triumphed with good over evil and life over death. Yes! There is so much to be learned from such an event!

> *"I have said these things to you, that in me you may have peace. In the world, you will have tribulation: but take heart; I have overcome the world." (John 16:33)*

That's triumph! God is the only One who can take evil actions and intentions of the enemy and make them work for our good. This tells us of God's goodness coming or that we will triumph over any tragedy if we give it over to God. That's right! All of our worries and concerns, give them to God.

You may be struggling with circumstances in your life, but stay close to Jesus and remember that God can be glorified in defeat. It doesn't matter what hurts may have been inflicted upon us or what circumstances are weighing us down. The greatest triumph in our lives sometimes occurs when the circumstances seem to be the hardest. I've walked through this; therefore, I can testify of it.

Remember, God says, *"Who can lay a hand on the Lord's anointed and be guiltless?" The Lord forbid that I should lay a hand on the Lord's anointed. (1 Samuel 26:9,11)* This reminds us never to act out of revenge but rather with love, honor, and respect.

If we are faithful followers of Jesus, we are called to be ambassadors to this broken and tangled world. Watching anyone suffer is a painful thing, but we can encourage others to press on in the name of Jesus and during the most challenging moments of their life. We can give the reminder of God's Word and the importance of it in their life. The significance of knowing the Savior on a more intimate level will bring provision and protection in a powerful way to your life. Triumph over all evil is only possible through the triumph on the cross.

* *

Diane Cheveldayoff is a successful business owner of 22 years and previously served 18 years in the hospitality industry. She has 40-years experience in Hospitality Sales and Marketing. Choices early in life led her to pursue her career and not God. There were many times she didn't see herself being married nor did she see any purpose in having children.

As God pursued her, He had other plans in mind including bringing her back to Him and with that, He brought in her life her husband Les. He blessed her with a wonderful strong Christian man, who has continued to keep God first in all he does. God changed her perspective completely and at the age of 32 married, now 27 years, with 3 beautiful girls in their early twenties.

Their family has always loved to travel together and see new places and things. Biking, hiking, nature, water and most anything to do with outside would be a draw to them. Even now bike rides are a family outing and they try to have quality time recognizing the importance of the family unit. God has created a desire and passion for Diane to mentor women of all ages, especially pre-marriage and newly married women.

Although, she said many times, she didn't deserve the family God blessed her with, she realized, His love is not conditional. At times, life comes at us hard. It's a constant reminder to depend on Him and be obedient, as He is always there for us in ALL, the good and the bad.

Healing After The Healing
Diane Cheveldayoff

It's hard to answer the question of why do bad things happen to good people. This is the question my husband was asked during an interview for the movie, Religulous, right after I became blind in one eye. When you're going through a trial, it's difficult to accept that God allows bad things to happen in our life for a good purpose. During those times, we have to hold steadfast to the scripture of James 1:2 – *"Consider it pure joy, my brothers and sisters, whenever you face trials of many kinds."* True, but not easy.

Years have passed since that time, and it's still hard to look back and pinpoint where my testimony begins. I do remember how, during my childhood, we went to church every time the doors opened, but we didn't bring church home. I went off to college, pursued my career, and chose my road. I made some bad choices, and like most of us, I have regrets. But, God had a plan I could not see, and He continued to pursue me. After many life and God experiences in my late twenties, God got my attention the hard way, and I walked back into a church. I never imagined all that would happen from that day forward, but to scroll ahead, God blessed me with my husband, three beautiful girls, my own business, and a beautiful life with great like-minded friends.

You see, at that time, I was very judgmental about some types of ministries that I couldn't relate to. It goes back to my believing in miracles, slaying of the spirit, and all those TV evangelists who I thought were overbearing, fake, goofy, or just overall weird. Involved with the ministry, my husband and some friends wanted to go and see a couple of these evangelists. So, I reluctantly went with arms crossed. To my surprise, I heard their hearts and didn't see them the same as I did before. As we were leaving the church that night, I heard such an audible voice. It was so clear to me that I thought everyone around me heard Him, too. He said, *"Who are you to judge who I choose to use in ministry? How they reach people is not up to you to judge!"* In hindsight, this was a time He was preparing me for what was ahead, and again, I could not see it at the time.

Did I believe in miracles, physical healing, spiritual battles, and being able to hear the Holy Spirit? I knew scripture, but did I truly believe? Many years after accepting Christ and my husband in full-time ministry, I still had questions. *My husband hears you, Holy Spirit, but what about ME? Where is MY ministry? Why do I question my salvation? I know You, trust in You, and believe in You, so why do I doubt? Am I on that narrow road that leads to life, but few will find? (Matthew 7:14)*

Satan planted so much turmoil and uncertainty within me. I never internalized how often the Holy Spirit spoke to me; I didn't stop and listen. But, be careful what you pray for, and I say that with all seriousness. You want to hear the Holy Spirit, feel Him close, and know your ministry, but are you ready regardless of how He chooses to show you, talk to you, and draw you closer to Him? Remember, His ways are not our ways. So, I had no idea what was ahead.

Now, some background will help you relate a bit. It all began with the conclusion of an intense Bible study. I was driving home that night, and the taillights in front of me were blurred. Having had Lasik surgery years prior, I remember being told the possibility of my vision regressing in future years. I wasn't too concerned until the next day when I noticed a black blob in the bottom corner of my computer screen. I made an appointment with the eye doctor, but within that time of three days, I had lost total vision in my right eye and was experiencing extreme regression in my other eye. It was November, during which time my husband was over three hours away doing another seasonal ministry. Under normal circumstances, that would not have been a big deal, except now I couldn't drive, had three children ages ten and under to care for, and no one local to count on to help me.

Trying to process this while juggling getting the kids to and from school, cooking, working, and now going to doctor appointments was overwhelming. My journey began with many local doctors, who, after performing many tests, quickly realized this was not a typical case. So, they sent me to Bascom Palmer Eye Institute in Miami. With them being rated the number one eye hospital in the States, one would think they would surely have answers. The many specialists reviewed every possible case they had ever seen, and after months of testing and research, it only led to the elimination of all the possible causes, such as multiple sclerosis, diabetes, a detached retina, etc. They had no idea what caused my blindness, but they also concluded there was no cure. My retina specialist determined, with color pictures to prove, only portions of my retina were still intact. The rest of the retina was gone, causing my blindness. Small pieces of the receptor layer had somehow been damaged, and I was told the retina is like brain tissue and cannot regenerate. So, as I left the hospital that day, they informed me that there was nothing they could do for me other than observe. They also added that the same would most likely happen to the other eye in about seven years.

If you think your world has been upside down for a few months, try to imagine anticipating living blind. It's not something most of us would even think could happen, yet for me, it did. I felt hopeless and afraid. My husband started trying to prepare himself and the girls for Mom being blind and how we needed to adjust our home life. He was shaken and disheartened with questions of his own, but he was committed to ministry, even playing that role of healing the blind. Still, this happened, and he could do nothing for me. I know people may have thought I did something wrong to deserve this happening to me. If asked, my answer would be that I had to take this as a compliment from God. He trusted me with this trial and knew I would give Him the glory through it all.

My husband and I knew the best thing to do was pray, and that's exactly what we did. We reached out to many believers, being very transparent of all that we were going through. Although many were praying, there was such fear that took hold of us. My heart was heavy with thoughts of not being able to do the most normal jobs around the house or for my business. Please, God, let me see my girls grow up, graduate, get married, have children, and all the other joys of being a mother," I would pray. The tears flowed as questions of how I could adapt to such expectations without seeing any hope or possibility of correction flooded my mind.

Months passed, and I received many prayers from all across the country, laying of hands on me, and anointing of oil. Hundreds asked for my healing, but ultimately, it was God's will. This southern Baptist girl was experiencing all the extremes that only now I can see as God preparing me. Go back to when I went to see the TV evangelists. I now see Him preparing me to be open to how He chooses to use people's gifts. I believed in miracles. After all, not only was my husband in ministry, but my in-laws were missionaries who personally saw multiple healings and the releasing of demonic possession. But, if I were honest, did I believe He could heal me? Or did I question IF He would heal me?

During this time, my lack of vision caused reading the Bible to be frustrating and a challenge. Praying and worship music became my source of strength. I felt God's presence and knew He was speaking to me. When people say there is peace in the storm, I now understood the statement. In this process, my prayers changed from asking God to heal me to telling Him that His grace was sufficient. I internalized Paul's quote in 2 Corinthians 12:9 – *"My grace is all you need. My power works best in weakness."* This scripture came alive, and I realized it was only by His grace that I was able to see for over forty years when I didn't deserve it. Now I prayed, "God, whether you choose to spare my physical vision, please give me Your vision. God, I'll love you anyway!" That was not an easy place to get to, and it was indeed a journey.

Each day, many times a day, I would place my hand over my good eye to see if there was any change in my blind eye. One of my gauges was not being able to see all the colored lights on our Christmas tree. Of course, my husband loves the decorations of Christmas and used this as a good excuse not to take down the tree. The months passed into March, and one day, I did my test and saw clear lights on the tree. A few days later, I saw all the colored lights on the tree! So, I immediately made an unsuccessful attempt to change my follow-up appointment before realizing it was appropriately set on Good Friday. Now, who doesn't think God has a unique sense of humor?

Again, my specialist repeated all the non-subjective tests, creating new pictures that showed a complete receptor layer in my retina. "It's like someone reformed your entire strand," said the specialist. What glorious words! Not being a believer, he had no idea, but our response was, "We know who did." We asked him to share God's healing to all the other specialists, as they knew there was no medical explanation for how this happened. The good news spread quickly, praise and worship times were scheduled, and there was even an interview with TBN for a segment called "Night of Miracles". I was able to do a reenactment and share my testimony, giving God all the Glory. Hallelujah and thank you, Jesus!

I wish the story ended here. Ten months later, when telling the story to friends and doing the usual hand-to-eye example, the blob was back. No vision in that eye AGAIN! My heart sank, and the questions swallowed me again as Satan planted even more in my mind. *Did God really heal me? How am I going to tell people this happened after I've been on TV claiming to be healed? What are they going to think? They'll think I was lying, or worse, they'll think I'm like those evangelists I use to think were faking it on TV. God, what kind of sick trick is this?*

I returned to Bascom to undergo the same excruciating testing. I'm sure skepticism and doubt entered the doctors' minds. The results were all the same, except for a minor change in one of the pictures. The Doctor in Fellowship explained the different layers, and without getting into technical terms, the retina sits on an outer shell, which had small cracks. Those cracks were slightly larger this time, and in his research, the doctor concluded there was a possibility that the cracks enlarged, causing damage to my retina. My question to him then was, "We know by the grace of God the retina can be healed, but what about those cracks?" His answer was yes.

I felt if we prayed specific and intentional prayers, God could not only heal the retina again but also the cracks so that it would not happen again.

Although embarrassed and scared, the very specific prayer request was launched. Regardless of how difficult it was to be open and then exposed to the comments from non-believers, I believed that God was at work. I just couldn't see it. (Bad joke!) However, the hard fact was, I was again faced with the challenges of not being able to care for my family or run my business. All those doubts and fears came flooding back into my mind. *After I've given you so much glory, why must I go through this again, Lord? What do You want from me? What am I supposed to learn from this?* I just wanted Him to tell me so I could learn it and move on again.

One day, my husband asked me, "Do you think He would bring you this far and then just leave you?" To be honest, yes. There were times when I asked, "Why me?" Yet, I knew the answer and needed to believe that He could heal me again. We chose to trust and claim that God was building a bigger platform for us to give Him more glory.

The doctors and medicine offered no cure, but He did. About three months later, my vision was restored through God's healing. God not only healed my retina for the second time, but He also healed those cracks so it would not happen again. It's now ten years later, and I haven't needed any corrective surgery or had any problems. Praise God!

I believe it's important to ask for prayer so others can be a part of the blessing when God answers those prayers. Many saw and shared in my healing, which strengthened their faith just as it did mine. Many people feel they've done something wrong and are being punished, or that God will only heal them once. However, I can testify that He is not conditional, nor is He limited. He can and will heal the same person multiple times if He so chooses, and if He doesn't, we have to understand that it isn't something we've done to deserve it.

I would never want anyone to go through what I went through, but at the same time, I wouldn't trade how close I felt to the presence of the Holy Spirit during that time. I can relate to King David when he asked the Holy Spirit never to leave him. I remember in Bible study discussing that we will have fires in our life, but if you allow Him, God will take you through the fire and bring you out on the other side. So, for me, I believe He created a bigger platform to show His glory. I believe God gives second chances and wants intentional, specific prayer. I also believe in healing after the healing!

. . . .

GRACE

Kimberly Ann Hobbs

God's grace to us is thrilling beyond words, but how can it be described? Grace is a word about God. The simplest definition of grace is unmerited favor or unconditional love.

Unmerited favor of God means to receive something we did not earn or deserve, and unconditional means something is not limited by conditions, such as good behavior. Grace is the love of God shown to the unlovely. Grace is all about getting what you don't deserve. It's most clearly expressed to us in the promises of God, which are revealed in scripture and manifested in Christ.

In grace, God gives nothing less than Himself as He did in Jesus Christ's act of redemption between God and sinners. If we are Christ's followers, we live every day by the grace of God. We receive forgiveness according to God's grace, and because of grace, we are able to forgive others. We can transform our desires and motivations and behaviors. "By the grace of God, I am what I am."

Things can challenge us and put us in difficult situations, or we could be suffering. But, God's Word tells us that *"He gives us grace to help us in our time of need." (Hebrews 4:16)*

The God of grace will restore you, confirm you, strengthen you, and establish you.

When we learn about the message of the "grace of God," we realize it is something everyone needs. Paul affirms that grace is accessed by faith in Romans 5:1-2, TPT. *"Our faith in Jesus transfers God's righteousness to us and he now declares us flawless in his eyes. This means we can now enjoy true and lasting peace with God, all because of what our Lord Jesus, the anointed one, has done for us. Our faith guarantees us permanent access into this marvelous kindness that he has given us a perfect relationship with God. What incredible joy bursts forth within us as we keep on celebrating our hope of experiencing God's glory."*

God shows us grace through His Son, Jesus Christ. When He was on the cross, He took all the punishment we deserved and placed it on Himself. God loves us so much that He shows us grace by Christ taking away all of the punishment that we deserve for disobeying God, and in return, He gives us good gifts.

This beautiful grace of God is the most powerful thing we will ever encounter in this lifetime. It's difficult to understand because it goes against what people feel is fair and what they think people deserve.

"For it was only through this wonderful grace that we believed in him. Nothing we did could ever earn this salvation, for it was the gracious gift from God that brought us to Christ! So no one will ever be able to boast, for salvation is never a reward for good works or human striving." (Ephesians 2:8-9, TPT)

Grace, grace, God's grace – a grace that is greater than ALL of our sins.

• •

Dr. Tasheka L. Green, servant leader, educator, inspirational speaker, transformational coach, six-time author, entrepreneur, philanthropist, and talk show host, is the Founder, President, and Chief Executive Officer of To Everything There is a Season, Inc. Her innovative coaching techniques influence personal, professional development and organizational change. She leads with a focus to support individuals and organizations in identifying their purpose.

Dr. Green's work garnered her a feature in the Harvard University School of Education, HarvardX Course, Introduction to Data Wise: A Collaborative Process to Improve Learning & Teaching.

A scholarly and virtuous woman, her extraordinary faith, vision, talents, presence, and accomplishments have allowed her to obtain a plethora of recognitions and awards. Dr. Green is an example of when preparation meets opportunity, the end result is success. She loves God and radiates with the joy of the Lord.

Dr. Green is married to William Z. Green, Sr., and they have three beautiful children, Marquis (21), Mikayla (8), and William Jr. (6).

In Due Season, You Will Reap If You Faint Not

Tasheka Green

Trial

The safest place in the world is in the will of God. Though trials, heartaches, burdens, and depression come to wear you down, you hold on to your faith and know that God is in control of your life. Who can save me? Who can heal me? Who can rescue me from where I am? God can heal, deliver, and break you free from all of your pain, hurt, and misery. A change, a season, a test, what is this?

> *"Though he slay me, yet will I trust in him: but I will maintain mine own ways before him." (Job 13:15, KJV)*

As I seek for the answers, I must endure to see the reward. *"The race is not to the swift, nor the battle to the strong, but to the one that endures until the end." (Ecclesiastes 9:11, KJV)* I know that God is close to me; yet, some days, he seems so far away. Lord, I need you more than I have ever before. God, help me, heal me, rescue me from me – from my way of thinking and the bondage that I have placed myself in.

> *"Many are the afflictions of the righteous: but the Lord deliv-*
> *ereth him out of them all." (Psalms 34:19, KJV)*

Only You can. Only You can. There is nobody greater than You. I cry out to You, "Oh God, please turn your ear towards my voice. I need you now."

> *In my distress, I called upon the Lord and cried unto my God:*
> *he heard my voice out of his temple, and my cry came before*
> *him, even into his ears." (Psalms 18:6, KJV)*

> *"And said, I cried by reason of mine affliction unto the Lord,*
> *and he heard me; out of the belly of hell cried I, and thou heard-*
> *est my voice." (Jonah 2:2, KJV)*

My entire life changed nine years ago. Life was going as normal, but God decided to interrupt my plans. I remember so clearly when God whispered to me that my mother's body was stricken with cancer. No one knew, not even my mother, but God told me. Why did He trust me with this? They were words I didn't want to hear, but it was God's way of preparing me and showing me what she was going through and about to endure. I battled with what God told me and did not share it with anyone, including my mother. Was it my fault? Am I to blame? What was I to do with the message that God gave me?

As time passed, my mother developed symptoms that were suppressed by ignorance and medicine. The doctors were only dealing with the symptoms and not evaluating the cause. Never getting to the core of the problem, things began to get worse as time went on. She went from being severely anemic to having rheumatoid arthritis, never acknowledging the real problem. A bleeding ulcer told it all. This bleeding ulcer manifested itself with the symptoms of chronic vomiting, weight loss, and severe nausea. I remember telling my mother to visit a doctor, and she said she would as soon as she could get an appointment. I told her not to put it off and to go to the doctor promptly. Again, she said she would.

After a phone call one night with my mother, I remember dropping the phone and weeping to my husband. "My mother is sick," I painfully said. "She is sicker than she even knows." Why didn't I tell her? Why didn't I adhere to the voice of the Lord? No one will ever know the pain she endured, the nights she cried while praying to the Lord, the fear that overcame her, the anxiety that shook her, and the heartache that crushed her. No one will ever know.

I remember the call like it was yesterday. My mother only confirmed what God had already told me. In a still calm voice, she shared with me that she had stomach cancer. We had never ended a telephone conversation so quickly. Silence filled the air of my living room, and then a stream of tears flowed out of my eyes and down my pale face. Why? Why didn't I do something? The Lord had revealed it to me, and I did nothing. At that moment, I didn't share it with her. I didn't pray, and I didn't ask for healing. I did nothing. Why didn't I take heed to the voice of the Lord? It was not comfortable, nor was it what I wanted to hear. Why is it so important to know God's voice and to take heed? Because knowing God's voice is important and critical in our life. We need to know God's voice so that we make the right choices for our life and can help someone else with their life.

God called Samuel each night, but he did not answer. Instead, he answered Eli and responded, "Here I am." Eli made it known to Samuel that he did not call him. On the third encounter, when Samuel ran to Eli, it was then that Eli informed Samuel it was the Lord calling him. Therefore, Eli instructed and taught Samuel to know and respond to the Lord's voice by saying, *"Speak Lord for thou servant heareth." (1 Samuel 3: 9, KJV)* This time when the Lord spoke, Samuel responded and tuned his ear and heart to the Lord. The Lord trusted Samuel with a word about what was going to transpire in Israel, as well as the plans that were going to be carried out against Eli. Samuel was fearful and did not want to tell Eli what the Lord had told him. However, Eli asked Samuel to tell him what the Lord had said and not to hold any words from him. Samuel proceeded to share with Eli the vision from the Lord. God used Samuel to save Eli's life. Eli was Samuel's teacher and taught him how to acknowledge and take heed to the voice of God. Eli told Samuel, "If you do not tell me, something severe will happen to you."

When God gives you a word for yourself or someone else's life, take heed and do what the Lord sayeth. Fear not the voice of the Lord when He is speaking to you or has given you a word that tingles your ear rather than soothes it. Eliminate the noise and pay attention to the sound. Noises irritate, and sounds resonate. The sound that resonates is the sound of God's voice in your ear.

Triumph

Going from trial to triumph meant I had to lose what I loved the most to walk into a life of purpose. My mother had to die so that I could live. I was living an ordinary life that was not aligned with the plans God had for me. Unexpectedly losing my mother was the most tragic encounter I have ever experienced. Although it lowered me into a lowly place, it elevated me into a new position in God and purpose. It taught me how to pray, trust God, activate my faith, lean not to my own understanding, and that God is the joy of my strength. Most importantly, it taught me that To Everything There is a Season, and in due season, I will reap if I faint not. The death of my mother birthed me into purpose, where I can now help, serve, and love others to greatness.

Nine years later, I have gone through many different seasons, but the best part about it all is that God has been with me through it all. The seasons have brought forth fruit, life, joy, happiness, and peace. I started a business, created a memorial foundation in memory of my mother, started a young girls mentoring group, became an author of ten published books and a talk-show host, was featured with Harvard School of Education Leadership Institute along with other entities and magazines, and have received a plethora of recognition and awards. Those seasons brought me to a place in God knowing that with men things are impossible, but with God all things are possible.

"But Jesus beheld them, and said unto them, with men this is impossible; but with God all things are possible" (Matthew 19:26, KJV)

I still ask God, "Why do you trust me with so much and with other people's situations?" His voice resonates in my ear, *"Many are called, but few are chosen." (Matthew 22:14, KJV)* "And you were chosen to do this even before you entered into your mother's womb. *"Before I formed thee in the belly, I knew thee; and before thou camest forth out of the womb, I sanctified thee and ordained thee a prophet unto all nations." (Jeremiah 1:5, KJV)*

In life, you will encounter trials, but I am a witness that God will take your trials and turn them into your triumphs. Regardless of what the trial may be, you must be confident and know that you are an overcomer. You can and will overcome any trial that comes your way. Most importantly, understand that for everything there is a season and a time for every purpose under heaven. You must press toward the mark each day and run after all that God has for you. If you are still here, go and live a purposeful life!

"To everything there is a season, and a time to every purpose under the heaven: A time to be born, and a time to die; a time to plant, and a time to pluck up that which is planted; A time to kill, and a time to heal; a time to break down, and a time to build up; A time to weep, and a time to laugh; a time to mourn, and a time to dance; A time to cast away stones, and a time to gather stones together; a time to embrace, and a time to refrain from embracing; A time to get, and a time to lose; a time to keep, and a time to cast away; A time to rend, and a time to sew; a time to keep silence, and a time to speak; A time to love, and a time to hate; a time of war, and a time of peace. What profit hath he that worketh in that wherein he laboureth? I have seen the travail, which God hath given to the sons of men

to be exercised in it. He hath made everything beautiful in his time: also, he hath set the world in their heart, so that no man can find out the work that God maketh from the beginning to the end. I know that there is no good in them, but for a man to rejoice, and to do good in his life. And also that every man should eat and drink, and enjoy the good of all his labour, it is the gift of God. I know that, whatsoever God doeth, it shall be forever: nothing can be put to it, nor any thing taken from it: and God doeth it, that men should fear before him. That which hath been is now; and that which is to be hath already been; and God requireth that which is past." (Ecclesiastes 3:1-15, KJV)

. . . .

PROMISES
Kimberly Ann Hobbs

There are many promises in God's Word, but how do you know which ones are for you?

Some are general promises and some specific. To give an example, I'll use the general promise of 1 John 1:9, which explains, *"If we make it our habit to confess our sins, in his faithfulness righteousness, he forgives us for those sins and cleanses us from all unrighteousness."* Then there are specific promises, such as in 1 Kings 9:5, where it is written to King Solomon, *"Then I'll make your royal throne secure forever."*

Promises of God are special and should matter to us. God gives us promises to help us "submit" to His will, not to make us "bend" to our own will. God's promises are spoken or written commitments, and if God says He will do something, we can rest assured that He will. If God says He will refrain from doing something, then that applies, too. Whether God says He will or will not do something, we can trust Him at His Word.

Joshua 1:25 says, *"Not one of the promises that the Lord has made to the house of Israel failed; all of them came about."* Often, we look to people to hold the same commitments or promises as God does. We shouldn't put our faith in human behavior. We must place it in a God who is faithful to keep that which He's committed to. God makes two types of promises to us in His Word: unconditional promises made without any conditions whatsoever, and conditional promises that are subject to certain qualifications or requirements. We need to understand the context of God's promise for our lives and not just pick a random promise, claiming it for our own. Maybe the promise was conditional, and therefore, we do not meet the requirements.

There are five biblical promises you can rely on:

- Promise #1: God loves you unconditionally. *So now I live with the confidence that there is nothing in the universe with the power to separate us from God's love. I am convinced that his love will triumph over death, life's troubles, fallen angels, or dark rulers in the heavens. There is nothing in our present or future circumstances that can weaken his love. There is no power above us or beneath us – no power that could ever be found in the universe that can distance us from God's passionate love, which is lavished upon us through our Lord Jesus, the Anointed One! (Romans 8:38-39, TPT)*
- Promise #2: You are redeemed and have an eternal home in heaven.
- Promise #3: God formed you with intentions and knows you intimately. (Psalm 139)
- Promise #4: God's plan for your life is to prosper you, not to harm you. (Jeremiah 29:11)
- Promise #5: You have special strength that is available to you through faith, through the power of Christ. (Philippians 4:13)

Standing on the promises of God and not men will prove stability in our hearts and assurance to our souls in a world where it is so easy to fall. Stand firm on the promises of God.

• •

Christine Mallek has a passion for helping people – from providing education on fundamental financial principles that aren't taught in school; to helping people take practical steps towards successful money management; and helping women acquire job search skills

After receiving her miracle of healing, Chris knew she wanted to use her experience to help others. She felt her purpose was somehow connected but didn't know what that looked like. She believes God led her to a leadership role in the Women World Leaders, a ministry which empowers women to find their beautiful purpose God has designed for them, to strengthen her faith and share her story, healing and faith journey, to inspire others who may be battling cancer or another serious illness.

Prior to launching her financial coaching business, Chris spent most of her career with Deloitte, one of the leading professional services organizations in the United States, specializing in audit, tax, consulting, and financial advisory services.

Chris has been active throughout her adult life in Girl Scout activities. She is a former Girl Scout Council Board and Audit Committee member. While at Deloitte, Chris took this passion to her community and facilitated programs aimed at assisting women to acquire job search skills needed to achieve gainful employment. She also facilitated financial wellness workshops for adults and *How Money Works* programs for kids. She currently leads the Women World Leaders ministry Finance Team.

Chris holds financial services licenses and is a graduate of Montclair State University with a Bachelor of Arts in Mathematics and Accounting. Originally from New Jersey, she and her husband of 45 years, Marty Mallek, now reside in Hobe Sound, Florida, have two grown children and one grandson. Chris loves being a grandmother and in her spare time enjoys yoga, keeping fit, deep sea fishing, being outdoors and traveling.

Journey To A
New Beginning
Christine Mallek

> *"I will not die; instead, I will live to tell what the Lord has done." (Psalms 118:17)*

I am a cancer survivor for no other reason than the grace of God. Who would have ever thought I would go through something like this at that point in my life? Let me start by giving you a bit of the backstory.

I am so blessed. When I think back on my childhood and growing up, I have beautiful memories of my family. I grew up Roman Catholic with two loving parents and a brother. My mother, who was one of my biggest supporters, said I could do anything I put my mind to. So, I did. I married a good man, birthed two wonderful children, and had a successful career in Corporate America. Throughout my early life, I went to church on Sundays, sent my children to catechism so they could receive all the sacraments, and did what I thought every good woman should do. As the years went on, my parents passed away, my children grew up, and little by little, I stopped going to church. Honestly, I never really felt like I had a relationship with God. I just followed the prescribed calendar of things to say and do, but never had a personal relationship with the Lord. That is until my cancer diagnosis changed everything!

After thirty years, my position was eliminated with my employer in 2014, and I needed to move on. Not easy for someone who is over the age of sixty. I remember talking to colleagues about anticipating this new chapter of my life, but never in a million years did I think it would bring me here. Wanting to do something that would help people and make a difference, I went into the field of financial literacy coaching.

In May 2015, I started feeling like something wasn't right with me medically. I had already gone through menopause, so any spotting should have been a red flag that something was not quite right. But, I procrastinated before finally going to my gynecologist right before Christmas of that same year. The biopsy came back positive for endometrial uterine cancer, and she referred me to a gynecologic oncologist. *What!?!* At this point, it seemed surreal.

In hindsight, I feel like the financial coaching I began in 2015 was a path to introduce me to the Lord and some new friends in my life who would walk with me on this new journey. I became part of a Life Group that loves and supports each other through Jesus Christ. It was through this Life Group that, for the first time in early January 2016, people laid hands on and prayed over me. They prayed that the surgery would be a success, my treatments would go well, I would be healed from cancer, and all would be okay.

I ended up having a complete hysterectomy and underwent a series of brachytherapy radiation treatments. I took it all in stride and thought no more of it. Feeling better, I went back to working, and life moved on. I didn't get it, so I guess God needed to shake me up again. Eleven months later, the cancer returned, and this time, I was scared! The real possibility of me dying hit me hard.

From a medical standpoint, my oncologist recommended that chemotherapy treatment start ASAP, but I struggled with if that was the route I wanted to take. I was learning so much about natural healing alternatives and God's power for healing, and I felt like I was being pushed in a direction I was not ready to go. I needed time to sort it out.

January 2017

> *"If you believe, you will receive whatever you ask for in prayer."*
> *(Matthew 21:22)*

When friends learned that my cancer had returned, they again prayed with me. One night, they really introduced me to the healing power of Jesus. For some time, I had been feeling like something was missing in my life; I wanted a relationship with God. That night, my eyes started to open. I got a glimpse of the healing power of the Lord and began thanking Him for healing me. I used strong affirmations for healing. Not that He *would* heal me, but I was introduced to the fact that He had *already* healed me! *Psalm 107:20* tells us that God sent His Word and healed them. It didn't say God sent His word to heal them, but He sent His Word and healed! God considers it done. I began regularly speaking healing declarations as God's medicine, such as: *"Every organ and tissue of my body functions in the perfection that God created it to function. I forbid any malfunction in my body in Jesus' name." (Genesis 1:28-31)*

A dear friend introduced me to John Hagee's "Healing Scripture" YouTube video. I listened to it every night before going to bed, and it gave me hope and comfort.

I also spoke with a natural cancer survivor who told me that my body created the cancer, so my body could heal it. I began to learn what that entailed and was presented with a whole new world of juicing, eating a plant-based diet, eliminating sugar and dairy, using essential oils, managing stress, and the benefits of using turmeric, Essiac tea, and the list goes on. Up to this point in my life, I thought I followed a pretty healthy diet, but I embraced this nutritional change immediately to strengthen my body's defenses and help fight the cancer. Fighting cancer became a 3-pronged approach for me – spiritual, nutritional, medical – and what a journey this has been.

For the next month, my husband Marty and I researched chemotherapy and other treatment alternatives, while I kept up with what I called my cancer-fighting lifestyle and diet. I got a second opinion from Moffitt Cancer Center in Tampa, who agreed with the chemo route. They stressed that my condition was serious, and I would probably be gone in a year if I chose to "do nothing". At this point, my cancer was staged at 3C, one step below Stage 4. Yes, that petrified me! I'm not typically an emotional person, but the tears flowed, both mine and Marty's. It was unfair! I did not want to die yet!

After much praying, I decided to incorporate the chemo into my treatment plan and prayed that God would work through the doctors while I stayed close to God. I prayed and gave Him praise daily, listened to the healing scriptures every night, and maintained the good nutritional lifestyle I had begun weeks earlier.

The day before I was scheduled to start chemo, my dear friend prayed with me, and I accepted the Lord as my Savior. I never felt more at peace than I did then! I felt a huge weight was lifted from my shoulders, and I believed whatever decision I made regarding how I would treat this disease would be the right one. Because no matter what, I would have eternal life with God.

"Your own ears will hear him. Right behind you a voice will say, 'This is the way you should go,' whether to the right or to the left." (Isaiah 30:21)

As I left this friend's house, my oncologist's office called to confirm everything was a go for me to start chemo the following day, but I decided to put it all on hold for a month. In my heart, I knew it was the right decision, and I truly believe God spoke to me through this friend.

March 2017

I think God has a sense of humor. As things got underway with the chemo treatments, I prayed that I would be an exception and not lose my hair. While I lost most of it, God left me with a little peach fuzz. I still smile about this.

March 10, 2017 – Just another ordinary day, or so I thought. Yet, it would turn out to be an incredible day that would change both Marty's and my life forever.

Marty had been attending a 6-week men's program at the office of his friend Mark. Friday, March 10th was the last session, and it went along uneventfully. Towards the end of the session, Mark said he was going to go through some Bible verses if anyone was interested in staying an extra thirty minutes. Marty immediately said yes. He thinks Mark sensed his need for prayer because he and I had some important decisions to make regarding my cancer reoccurrence.

As Mark prayed over him, Marty experienced an intense rush of heat. Even though the room was air-conditioned, he was perspiring all over. The next thing he knew, he was speaking strange words, not English or any language he had ever heard. The words came out as, "In a ma gauch sa tee, a a tee in ma sa." He kept repeating those words as Mark continued to pray. At some point, he didn't hear Mark anymore nor the others in the room. It was as if his senses had been paused, and he felt like he was in a zone of peace for a few moments. Then he began to hear Mark again and the others, but he was exhausted. It took him ten to fifteen minutes to recover to the point that he could stand up. Something had happened that he never experienced before. Mark said he had received the Holy Spirit, but Marty didn't know what that meant. He kept asking himself what those words meant. He would soon come to realize they were powerful words indeed!

As he left the office and walked to his car, Marty was struck by what he saw and heard. If he looked at a tree or the clouds in the sky, the level of detail he could see was incredible. Birds chirping in the distance became the most beautiful sound. On the way home, he made a stop at a large fruit and vegetable market. When he entered the market, it was as if he could see into the hearts and souls of each individual. Many were sad, and some were lonely. Others seemed happy and positive. He smiled at everyone and said hello as he walked through the store. Some responded, and some did not. But, for Marty, it was indeed a unique experience.

When he returned home and relayed his experience to me, I said it sounded like God was talking to him. He agreed, but wondered why? That night, he found out why.

He went to bed at his usual time. Please know that Marty very rarely dreams, and when he does, he can't remember them. This night would be different, though. His dream this night was to take me to the beach on Sunday morning at sunrise. We were to take with us a Bible and an anointing oil called Frankincense. It just so happened that a week before all this transpired, I had ordered some Frankincense essential oil. Coincidence? I think not! His dream ended with these instructions:

- Be at the beach for sunrise.
- Bring a Bible.
- Bring Frankincense oil.
- Christine will go into the ocean and immerse the areas of cancer.
- When she comes out of the water, anoint her with Frankincense oil over her lungs and abdominal lymph nodes. Repeat 3 times the words experienced on Friday.

As we left home for the beach Sunday morning, Marty happened to look up in the sky and saw three cloud formations in the shapes of running lions. He immediately thought about the Book of Daniel. As we drove, Marty asked me to open the Bible to Daniel and find the verses dealing with the lions' den and furnace. He knew in his heart that I would be healed. I would have to face the lions and the furnace, but God would protect and heal me.

We went to the beach as instructed and did what the dream told us to do. As we performed these steps, the sun broke through the clouds, and the wind began to blow, creating an amazing formation in the clouds that appeared to us as the face of God. The sun shone through His eyes and mouth as if directly on us. As the sun came up, Marty said to me, "You are in remission. You will be fine." People said it was the most spectacular sunrise they had seen in weeks. We looked at each other and smiled because that sunrise was meant for us!

While we were there, a woman approached us. We learned her name was Karen. She was quite a good photographer and said that of all the people on the beach that morning, she was particularly drawn to us. She didn't know why, but she said there was something about the sunrise that was special and knew it had something to do with us. We told her our story, and when we learned that her last name was Lamb, we were astounded because it made us think of "The Lamb of God."

April 2017

I was blessed with nothing short of a miracle. I had very few side effects from the chemo, and what I did have was manageable. Each time I received chemo or went for a new test, I felt at ease and not afraid. I recall telling the women in the infusion room with me one day that I believed God was sitting right next to me, protecting me. Halfway through the chemo treatments, a CAT scan at Moffitt of my abdominal lymph nodes showed nothing abnormal when doctors went to do a biopsy, so they could not proceed. They removed the IV and let me leave. The medical professionals that day said they rarely, if ever, see that happen. All glory and praise to God! Then a PET scan a few weeks later showed there was no cancer anywhere. Whatever had been there in January was gone! I was in remission, and my doctor said to keep doing what I was doing! I remember sitting in the doctor's office after hearing this news and high-fiving with Marty. When we got home, we joined hands and praised God! It was truly a gift of healing from God. Thank you, Jesus! I also thanked many people for their prayers. The power of prayer is amazing.

For the next two years, I felt great. Juicing and a plant-based diet became my norm. All cancer tumor markers were good, and my hair grew back a beautiful shade of silver. Every chance I got, I told people portions of my story, the signs we received from God, my belief in the power of prayer, and the healing power of the Lord. After experiencing this miracle, I wanted to help others and felt my purpose was somehow connected. I believe God brought me to a leadership role in a women's ministry to strengthen my faith and share my story of healing and faith to encourage others who may be battling cancer or another serious illness.

Two years later – July 2019

Everything was going well. My tumor markers and scans were consistently good. I continued to eat well and started working with a functional/integrative medicine doctor to help my body stay healthy so the cancer would not return. Then, the hammer fell. I started experiencing some bleeding again, and in a regular follow-up exam on July 3rd, the doctor found a vaginal tumor that turned out to be cancerous, as well as some larger cancer lesions that had metastasized to my lungs. Now Stage 4. Strangely enough, I did not panic when I heard this news, but then I thought maybe I should have.

Why did I have to go through this again? No matter what diet I had, no matter what drugs or medical procedures I used, I believed it was the Lord who healed me. So why was this happening again? I felt I was a new person, and I had a much closer relationship with the Lord. So why?

Things were starting to move fast again. I needed to decide how I would attack this. My prayers and those of my friends went back on high alert. As I write this testimony, I have started chemo treatments again, have undergone several external radiation treatments, and believe I will be healed again. Or more accurately, I already have been healed. The medical tests just haven't caught up to God's reality yet. I've received many signs from God that he has everything under control. Do I sometimes doubt and feel that I'm just reading what I want into what's happening? Sure, but then I step back again and put all my faith in Him, and I see more signs.

Such as the time Marty and I decided to go back to the beach at sunrise on July 13th as we did two years earlier, even though we hadn't received another specific direction from God to do so. What could it hurt, right? The night before, in the early morning hours before I woke, I had a dream where I was going to pick up Marty and a neighbor to go to the sunrise. The neighborhood looked like the one where I grew up. Inside the house, which looked more like an airport walkway to flight departure gates, a large, dark-skinned woman dressed in a stretchy purple/violet covering kept bumping into me and blocking my way so I could not proceed. I had to turn around and run out of the "house". I looked around outside for a bat or metal stick to use as a weapon if she came after me. I called 911 and was on top of a hill a little way from where this all took place, when a police car pulled up and asked if I called them. As I said yes, my alarm went off, and I woke up.

Could this woman have been Satan trying to stop me from going to the sunrise and speaking with God again? Or was she a gift from heaven dressed in purple, symbolically keeping me from going all the way down the runway because it is not my time yet?

Many other signs have happened, as well. Based on our experience in 2017, I believe God speaks to Marty, so I have come to rely heavily on what he hears. A few weeks ago, Marty had a medical exam for an issue that turned out to be okay. While driving home after his appointment, he thanked the Lord for his healing and the good results, then prayed that God would give me the same. Marty again felt that feeling from God telling him that I would be okay, but that I needed to go through this because it is part of my story. Maybe God's not done with me.

During recent radiation treatment, I not only prayed during the procedure as I always do, but I very specifically asked God to send me his Holy Spirit to guide and protect me and to help me to hear and feel the Spirit. Even though I had asked something similar several times in the past, I was never sure that he heard me. This time, I felt a warm tingly feeling starting in my head and traveling down to my toes. In my heart, I believe God heard me and sent his Holy Spirit to me. Since that day, songs on the radio, music in the radiation treatment room, and even the whiteboard message in my chiropractor's office have all spoken directly to me.

> *"If you go to Jesus, He may ask of you far more than you originally planned to give. But He can give you infinitely more than you dared to ask or think!" (Ephesians 3:20)*

I certainly hadn't planned to go through this again, but God's got this. I will be healed! I am a work in progress and believe that with every new step I take, I am heading in the right direction. I am learning to give it all to the Lord and to lean on Him for peace, wisdom, and comfort. And it feels so right!

Since all this began, I have been blessed with a new and beautiful reason to live a long and purposeful life – my baby grandson. I so want my grandson and my children to come to know the Lord as I have – and to ensure we will all be together in Heaven when we leave this earth.

"When you're going through something difficult and you wonder where God is, remember the teacher is always silent during the test." ~ Author Unknown

NEW/NEWNESS
Kimberly Ann Hobbs

Walking in "newness of life" is not just a matter of changing our behaviors but of gaining a new heart and a new spirit. To walk in newness of life requires us to abandon our judging ways and move to do God's justice rather than our self-serving habits. God's grace came into the world to bring reconciliation and justice, but there are still evil spiritual powers at work opposing the life-giving power of God's grace. We would be wise to partner with God through Christ against these evil forces and walk in newness of life as Paul talks about in Romans 6:4.

Walking in newness of life requires we abandon our old way of living, leave our self-serving habits, and follow God's justice through the life-giving POWER of God's grace as it builds us up within the community of Christ. God's grace does not want us to resort back to our old ways; He wants us to permanently choose to stay in the "new life" in Christ.

Walking in this newness of life may feel challenging at first. However, when God brings us into union with Christ, transferring us from the reign of sin to the reign of grace, it causes us to be baptized into Christ and have identification with Him that brings indescribable change. It means our sinful inclinations may be "done away with" and "rendered powerless". We are no longer slaves to sin; it is no longer our master. It does not mean sin is completely wiped out of our lives, but the power of sin in our lives is broken forever. We are now free, by God's grace, to grow in holiness – sinning less and obeying God more. Thus, bringing us into a "newness" of life. (Romans 6:4, TPT)

Sharing in his death by our baptism means that we were co-buried and entombed with him. When the Father's glory raised Christ from the dead, we were also raised with him. We have been co-resurrected with him so we could be empowered to walk in the freshness of new life.

Until the day when God will provide a new heaven and new earth to live in (Revelation 21:1), enjoy your "newness of life" through your "newness of spirit". Thank God – the only able One – for making you new.

* *

Josy Cartland is a Cuban American Florida Native whose passion is evident when it comes to people and healthy relationships. She personally knows the struggles that come with relationships, marriage and family-life. She is the happy wife of Brian Cartland and together they have a blended family. She is a mother to five wonderful adult children, one handsome son in law, and grandmother of two beautiful grandchildren.

She and her husband are certified pre-marital and relationship coaches as well as licensed financial coaches. They enjoy serving in lay-ministry within their local church community. They are the founders of their coaching practice BlessedLifeCoaching.com in Palm Beach County, Florida where she provides relationship coaching to single women, and together they mentor couples. They have been involved with several ministries throughout the country conducting workshops, bootcamps and couples' groups. They are not only passionate about educating families in relationships, but with finances as well.

Abandonment & Rejection
Josy Cartland

My story starts with the earliest memory of abandonment at the age of two years old. I remember it vividly, like a movie playing in my mind, watching as my father packed his belongings with a buddy while my mother carried me in her arms and wept. I recall her pain and helplessness because I felt it. She rocked me back and forth in total confusion for what was tragically about to take place in our lives – her high school sweetheart was leaving and divorcing her.

I grew up in the city of Miami in a Cuban American culture where God was mentioned, but there was no biblical teaching or under-standing whatsoever. A gorgeous, green-eyed, blonde-haired, single mother with an impeccable work ethic raised me, and I visited with my father every other weekend from about two to nine years old. By the age of five, my father was married to his third wife. My mother was in and out of non-committal relationships until I was nine, and she married my stepdad. My stepdad suffered from mental illness and took his life twenty-seven years later. I think my parents did the best they could. However, I experienced so much brokenness in their lives that it later became the dysfunctional norm in mine.

Ever heard of the saying "she has daddy or mommy issues?" Well, it's a fact. According to a conversation between God and Moses in the Bible, *Exodus 34:7* mentions that the sins of the parents can be passed down to three and four generations. I've learned that we inherit generational choices, known as generational curses. The choices made by our ancestors, parents, and even ourselves will affect our future and our children's future.

Some of the damage I experienced firsthand was my parents' divorce, which later in life became a big influence on how I handled relationships. I had no foundation on what was emotionally and spiritually healthy in my life. Therefore, I had no idea what a healthy or normal relationship resembled. As a child, I was skinny, hyper, insecure, and looked nothing like my beautiful mother. I was rejected by kids constantly, while my sister was the popular one. Once I blossomed into my teen years, the ugly duckling began to use her charm and beauty to gain attention and acceptance, especially from the boys. My teenage years were very destructive. Besides all the dysfunction taking place in my home environment, I had no parental guidance or emotional connection with my parents. I sought out older male relationships because I desperately wanted to be loved and accepted, which later led to a life of promiscuity and brokenness.

Although my mother and I came to know and accept Jesus when I was sixteen years old, the seed of abandonment and rejection continued to pop up in my life in many forms. I was married one month after my nineteenth birthday to a young man who I met in church. At twenty-one, I was already serving in full-time ministry as a missionary and a pastor's wife. I had three children by age twenty-five, and at twenty-nine years old, I found myself alone fighting one of the toughest battles I've ever fought in my life because my husband walked out on us, divorced me, and dragged me through the legal system for several years. It was history repeating itself in my life once again.

Feeling like I failed in life and marriage, my past and shame caught up to me again. That insecure little girl was still inside, crying out to be loved and accepted. Instead, she found herself abandoned and rejected over and over. I developed this false self-belief of unworthiness to the point where abandonment and rejection was something I thought I deserved. For several years, I found myself enduring destructive behaviors, unhealthy and meaningless relationships. As a young single mother of three, I made many poor choices. While I searched to be loved and accepted, I didn't realize I was not connecting with my children emotionally during the most vulnerable years that they so desperately needed me. Not to mention, I was dealing with an abusive, narcissistic, and competitive ex-husband who didn't promote love and peace between our children.

Looking back now, fifty years later, I can see two things that occurred in my life. The seed of abandonment and rejection was planted deep within my heart at a very young age. On the other hand, I can recall growing up with the constant feeling that someone was watching over me. Understanding some of the complex dynamics my grandparents and parents had to endure – such as families splitting up, fleeing from Cuba, divorces, adultery, abuse, my grandmother giving up my mother because she was poor and birthed her out of wedlock, and my father losing his father at a young age – helps me understand why they made some of the choices they did. Now that I am in Christ, I do not need to blame them for my issues. Instead, I can forever change the future for my children and grandchildren by choosing to follow Christ and teach them to live a life God has intended for them without a generational curse.

It was in my journey of seeking God for answers many years later, where I discovered God fearfully and wonderfully made the little two-year-old girl. It was then the healing process began, not at a surface level, but deep within my heart. And finally, for the very first time, I believed with all my existence that I was worthy of God's affection. My life has never been the same. *Psalms 139:13-14* says: *"For you created my inmost being; you knit me together in my mother's womb. I praise you because I am fearfully and wonderfully made; your works are wonderful; I know that full well."*

You see, when we walk through life with all our childhood damage, broken relationships, and unresolved issues without truly knowing God, we subconsciously seek out unhealthy, detached, and non-committed relationships that imitate the emotional abandonment we experienced in our younger lives. In this condition of abandonment, we attract people who avoid intimacy and God because they provide the distance we need to feel safe. Then we neglect our feelings and needs for fear of being rejected. We need to STOP losing ourselves just because we want others' love and approval. God already said we are made in His image, and we have been given the privilege to be His children. But, the problem is our BELIEF system. We hear these scriptures and know they are true, but are we truly BELIEVING God, or are we believing the lies that have been rooted deep within our lives?

John 1:12 – "Yet to all who did receive him, to those who believed in his name, he gave the right to become children of God."

Ephesians 2:4-5 – "But because of his great love for us, God, who is rich in mercy, made us alive with Christ even when we were dead in transgressions – it is by grace you have been saved."

Once I began to identify the lies, I was believing and accepting in my life. I then was able to turn to God for His truth. I began to see, walk, and live differently. My faith grew as I leaned closer to the One who created me and knew my heart more than any living being – Jesus! I look back now and see that I accepted Jesus as my Lord and Savior, but I never truly surrendered my false self-belief. There is a difference between experiencing God on a surface level and experiencing Him on a deeper, more intimate level. I thought surrender was just giving up sin and doing good for God. I realized I had to come face to face with those generational choices, lies, and curses that had been deeply rooted within me, which needed to be uprooted from my life and sent back to where they came from – the Father of Lies, Satan.

> *2 Corinthians 5:17 – Therefore, if anyone is in Christ, the new creation has come: The old has gone, the new is here!" I love this scripture! God makes ALL things new.*

Understanding who I now was in Christ allowed God's purpose and perfect will to surface in my life finally. Wow! My God truly knew the desires and dreams within my heart because, after all, He planted them there when He created me. On a practical level, I learned how important it was to understand myself, how God viewed and made me, as well as what my emotional and spiritual needs were before entering any relationship. Without a doubt, I identified that God created me to experience true affection, love, nurturing, companionship, and to be understood, appreciated, and valued. These are some of the ingredients I go to God for before I go to anyone else. God knows what we need, and He is more than able to meet our needs.

Psalms 147:3 – "He heals the brokenhearted and binds up their wounds."

Once I experienced God's inner healing in my life, I waited patiently for His direction and perfect will. He knew I longed for a healthy companion, and I relied on God's timing for it. Today, I am married to one of the most amazing human beings I have ever met. When I met my husband, Brian, it was truly a divine appointment and God-ordained. He has been a precious gift from God. I can now say I have experienced what it is to be in a healthy, God-fearing, and loving relationship because God is the center of our marriage.

Psalms 20:4 – "May he give you the desire of your heart and make all your plans succeed."

Psalms 37:4 – "Delight yourself in the LORD, and he will give you the desires of your heart."

Jeremiah 29:11 – "For I know the plans I have for you, declares the LORD, plans for welfare and not for evil, to give you a future and a hope."

In the end, my intention to break any generational curses for my children, my grandchildren, and myself will come to pass by God's mercy and grace. And to my surprise, God gave me an amazing gift when I had the privilege to present the gospel to both my grandfather and grandmother on separate occasions. And, yes, they both accepted Jesus as their Savior before they died. Wow!

I cannot tell you these feelings of insecurity, unworthiness, abandonment, and rejection don't creep up on me, because they still try to in various forms and through people, especially some who I dearly love. But, knowing and believing God's Word is what compels me to walk in His truth about me! God has called us for such a time as this to live holy and surrendered lives unto Him.

> *Romans 12:2 – "Do not conform to the pattern of this world, but be transformed by the renewing of your mind. Then you will be able to test and approve what God's will is – his good, pleasing, and perfect will."*

> *Philippians 3:12-14 – "Not that I have already obtained all this, or have already arrived at my goal, but I press on to take hold of that for which Christ Jesus took hold of me."*

Brothers and sisters, I do not consider myself yet to have taken hold of it. But, one thing I do: Forgetting what is behind and straining toward what is ahead, I press on toward the goal to win the prize for which God has called me heavenward in Christ Jesus.

Today, I am a simple woman who walks by the grace of God, imperfectly with a perfect God. My heart is to serve, love, and show those who are in need of knowing the heart and character of God, His great love, mercy, and forgiveness.

. . . .

COMPASSION
Kimberly Ann Hobbs

Compassion is our human disposition that fuels acts of kindness and mercy. It's a form of love, and it ignites within us when we are confronted with those who suffer and are vulnerable. Compassion will often produce action to alleviate the suffering another person may be feeling, but compassion is not an act that flows freely from everyone.

If we are followers of Christ, we learn about compassion through example. The scriptures show us and exhort us to make compassion an integral part of our lives. *(Colossians 3:12 and Zephaniah 7:9)* But, our clumsy attempts to please God and our works of religion are truly unable to make us holy or come anywhere close to His holiness. God is so kind and compassionate and gracious with all who receive His Son, Jesus Christ, He provided for us the way.

Compassion is evident of God's very being. *"The Lord, the Lord, the compassionate and gracious God." (Exodus 34:6)* Compassion begins with God. Echoes of God's compassion are found throughout His Word.

It is God's compassion we should long for when we need to be consoled. We should find it essential and reproduce it in our lives toward others. God's compassion never fails. *(Lamentations 3:22)* He will never let go, never turn away, and He will always see you through. When we are hurting and feeling alone, rejected, abandoned, or despised, the Lord God will comfort His people and have compassion on the afflicted ones. What a comforting thought to know the God of our galaxies, Creator of the universe, wants to comfort each of us.

"But you, Lord, are a compassionate and gracious God, slow to anger, abounding in love and faithfulness." (Psalms 86:15)

God walks beside us and bears our suffering. He is with us and He is for us! We should want the world to know what it means to be loved by God. We can do this, but not by showing how strong we are. Instead, show them how weak we are, and then show them God's strength, God's mercy, and God's compassion. It's not in waiting; it's in doing. It's not in watching; it's in helping. It's not in leaving one alone; it's drawing others to be together.

God's love motivates us to love one another and show compassion just as He shows us. *(Psalm 116:5)* He was so kind, so gracious to me. Because of His compassion toward me, He made everything right and restored me. How wonderful to know where to go for our compassion, God.

* *

Catherine Hamilton loves the Lord and strives to serve Him with purpose in work and ministry as the Outreach Team Leader in the Global Office of Women World Leaders and as President of Two Sisters Compassion Project. Both organizations encourage and support women in gaining confidence and reaching for their purpose in the Lord. She also works as a financial coach, educating others in responsible stewardship.

Catherine is the mother of four grown children, which she home-schooled, and they inherited her love of world culture, family history, and living with passion and purpose through Christ. She lives in South Florida and enjoys her time at the beach and anything on, in, or around the water.

Mercy: He Hears Our Cries
Catherine Hamilton

The word was whispered in the school bathrooms and at sleepovers again and again. Abortion. We all knew someone who'd had one, but I never thought it would be me. However, when I was fifteen years old, I became pregnant while on "the pill." I was in frozen, silent shock. This was before home pregnancy tests existed. So, I hoped I was just late. As that became less and less likely, I had to face facts and find a family planning clinic to confirm my worst fears and find out the truth. The very hard truth.

In all honesty, I have to say it was not a baby to me at that point. It was an inconvenience that could get me thrown out of my home, and I would become the laughingstock of my school. I would be homeless and a high school dropout – the first in our nice mid-dle-class neighborhood. I don't remember any options being discussed between the two of us, and as far as I knew, God was not in the mix. Oh, I prayed, but I didn't know I was supposed to listen for God. I didn't give this crisis to the Lord and leave it with Him.

I was ignorant, so I didn't realize the clinic I found in the Yellow Pages was a pro-life facility. The woman who met with me was a Christian, and she would gently counsel me to have the baby despite me not having any resources that would allow me to care for a baby's needs. Like Proverbs 12:15 states, "Fools think their own way is right, but the wise listen to others," and sadly, I ignored her. I didn't believe I was good enough for God to care about or spend His time on me. Nobody ever explained to me that "God proves His love for us by the fact that the Messiah died for us while we were still sinners, Christ died for us." (Romans 5:8 HCSB) I just knew it needed to be over, and any nervousness I felt was about getting caught and possibly having an excruciating procedure. I received not a nudge from the Holy Spirit, whom I would not know for many years yet. So, my boyfriend got the money, and we went. Quietly.

My boyfriend borrowed money from a friend, a parent in my neighborhood. That same man told him where to make the appointment. I remember thinking, why is this man friends with my boyfriend, and why does he know anything about this? Did he take his daughter? Would he urge his son to do the same thing if he was in our shoes? Later, I thought, why didn't our parents teach us anything about this before it got to the point of having the "cool dad" telling us where to get an abortion?

I remember the dread and anxiousness leading up to the day – lying to my mother, hiding my sickening secret, just wanting it to be over. So many emotions and visceral physical sensations went through me on that seemingly long car ride. It was all I could do not to groan and cry out loud. When we arrived, and I stopped staring at my hands in my lap, I looked up to see the twin buildings that housed my family's dentist's office. No way! I couldn't go in there! Somebody might see me, and they were friends of my parents. At this point, I was starting to get extremely anxious, and my boyfriend had to coax me out of the passenger seat.

We walked through the parking lot toward the closest building where both my dentist and the doctor I would be seeing were housed. Oh, joy! And better still, there were news crews outside, which it took me a minute to realize were there for the protesters who were yelling angrily and waving big graphic posters against abortion. I remember being horrified and so afraid that we'd end up on the local news or someone I knew would see us in the building. I believed the pictures of various stages of fetal development on the signs were fake, and I hated those awful people yelling horrible things at us, judging us – two scared teenagers. Walk a mile, I thought as we skulked past them all, never knowing that God was waving stop signs and red flags in my face.

We walked in together and sat looking at magazines without talking. When I was called back, and for the rest of the procedure, I was alone. A damaged child from years of horrifying events, I appeared hard and older. I had grown up too fast. I was too old to cry, to admit fear, to even ask questions. I just nodded my head as I went from one area to another in the medical office. There was no ultrasound. There was no counseling. There was no warmth. I recall the abortionist being gruff, and I felt very alone and humiliated in that sterile room, and then relief when it was over. I ashamedly must admit that I was thrilled to be done with it and out of there once I was able to leave.

My boyfriend was coming in the front door as I entered the waiting room from the office. I could see he'd been crying. He still had tears in his eyes, and his face was red. He looked at me with such bewilderment that I was smiling slightly and seemed fine. I was ready to leave and get something to eat finally after barely eating anything for weeks. There was pain, but I knew it was temporary as opposed to going forward with the pregnancy. I couldn't even imagine the pain of labor and delivery. And what if I had decided on adoption? I still would've been homeless and alone and then giving up this little person who had turned my life upside down. No way! That pain would have been too much to bear, I thought selfishly. I look back now and think, that poor girl had no idea that she added another layer of trauma that she would have to dig through one day to find real healing from that appalling act.

This pain was buried with many other acts and events that preceded it and came after. I didn't realize how everything was connected until decades later. I didn't know there was help then or after. And even though I wasn't the only one and knew of others who had an abortion, I felt isolated and alone. I didn't have any idea that, according to an article by Life News, the National Right to Life Committee (NRLC) sited, "there are more than 3,300 abortions daily and 137 abortions per hour every hour in the United States. Translated another way, an abortion is done about every 30 seconds in the United States." But, because I didn't understand the horrible reality, I walked brazenly through that dark door. As Billy Graham once stated, "You may be one of a crowd now, but the day is coming when every person must stand alone before Almighty God and be judged. That will be the climax of all the loneliness of earth for you and just a preview of the loneliness of hell."

Of course, I thought I was already in hell on earth. What stuck in my mind was the older woman in the recovery room with me. She was probably in her 30's and beautiful but so miserable. I couldn't fathom why a woman her age would need or want an abortion. She stayed planted in my mind's eye all these years. Looking back, I know now age doesn't matter. She was in her own hell and searching for her own escape just as I had been. She had no spiritual maturity either, and neither of us found our escape in that place. I didn't know at the time, but Jesus said, "Truly, truly, I say to you, everyone who commits sin is a slave to sin." (John 8:34, ESV) And so it continued.

When I was twenty-four and dating the man I would soon marry, I again became pregnant while using another form of birth control known as "the sponge." By this time, I had one child delivered during what was a very distressing birth. I had no intention of going through anything like that – or putting another child through anything like that – again. Yes, I was quite the martyr.

> *"Do nothing out of rivalry or conceit, but in humility consider others as more important than yourselves." (Philippians 2:3-4, HCSB)*

Everyone should look out not only for his/her interests but also for the interests of others. I still had not fully learned to do that yet, although I did know what it felt like to have life grow inside of me, of bringing that life forward into the world, and then being responsible for this tiny beautiful person. I still didn't know Jesus and did not believe God had ever heard my cries or been there for me. I didn't believe He cared about me at all. I didn't realize He had saved my daughter, and as I became more responsible, He kept me from my self-destructive behaviors. But, here I was again, and sadly, He didn't factor into this decision any more than the first time this happened when I was a teenager. I was so oblivious to His truth!

I went to my boyfriend and told him through tears that I was pregnant. I laid crying in the crook of his arm while he said nothing.

I said I would go the following weekend to have an abortion. I don't recall him saying anything at all. I could not imagine being a single mother of two, as I was still afraid, foolish, and making my interests a priority, opposing Philippians 2:21.

I found a clinic, and this time, my best friend went with me. As we drove up, we could see people holding signs and blocking the entrance to the parking lot. I shut down; I completely froze. "No, no! I can't!" I said, panicking over what to do. If I had known Christ, I would have seen this as a clear sign and given the situation to God right then and there, trusting that He would've taken care of me, my toddler, and this new life growing inside me. However, that wasn't the case. I was on my own, or so I believed.

We returned the following week, and this time, the path was seemingly clear. I was able to block the protesters out as if I had blinders on, and I went in. I honestly cannot tell you where it was located or what the building looked like outside or inside. I don't remember the people there. However, I do remember some aspects of the procedure itself: the cold room; the hard, steel instruments scraping against each other on the surgical table right before they were inserted inside of me; the pulling and tugging pressure; the sounds of the equipment whirring. Me, seemingly so small and insignificant with no voice, wanting to stop it. The words, a shout behind closed lips, and tears trailing from my eyes and slowly down my temples, soaking my hair. Then there were the words of the abortionist that have stayed with me from that day, calling it a "he" and approximating him to be a 12-week-old fetus. Frozen shock stopped my breath. My eyes darted wildly back and forth. Too late! Those posters flashed before me, and I realized those photos waving in my face had been real. Then there was a sense of plunging downward into an abyss while calling out, "Oh, God, what have I done?" There was no relief. I was utterly alone, and it was done.

For all of those who travel the pathway of sin, there is an engulfing pall of night that isolates them from all good and true fellowship. Sin always has been darkness. Sin always will be darkness. Judas was lonely because of his sin.

"There are thousands of lonely people in the city and in the country, who carry heavy and difficult burdens of grief, anxiety, pain and disappointment; but the loneliest soul of all is the man or woman whose life is steeped in sin." – Billy Graham

I held this deep, dark secret for years, not knowing that "whoever calls on the name of the Lord shall be saved." (Romans 10:13) But, in His timing, we gave our hearts to Jesus. He showed us his infinite mercy and forgave us of our sins. It was a tumultuous marriage at times, and while we agreed we were meant to serve and build a ministry, we did not agree on sharing our very personal stories of sin and redemption. I have always believed our testimony is to be shared to help others, and keeping sins a secret caused me to become physically, emotionally, and spiritually ill, because as David said in Psalm 32:3-4, "When I kept silent, my bones became brittle from my groaning all day long. For day and night Your hand was heavy on me; my strength was drained as in the summer's heat."

After twenty-five years of marriage and a bitter divorce, God has brought me to this point of sharing this portion of my story to help those who are considering abortion. Know it is not a quick fix. There are also lifelong ramifications to this and any sinful choices regarding physical and spiritual health, future relationships, and your walk with God. For those who have experienced this, know that God forgives all sin when asked from a humble, sincere heart. He loves you and wants you to rejoice in your salvation and redemption today!

> "But if we confess our sins to God, he will keep his promise and do what is right: He will forgive us our sins and purify us from all our wrongdoing." (1 John 1:9, Good News Translation)

I pray that you understand this is not a coincidence that this book is in your hands, and you're in this chapter on this page. I pray that whatever your situation, you acknowledge your sin to the Lord and not conceal your iniquity, and as you confess your transgressions to the Lord, He will forgive the guilt of sin as promised in Psalm 32:5. I pray we can all be more empathetic toward women who've had abortions – or are bound by some other sin – and understand that God is our judge, not each other. I pray many more will find God's grace and healing from their past misguided decisions, whether it be abortion or some other sin for which they have not sought forgiveness or forgiven themselves. There is no end to God's mercy. Sin loses all power over us once confessed! (Psalm 6:9)

God saw me safely through these decisions, forgave me, showed me much grace and mercy, made me a mother four times over, and gave me such a heart for my children, single mothers, and women who've lived alone and apart from God because they believe they are unforgivable. Somewhere deep inside, I knew hope and longed to be set free but was kept quiet by fear. No longer! God wants women to speak up and help others and help the unborn. We cannot stay silent anymore. God commands us, "Don't participate in the fruitless works of darkness, but instead expose them." (Ephesians 5:11)

Nothing in my past, present, or future can ever take me from the love of God.

"And from His fullness, we have all received grace upon grace." *(John 1:16)*

He has plans and a purpose, and I am seeking Him with my whole heart and surrendering everything to Him every minute of every day. He has found me, and He will never leave me or forsake me (Deuteronomy 31:8), no matter what I've done. And He seeks you. He waits for you with all the mercy and grace and forgiveness any good father would want to bestow on His child.

"Praise be to the LORD, for he has heard my cry for mercy." *(Psalm 28:6)*

Ask Him. He and all the saints will rejoice in your surrender and salvation and forgiveness and redemption. Give it to Him.

"Yet, Lord my God, give attention to your servant's prayer and his plea for mercy. Hear the cry and the prayer that your servant is praying in your presence." (2 Chronicles 6:19)

Free yourself. Accept His unconditional love and be victorious! Experience the triumph that awaits you in His arms.

"For I know the plans I have for you," declares the LORD, "plans to prosper you and not to harm you, plans to give you hope and a future. Then you will call on me and come and pray to me, and I will listen to you. You will seek me and find me when you seek me with all your heart." (Jeremiah 29:11-13)

https://www.lifenews.com/2012/01/23/54559615-abortions-since-roe-vs-wade-decision-in-1973/

Indented quotes from Billy Graham: "The Despair of Loneliness: A Classic Message from Billy Graham" January 31, 2017, Billy Graham Evangelistic Association; billygraham.org

MERCY

Kimberly Ann Hobbs

Mercy is God's gift to the repentant heart. We can see this throughout scriptures. "You, Lord, are forgiving and good, abounding in love to all who call to you." (Psalm 86:5, NIV)

Mercy, as described in the dictionary, is compassion or forgiveness shown towards someone whom it is within one's power to punish or harm.

As we look to God and His Word, we see our natural tendencies are to act in sinful, selfish ways. It is only with a transformed heart that we can truly be merciful to another. Mercy is a word that feels compassion. Mercy is kindness, forgiveness, and empathy. Mercy chooses not to be offended and compassionately sees the hurting heart.

God's mercy is reflected in the cross of Christ, a direct reflection of His love for us. How often do we mess up, making painful mistakes that bring hurt or harm to ourselves and others and God? Because of God's mercy, it is reflected in the cross of His Son, and we see a direct reflection of His love for us. How beautiful is this? He extends mercy to the repentant heart because of His love for us. It's undeserved; we did nothing to earn it. It's a direct act of kindness and compassion from a God who loves us unconditionally. Mercy is a characteristic of the one true God.

Because God is love and his mercies endure eternally, we can show His love through our lives and be merciful toward others. This act of love can bring joy to their hearts as well as ours. When we choose to submit to God's merciful ways, we choose to acknowledge peace. This is something we can't do without God.

Mercy is mentioned hundreds of times in various forms throughout God's Word, but because of mercy within God's Word, it allows us to experience love, forgiveness, compassion, peace, and joy, whether we deserve it or not.

"Let us then with confidence draw near to the throne of grace, that we may receive mercy and find grace to help in our time of need." (Hebrews 4:16)

Since we have received mercy from God, we are called to be merciful in all things and to all people. Mercy cannot save someone. Only God can, and God's mercy must be shared through His Word.

. . . .

Michelle Redden is the founder of Mae Dae Mentoring. She is an established international life coach and mentor, using Quantum Biofeedback to help her clients create new patterns in their brains and lives. She has managed multiple million dollars business in many different industries which she uses to guide her clients in business growth. She has extensive experience with personal and spiritual growth.

Michelle has been a guest on the radio show All in for Jesus WFYL1180 AM. She has a passion for helping people to grow. She is married to her husband Donald. His career has provided many opportunities for them to live in multiple states.

World Beliefs ~ Kingdom Truths

Michelle Redden

The world has a way of burrowing false belief systems into your soul without you even knowing. Satan has the world believing he is not real and can't have an effect on your daily life. He uses deception to lay the groundwork for false belief systems. One particular false belief is that men have authority over women, and they can treat us how they want, and we should tolerate whatever they do. There are two lies in this statement. One, not all men use their authority in that way. The other false belief is that we must tolerate their treatment and don't have the right to stop the men who are misusing their authority.

Another falsity I was taught was in my 6th grade sex-ed class was to "practice" safe sex, which meant to use a condom. What the educators failed to explain was that when you have sex with someone for the first time, you are making a blood covenant with that person. (The hymen is the blood membrane that is penetrated by the penis.) This is the most important part of sex, and it is not mentioned. So, the energies/spirits of the person who you are having sex with possesses can penetrate you, which means you have opened the door for Satan to attack you. They were hypervigilant about safe sex practices, which is deceptive. Because they are using the word "safe", it is insinuating that sex outside of marriage is safe. To use the word "safe" in context with sex is deceptive to the children who are hearing this. It should be called "protection from sexual disease". That would be more accurate. And since they did not address the spiritual or emotional effects of sex outside of marriage, that is also deceptive. Even if it is not your first time, every time you have sex with a person – willingly or unwillingly – you are becoming one with that person, which means you are now energetically connected. You are making a covenant with the person, and whatever energies or spirits they have now have access to you. When a person doesn't give the other person permission to have sex with them, and they do it anyway, it causes trauma. It's why sexual assault is so damaging. They have spiritually injured you.

My story starts in Florida. I was happy with my career and my life. The only other thing I wanted was to have a husband and a family. I had just bought a house and felt like I was in a good place. I walked every morning before work with a woman in my development, and she wanted to introduce me to her new neighbor. Thinking she was a smart, wise woman, I trusted her judgement. I decided to give him a shot and go out with him. We dated for a few months. We weren't together all the time and didn't spend long periods together. I don't remember exactly how many times we went out, maybe five or six times. He was about ten years my senior and owned a successful business in our town, so I assumed he was a mature man and a good guy.

After having some dates, he sat me down and expressed that he just wanted to be friends. He said he thought I was too good of a person for him, and I flippantly replied, "Yeah, okay. Whatever." He said I had too many morals, which I thought meant I was ugly. A few days later, he called and invited me to hang out with him at the beach for the day, and I accepted. Of course, at that point, I thought he only wanted to be my friend. I assumed he was not attracted to me, so I never thought he was entertaining the idea of having sex with me. And I'm not sure he was thinking of sex when he called me. There was no indication whatsoever that he sexually wanted me. We didn't even talk or joke about sex on the way to the beach.

We arrived at the beach, and it was sunny and beautiful. My happy place has always been on the beach. While at the beach, I was so relaxed getting some sun and enjoying the water. I am usually tan more on the front of me than on my back, so I decided to lie on my stomach to even out my tan. As I lay on my belly, I started to doze off, and then he just penetrated me. By the time I realized what was happening, it was over.

I struggled with calling it rape. However, when I looked up the definition, Merriam-Webster Dictionary defines rape as any unlawful sexual activity, usually intercourse, carried out forcibly or under threat of injury against a person's will or with a person who is beneath a certain age or incapable of valid consent because of mental illness, mental deficiency, intoxication, unconsciousness, or deception. Because it was not violent, I was not sure if he had raped me, but I did not give him permission. He was acting deceptively, and I hadn't had the opportunity to say no.

I was so shocked and confused that I jumped up, looked around, and then started swiftly walking to my vehicle. He followed and jumped in my car. I was shaken up, so I didn't speak. I was trying to figure out what I had done wrong. I was angry with myself for not seeing it was something that could happen. I kept questioning myself as to did it really happen or was I dreaming. I could not rationalize what had happened because I was traumatized. So, I pushed it down inside of me.

After arriving home, I ignored what happened. My motto when bad things happen to me is, I refuse to let the bad take control of me. So, I thought by ignoring it that I had dealt with it. I did not understand that trauma has to be processed. I refused to let a negative situation hold me back. I felt if I did not let my brain go over the bad things that happened to me, then I had processed it.

About three weeks later, I started experiencing intense pain in my lower abdomen and groin area. It was so intense that I decided to go to the doctor, and they took a pregnancy test. The results were positive, and the symptoms indicated I might have an ectopic pregnancy. At that point, I was scared but excited at the same time. Not knowing what to do, I called my brother. He is a kind and gentle man, and he told me that whatever I decided to do, he would support me in any way that he can. He ended the call by saying he loved me. He gave me great comfort in a time when I felt alone.

After doing an ultrasound, they found out that it was not an ectopic pregnancy. So, at that point, I decided I wanted to keep the baby, and I called the man to tell him the news. He flew into a rage, which immediately scared me. At that point in life, I had not realized people use anger as a way of controlling the people around them. He had some influence in the community, which could have affected my career at the time. He also told me that if I decided to have the baby, not only would he deny it, but he would come after us, and I believed him. He wanted me to have an abortion. This, of course, terrified me. At the same time, my daily career life consisted of thirteen-hour days, and after a few weeks of battling with him, I was exhausted and afraid. So, I decided to have an abortion.

Since I had gone to Planned Parenthood from sixteen years old to the age of thirty for exams and birth control, I was exposed to information and more false beliefs. The world said if the baby didn't have a heartbeat, it was not murder. I also believed if the baby did not have a pulse, then it did not have a soul attached. Also, how many times have we heard it's our body and our choice? Those were more false beliefs that burrowed into my soul.

Once I decided to have an abortion, I shut my feelings off. Therefore, I did not have any emotions while driving to the clinic, which was set up like a typical doctor's office. The atmosphere was relaxed. When I came out of the anesthesia, the spirit of the child came to me. It was a baby boy. He came to my right shoulder and whispered, "It's okay, Mommy. I forgive you." It completely crushed my soul. I kept saying sorry while looking up to see if the nurses and doctor had heard what I heard. They must have because they were emotional; some were even tearful. After they left the room to gather their composure, the room was empty as I went back under the influence of the anesthesia.

The next thing I remember is being at home feeling nothing. I was numb. I remember having a conversation with myself, saying I know I should feel something but don't. My neighbor and good friend, Angie, came over. When I told her what I had done, she showed compassion.

I shut my feelings down until years later when I could not keep it inside. The pain of what I had done was eating at my soul. I had no idea how to stop the pain and thoughts. Most of the time, I would tell myself how worthless I was and how I couldn't forgive myself. Other times, I would try to justify it was better the baby did not have to live in this horrible world. It caused me to shut my heart off. I felt like I could not connect to people properly anymore. I did not trust people and what they said. I was suspicious of all people and their motives. I also wanted desperately for someone to love me.

At this point, I was working at an acupuncture office, and on this particular day, it was extremely difficult for me. I went to lunch and could not stop crying. While sitting in my car, I said out loud, "God, I broke one of the ten commandments, so I guess this is what I have to deal with. I hear people say that You help them, but I don't know if You are real." After that talk with God, I gathered my composure and went back to work.

The doctor who I worked for said she wanted to do a treatment on me, and I agreed to it. She put the needles in and walked out of the room. When she left, a cloud figure in the shape of a gigantic person came out of the ceiling, and I knew it was God. He had my baby with him, and He pulled me from my body to them. We all embraced for what felt like a moment. I have never experienced love with no conditions until that moment. He came to forgive me and wanted to relieve the pain I was carrying. It was unimaginable to me what true love felt like, but at that moment, I was feeling it. Once God was finished, He put me back in my body. Then, the doctor entered the room. She was excited and crying at the same time.

"What are you crying about?" I asked her.

"God was here," she replied.

"How do you know?" I questioned.

"Because a cloud figure embraced me and said not to come into the room because He was having a conversation with you," she told me. "God said that He would tell me when He was finished."

Of course, I thought about this meeting for about a year and was amazed at how God is real. Time passed, and a year later, I was driving down route 78 in Pennsylvania, when I heard a voice say, "Today is the day."

After looking around the car and seeing no one, I said, "Today is the day for what?"

God replied, "Today is the day you will accept my Son as Lord and Savior."

"I don't know how to do that," I said. Then He instructed me to turn the radio on. So, I did, and the minister said if anyone wanted to accept Jesus as their Lord and Savior to say Romans 10:9-10: *"If you declare with your mouth, "Jesus is Lord," and believe in your heart that God raised him from the dead, you will be saved. For it is with your heart that you believe and are justified, and it is with your mouth that you profess your faith and are saved."* I immediately pulled over and cried for a while.

A few days later, I was digging in a closet, but I didn't know what I was looking for. When my husband asked what I was doing, I told him, "I'm not sure what I am looking for, but I can't stop looking." Then, all of a sudden, there it was – a Bible. I got it out and started to read it. I had never read the Bible before. I only knew what was told to me the times I went to church as a child. I began to ask God questions, and He answered me. This process lasted for three years.

Jesus started to deal with my broken heart. He revealed to me that He was the healer of the heart. So, every day, I prayed, "Jesus, please heal my heart." Jesus let me know it would come with pain and lots of crying, which would help me process the traumas of my past. I have a cross above my bed that depicts Jesus being crucified. One night, I had a dream that I was talking to my husband, who was standing across from me. Behind him, I noticed a life-size cross like the one in my bedroom, but Jesus was not on it. Just then, a man, who was dressed as a contractor, walked in between my husband and me, and when I looked at him, we made eye contact. Instantly, I knew it was Jesus.

Jesus did not speak. He looked at my husband and me with love in his eyes. I heard a deep voice from above (God) say to Jesus, "Will you die for her?" Jesus nodded his head. Then God said, "She will have an abortion, drink, and behave ungodly."

Jesus still replied that He would die for me. At that moment, it felt like it was actually happening. It did not seem like a dream anymore; it felt and looked real. Jesus climbed up on the cross and was crucified in front of me. I sobbed hard because I now had a better understanding of what He did for us. He WANTS to forgive us. He wants us to run to Him so that He can take the pain of our mistakes. God is a forgiving Father, Abba.

Sometimes we don't realize the false belief systems we believe until we have made a mistake. That is the exact reason I am writing this. There are thousands of women who don't know if they can be forgiven for abortions or other sins. YES, you can! Jesus is willing and waiting for you. Isaiah 43:25 says, *"I alone am he who blots out your transgressions, for my sake and remembers your sins no more."* This is what Jesus died for – us! God's love for us is not conditional, like some of our family and friends display to us. I can tell you firsthand that He loves us and wants to spend his eternal life with us.

Since God presented himself to me, and I started reading the Bible, my life has changed. He has shown me that all I need is to come to Him and say I need His help. He reveals the lies that we believe about ourselves, the world, and Him. He cleans us up from the inside out. Jesus repairs our hearts, and then we are not to continue sinning because he teaches us how to love ourselves through Him loving us. He is real, and He is waiting for us to come to Him. His love takes away the torment from our emotions and thoughts. In Acts 10:34, Peter says, *"I now realize how true it is that God does not show favoritism."* That means He does not show favoritism to ANYONE.

Romans 10:13 says, *"Everyone who calls on the name of the Lord will be saved."* See, that is what I did. I called His name, and He came to me – to help me receive what Jesus did on the cross, to bring me forgiveness. As you finish reading this chapter, I want you to know that no matter what you have done, Jesus is waiting for you. You can be forgiven, and God LOVES you. It is why you're reading this. He is asking you to receive Him. He's just waiting for you to call out to Him.

. . . .

REDEEMED
Kimberly Ann Hobbs

When life gets hard, we tend to say we need a break, but what we need is to be redeemed. Redemption is the promise of God to deliver us from the power and presence of sin. The Bible envisions a day when broken relationships will be forever restored, and tears will be eternally wiped away. What a day of triumph that will be!

If you belong to God, He encircles each one of His saints and claims us as His very own. We are unique in that we belong only to Him. Uniquely His, we are monopolized by God, taken to Himself by grace and through faith, and surrounded by His love.

God is a loving God. God is a forgiving God. He sent his son, who is the image of the invisible God – the firstborn over all creation to be our rescuer and redeemer. (Colossians 1:15)

God wants to make His presence known in your life, but He needs you to open your heart so you can hear from Him. He wants to redeem you and rescue you from the dominion of lurking darkness in your life. (Colossians 1:13-14)

You may have the hauntings of past mistakes embedded in your thoughts, or hurts that are a result of inflicted behavior from another, or the damage of your mortal bodies from breakdown or decay due to various causes. Whatever the reason, redemption is yours for the taking. Your bondage has been bought with Christ's blood and life.

> *"Christ saves us neither by the mere exercise of power, nor by any subjective influence on his people, whether natural or mystical, but as a satisfaction to divine justice, as an expiation for sin, and as a ransom from the curse and authority of the law, thus reconciling us to God by making it consistent with His perfection to exercise mercy towards sinners." (Thompson Nelson Bible Dictionary)*

The payment made for our hurts, our mistakes, our decay, our sin all comes from Christ, who shed His blood for us.

> *"...who gave himself for us to redeem us from all wickedness and to purify for himself a people that are his very own, eager to do what is good." (Titus 2:14, NIV)*

We have hope because God himself promised to redeem all of creation. Redemption involves deliverance from bondage based on the payment of price from the redeemer, Jesus Christ. Whatever bondage is holding you and suppressing you from being fully alive in your life, surrender it to the Savior. He will cover you and return you from your alienation back toward God! (Romans 4:25) Only the atoning death of Jesus Christ can genuinely liberate and bring you to a life of freedom. Respond to God's grace in your life, and open your heart to the One who loves you most.

* *

Cate Heck grew up in a loving Christian home in Southern California and is close to her extended family. She is married to Wayne Heck and they reside in Newport Beach. They have one beautiful daughter, a wonderful son-in-law, and two precious grandsons, the loves of their lives. After college, Cate taught junior high and high school at Christian schools in Orange County and loved every minute of it. Her passion for children and theater led to co-founding Camp Broadway, a children's summer theater program. For eight years she was the artistic director and choreographer. Additionally, the Hecks are entrepreneurs who have established several successful businesses in Orange County.

Cate has a heart for the Lord, prayer, and for encouraging and serving others. She is especially passionate about Kerus Global Education, founded by her two dear friends, with a mission to advance faith based public health initiatives in underdeveloped countries. As a board member, Cate raises funds for annual Kerus events in California and has traveled several times to South Africa to uplift the vulnerable children at the Kerus Orphan Care Center. Traveling, beach days, Broadway shows, entertaining, and spending time with family and friends are among Cate's favorite things. A day with her is filled with good conversation, lots of laughter, and planning new adventures.

The Prodigal
Cate Heck

If you're the mother of a daughter, you have probably dreamed of the day she would walk down the aisle to marry her prince and of the day she gives birth to your first grandchild. I had those beautiful dreams, but my story isn't exactly like a romantic Hallmark movie. Instead, this is the story of a prodigal, the mother of a prodigal, and a story of redemption.

Jeremiah 29:11 says, *"I know the plans I have for you,"* declares the *LORD, "plans to prosper you and not to harm you, plans to give you a hope and a future."* This is our daughter's Life Verse, proclaimed over her when she was very young. I had no idea how much I would cling to that verse in the coming years, and how faithful God would be to bring my family through trials and heartache... to victory!

My husband and I had been happily married for nine years and were busy with our careers. I was a junior high and high school teacher, and he was the owner of ice cream shops and sold residential real estate. In year ten of our marriage, the greatest blessing occurred! I gave birth to a beautiful daughter, Hayley. We were smitten from the moment we saw her! She was a precious little blond, blue-eyed cherub, and the love of our lives. Hayley was an easy baby and such a loving, joyful, spunky child to raise. We were a happy trio and went everywhere together. Just packed her up, and off we went on travels and outings! We loved the Lord and were involved in our church, and Hayley accepted Jesus as her Savior at an early age. She attended a Christian school and entertained us with her love of plays, dance, music, and soccer. We enjoyed family time. Life was sweet; however, it wouldn't remain sweet.

Upon Hayley entering high school, a series of events would spiral into a long season of difficulty and pain. Hayley wanted to attend the local public school with all of her friends after spending her freshman year unhappily at a Christian school where she knew few people. We are advocates of Christian education, so this was a tough spot. She felt we weren't hearing her and was hurt. Consequently, in her sophomore year, we agreed to let her attend the public high school. But, those years would be a challenge beyond anything we could have imagined.

At the new school, Hayley was doing well in her classes, played soccer, and was on the dance team. I was in a "Moms in Touch" prayer group each week, praying for the school and the individual needs of our teens. Things seemed to be going well, but then they took a disastrous turn. Hayley began drinking and partying with her new friends. She soon fell for the wrong guy, who took her down an ungodly path and set her up for years of dysfunction. We were devastated about this relationship and the direction Hayley was going. There were lies and hiding, worry and stress, and trust was broken over and over. My mother's heart was breaking as I watched our beautiful daughter make some poor choices that would dramatically affect her life. We deeply loved her and did all we could to help her. She began seeing a Christian counselor, and a dear pastor friend came alongside our family to support and help us.

All the while, Hayley never missed her church life group and attended the Fellowship of Christian Athletes meetings at her school. She never entirely left the Lord, but she was compromising, living in two different worlds, and those worlds were colliding. There were confusion and rebellion, faith and family. Clearly, a spiritual war was raging in her life. The battle was real, and we were praying and fighting the battle continually.

There were many nights when I found myself pacing upstairs in my home, looking out the window onto the street below while wondering where my precious daughter was. Was she safe? Who was she with? Would she come home? Why was she doing this to herself and us? I often felt like I couldn't take it anymore. I would sob and cry out to God. Sleepless nights seemed to be the norm as I prayed my way through the anguished hours. I felt inadequate as a mother and beat myself up emotionally. But, I knew God didn't condemn me. I knew He heard my cries and my fervent prayers.

I firmly believed this trap of rebellion, brokenness, and confusion did not define who our daughter truly was. This was not her identity or destiny. I was committed to Christ, to see our daughter restored, and I was determined to be there for her no matter what. Throughout her high school years, I never missed a soccer game or a dance performance, and we were always there to support and love her. I prayed for her and with her. In time, there were some areas of progress. Thankfully, Hayley finally broke up with the toxic boyfriend, graduated from high school making the honor roll, and was headed to a Christian college. My husband and I held an affirmation and blessing celebration for her with family and friends and sent her off with high hopes for her college experience.

College consisted of dorm life, academics, friends, football games, and freedom. Hayley had a wonderful guidance counselor who took a special interest in her, and she was applying herself in her classes. On an occasional weekend, she and her college friends would come home for a visit and spend some time at the beach. It was a joy meeting her friends and having her around. But, soon, we learned there was partying going on behind the scenes. Unfortunately, Hayley was kicked off the cheerleading squad after admitting to drinking at a party. She began struggling in her classes. There were apologies and tears, but the behavioral changes weren't lasting.

Problems began to escalate, much to our dismay. On a particular Valentine's weekend, my husband and I were having a romantic overnight getaway at a nearby hotel. During the night, I couldn't sleep because I had a nagging feeling that something was going on at our home. I felt disturbed and had no peace. My husband had fallen asleep, so I drove the short distance home. Sure enough, Hayley was having a party at our house, and the old boyfriend was even there! I broke up the festivities, and the next day, we had a confrontation with her. Again, there were heartfelt apologies, but true repentance wasn't there yet.

Sadly, her freshman year would end in major disappointment. Hayley came back home and felt the embarrassment and pain of it all. She felt like a failure. Once again, in my heart, I knew "failure" was not my daughter's name or her destiny. God's Word was true, and *Jeremiah 29:11* was my constant source of hope.

During the following year at home, Hayley went to the local community college, got a job, and began picking up the pieces of her life. We were still in a loving relationship, and I felt close to my daughter. We spent a lot of time together, did some traveling, and she was still such a devoted family girl. But, the drama wasn't over yet. There would be more partying and more nights of worrying, pacing, and crying out in prayer. Fear would sometimes feel like a death grip on me.

Hayley's life was still in turmoil, with those two worlds battling for her allegiance. My heartbreak was palpable. *Lord, when will this ever end?* My husband and I prayed the scriptures over her and pleaded with God. My beautiful sister, a prayer warrior, who was always there for me, prayed consistently for Hayley and loved her unconditionally. My dear Christian girlfriends prayed fervently and supported me. One friend and I anointed Hayley's entire room with oil as we prayed. I couldn't have gotten through this long journey without them.

One evening, we received one of those telephone calls no parent wants to get. It was from the police station. Hayley had gotten a DUI. Our hearts sank, and so did hers. But, we thanked God that she was safe. She attended the required classes and took responsibility for her actions. Not long after that, at twenty years of age, she was diagnosed with ADHD, and we soon learned of the correlation between ADHD and alcohol issues. She began seeing a new Christian counselor who specialized in ADHD. Although this was a challenging season for her, some significant insights and positive changes came as a result. The counselor was a godly man who poured godly wisdom into her.

Hayley was growing in the Lord and began leading a Bible study with a close girlfriend. She was always one to reach out to her friends, especially to anyone who was hurting, exercising her spiritual gift of mercy. It was wonderful to see these changes and her renewed passion for Jesus. By then, I was involved with Kerus

Global Education, a ministry founded by two amazing girlfriends. Hayley and I were privileged to travel twice to South Africa to uplift the precious children at the Kerus Orphan Care Center. Our lives were dramatically impacted, and so many beautiful things were happening.

Then, Hayley met a new young man. Three months into the relationship, she came to me one afternoon with a serious expression on her face. She sat me down and told me that she was pregnant. I was stunned and devastated. They didn't know each other very well, and he had a history of addiction. Yet, soon, they would be parents together. Hayley wanted our blessing. Although I never rejected my beloved daughter, later that evening, I called my sister and sobbed until there were no more tears. I wish I could say I jumped for joy, but I had been through so much, and my disappointment was deep. It felt as though my hopes and dreams for her were shattered. I was heartsick that she still battled those unhealthy patterns of compromise that led to this "out of sequence" scenario. Even so, we were grateful that she was choosing life, and she was determined to do what was right.

My husband and I came alongside our daughter and baby-to-be. This would be our first grandchild, and we desired to walk in God's love and joy. Family and friends rallied around us, and our Christian counselor traveled this road with us, as well. Hayley remained with her boyfriend, although they didn't marry due to unresolved serious issues.

Excitement about the baby was in the air. There were doctor appointments, baby showers, and nine months seemed to fly by. Soon, a precious baby boy was born, our beloved grandson. We immediately fell in love with our adorable little guy! The baby's father was involved in the first year of his life, but his addictions complicated the relationship between him and Hayley. In the end, she broke up with him, and they spent a long season with no contact.

Hayley was a single, working mom. We were her support team, and having them in our home was a joy and privilege. We grew very close to our little grandson. Hayley was an amazing, devoted, and loving mother, following Jesus without compromise. Today, she has a new life. We are so proud of her and praise God for her transformation! We have a close, beautiful relationship and are eternally grateful to our God.

Our story was like a roller coaster ride with many twists and turns. How did God rescue and redeem my beloved daughter? Hayley's transformation was a long journey. Sadly, as beautiful

as she is and as confident as she appeared, she often felt like a failure with no vision or a sense of purpose for her future. Her Christian life was inconsistent – two steps forward, one step back. When she felt down, she would escape into pleasures for the moment to anesthetize her feelings. Yet, during this entire season, she had powerful times with God, whether at a Christian confer-ence, a Bible study, or when a prophetic word was spoken over her. Always drawn to worship, she would experience His presence and have such a yearning for Jesus. Yet, these spiritual "breakthroughs" seemed temporary, as she was impulsive and drawn back into the world. Admittedly, Hayley was in bondage.

Her counselor warned that she was living outside of God's laws and, therefore, outside of His protection. That put a holy fear into her. Getting pregnant was Hayley's profound wake-up call. It became very real that sin has consequences. There had been many chances and warnings. This time, she did not want to continue disobeying God, but instead, she wanted to honor Him in her life. That's when a genuine breakthrough came.

Hayley sincerely repented and asked God to change her heart and desires. She heard His voice in whispers. Seeking fellowship with believers, she changed her friend group, which took courage. She became connected to the community where she could talk about her real life. Hayley learned to love God sincerely and love herself enough to forgive herself. Recognizing triggers and removing or changing them was also a bold step. One of her triggers was music, and changing what she listened to was highly significant. Leadership in Bible study developed a sense of purpose and a vision for her life. Spending time with God became her priority. These were momentous turning points in her life, and her new practice of spiritual disciplines led to healing, forgiveness, freedom, intimacy with God, and spiritual growth that continues to this day.

How did God heal this mother's heart? What did He show me? I liken my journey to two stories in the Bible. The first is found in *Luke 15: 3-7*, the parable of the shepherd and the one lost sheep.

When I was a little girl, my mother would sing a beautiful song to me called "The Ninety and Nine". I was teary-eyed as she sang the story of the shepherd who left his flock of ninety-nine sheep to look for the one sheep that was lost. The shepherd risked everything to find that little lost one and bring it home. That was my daughter. She belonged to Jesus all along but was lost for a while and faced great danger out there in the darkness. But, the Gentle Shepherd searched relentlessly until he found her. The parable ends, declaring, *"Rejoice with me! I have found my lost sheep! I tell you that in the same way there will be more rejoicing in heaven over one sinner who repents than the ninety-nine righteous persons who do not need to repent."* What extravagant love God has for His sheep!

Isn't this precisely how the father responded to his prodigal son when he returned home from his season of reckless living, squandering his entire inheritance? Scripture tells us that the father ran to his son when he saw him coming toward home. He embraced him, gave him gifts, and then threw a big party for him! In *Luke 15:32*, this grateful father proclaims, "But we had to celebrate and be glad, because this brother of yours was dead and is alive again; he was lost and is found." That is the heart of our God!

I can picture Jesus running to Hayley with open arms when she was returning home! And I felt His strength and joy as I was running with Him to embrace and love my daughter! Oh, how I rejoiced when she was found and came home! Jesus rescued Hayley and forgave every sin, every mistake. He healed every hurt, set her free, and redeemed her entire life. God had been wooing her back the whole time, even when she was running the other way, waiting for His prodigal to return home. And so was I.

As for my heart, when I was in despair and anguish, God met me. He gave me strength when I had none. He wiped away many tears. By faith, I received His love. He helped me endure the trial and gave me hope when I was at my lowest point. The Holy Spirit brought scriptures to mind to encourage me and to use in prayer. He brought loved ones around for support and proved that His Word is alive and does not return void. He never gave up on me, never gave up on Hayley, and He helped me do the same. Surely, God has forgiven me of much, and His glorious, loving-kindness draws me to Him time and time again. He helped me love

Hayley through her most difficult seasons. He is our supernatural God who did supernatural things in us. He ministered to us and through us.

If you are a mother who beats yourself up and feels like you've failed, I have been there. But, there is hope, forgiveness, and healing of hurts and broken hearts. Do not listen to the lies of the enemy who will prey upon you when you are weak and in pain. God is for you, not against you.

If you have a prodigal child, never give up, never stop loving, never stop praying, and know that the seeds of love and faith that you have planted in your child will bear fruit. Never give up on God, for He is our refuge and strength, an ever-present help in times of trouble. Call out to Him and tell Him your worries and fears. Cling to His Word. In times of spiritual battle, recognize who your real enemy is, and remember that the weapons of our warfare are not carnal but mighty through God for the pulling down of strongholds. Pray in the Spirit and pray Scripture over your child. Seek close fellowship for loving support and worship the Lord, listening to uplifting worship music whenever you can. God inhabits the praises of His people, and He will lift you up! I have experienced these powerful truths!

And if you are a prodigal who feels defined by past sins, remember that is a lie. We are not defined by our past, by our sins, or by our failures. There is always hope. You are forgiven, cleansed, and declared righteous by Jesus. Make Him your Lord. He is the Rescuer, Redeemer, and Restorer. His love is unconditional, and His grace amazing! His plans and destiny for you are beautiful. You can be completely set free, for she who is free in the Son is free indeed!

So, what about that Hallmark movie happy ending? It occurred after all! First and foremost, Hayley knows her past does not define her. Rather, she has been delivered and is an overcomer in Christ. She is a daughter of the King, and her destiny is marvelous and is in His hands. She is a woman of God, an excellent mother, and has a successful health and wellness business. God has used Hayley's story to encourage others and has given her the opportunity to counsel other young women who have found themselves pregnant, yet unmarried and choosing life. He has blessed her and has beautifully worked all things together for good in her life. But, there's more!

Nearly four years ago, Hayley met the love of her life, a handsome and godly young man. They dated, fell in love, and committed to purity until marriage. Soon, they had a magical, beautiful wedding in San Jose del Cabo, surrounded by family and friends. Both of them have a redemption story. So, together, they are a shining example of the transforming power of Christ's love. They serve the Lord and are training their children in godliness. Our precious first grandson just turned seven, and we can't imagine life without him and love him dearly. And we now have another adorable little grandson to love who just turned two. They are the most beautiful blessings, and being a grandmother is my greatest joy!

God has done exceedingly abundantly above all we could ask or think. To God be the glory! By His grace, *Jeremiah 29:11* has come full circle. Truly God has given us all a hope and a future. We praise Him for bringing us from tears, to transformation, to triumph!

. . . .

RESCUE

Kimberly Ann Hobbs

There are so many incredible stories in God's Word that speaks to us about rescue. They stir our emotions, and they can be dramatic and exciting at the same time.

Think about Daniel being rescued by God from the mouthwatering lion who wanted to devour him. Think about Jonah who was saved from death inside the belly of a whale after running from God. Then there was Rahab, who was rescued from the falling city of Jericho. What incredible stories God gives us as examples of His mighty rescue. One of the most incredible stories to me is the parable of the lost sheep as told by Jesus, when the Pharisees criticized Him for socializing with sinners. *(Luke 15:3-7)*

The parable begins with a straying sheep. A sheep apart from its Shepherd is defenseless and in grave danger. Jesus views any person apart from Him as lost. How is he lost? His sins alienate him from the Holy God. *(Isaiah 59:9)*

The Shepherd in the story didn't despise His sheep. Quite the contrary, with a heart of compassion, He rescued him. Jesus also values each sinner the Father entrusts to Him. *(John 6:39)* The parable also illustrates Christ's attitude toward the saved sinner. The parable gives no indication of the Shepherd ever rebuking or punishing. Instead, He hoists the sheep on His shoulders and takes him home.

The parable of the lost sheep offers an extraordinary glimpse of heavenly emotions as the Shepherd calls his friends and neighbors saying, "Rejoice with me." The rescue of the lost sheep was a proclamation, and the celebration we can learn from.

Jesus will rescue us as we stand firm in faith just as Daniel did. He will rescue us if we run from Him like Jonah did, and He will transform us from "garbage and dirt" like He did Rahab. But, how beautiful to understand that Jesus is our rescuer. He will leave the ninety-nine other sheep to come and find us and bring us home. It is because of His unconditional love for just one lost sheep that He does this. That's incredible love. That's true forgiveness. Jesus Christ is our rescuer.

 **Eurecka R. Christopher MBA**, is a wife, mother of 3, and an avid participant in her local and international community. Being a first-generation college graduate of her ancestry home of the Bahamas, Eurecka has obtained a double Masters of Science in Accounting and Finance Management.

Eurecka, based on her own personal experience, has dedicated her life to encouraging women who've survived or may be going through domestic/abusive relationships.

Eurecka volunteers through various community organizations, gathering supplies for backpacks in support of women in shelters, working with first-time home buying programs, and credit education and clean up. She has also volunteered with Habitat for humanity, March of Dimes walks, The Trayvonn Martin Foundation, Footprints across Haiti and IPAWs (animal rescue).

Eurecka's life purpose is, "setting up the next generation and putting them in a better position than the last". She strives to break generational curses and set young women in a, "nothing can stop you but you" mentality.

Until You Know My Story...
You Will Never Understand
My Praise

Eurecka R. Christopher

Some people have seen from where God has brought me. They don't understand it and may even be jealous of what they see now.

You don't know my story. You don't know the things I've come through. You cannot imagine the pain and the trials I've had to endure. You don't know my story, the day my eyes were opened and I was set free. You cannot imagine the strongholds and the walls that bound me. In all, God has been faithful to me. My story proves that God can use anyone. Deliverance is my testimony

Let me go back for a second. A Bahamian-born native, I was ten years old when I arrived in Miami, Florida, in early April of 1981 with my mother and brother. Brought up in a Baptist church, my grandmother made sure she gathered all the grandchildren together every Sunday, and she made it her mission that we were in Sunday school. We weren't allowed to miss vacation Bible school during the summer, and we sang in the children's choir along with participating in the church plays and other activities. I was baptized at sixteen and have always been a member of a church body.

Jumping forward to high school, I was astonished that God had not sent me a boyfriend. Graduating high school a virgin, I thought I was a freak. I was good looking enough to at least have a serious boyfriend by then, but that was not the case. Eager to have someone, I entered into a sexual relationship right after graduation with someone who, in all honesty, was more interested in one of my friends. But, I was convinced I could change his mind if I showered him with total adoration. Well, he showered me back with my first son and still moved on to be with my friend, who also had a child with him a year later. Life Lesson #1: You cannot make someone love you.

Life was a struggle for a single mother just shy of turning nineteen years old and trying to raise a child alone with no financial support and working a full-time job. Yet, I was determined to get that college education. I think I saw my baby four hours at night while he slept that first year of his young life. I went to work at 7:00 a.m. and straight to evening classes at 6:00 p.m. I had no transportation, so it took two buses and a train to pick him up from the second babysitter at 11:00 p.m. every night. Eventually, when he was about ten months old, I sent him to the Bahamas to live with my aunts. My family was very supportive as they saw my efforts to rise above my situation.

Thankful that God had provided a way for me to concentrate on my school, I moved to New Jersey to continue my college education, hoping a change of environment would be what I needed to forget the struggles I had endured thus far. My mother had just moved there and raved about how much she loved it there. So, off

I went to New Jersey in the fall of 1989. I registered at Fairleigh Dickinson University as a sophomore and continued my studies. I found another church home and engulfed myself in the choir ministry. From the sidelines, I watched as other young ladies married. I cried over the loneliness, wondering when my time would come. I smiled as I stood as a bridesmaid for some, wishing each a happy life and marriage. I felt maybe I was not good enough or pretty enough. Otherwise, I would be married, right? I had put on some weight after having my son, but I did not think I was too bad at a size 14.

As I neared my 21st birthday, I decided that I needed to move out of my mother's house and find my own place. She made it hard to date guys, as she was very inquisitive like a mother should be. Maybe I should have listened better, but I was headstrong and thought I knew it all. What young lady doesn't think that?

Right before my birthday, I visited the home of one of my high school friends, Patrice Williams, who lived with her mother in a nice two-family house. While I was there, a cousin of hers also stopped by to visit. For my story, I will call him G.P. He was new to the U.S. and showed an interest in me. *Could this be my time?* I thought.

Patrice told me that her landlord had an attic that he had converted to a sleeping space, but it was connected to the upper level of his living quarters on the 2nd floor. She thought maybe he would let me rent the space from him. I did not care about sharing a living area with the family. I only needed a room to rent. But, low and behold, the attic was huge with two nice-sized rooms, two smaller walk-in closet-sized rooms, and a full bath. G.P. went along with us to look at the space, and he let it be known that since he worked in the electrical/construction field, he could convert one small room into a makeshift kitchenette. Then I could use the one room as a living room space even though it had a slanted roofline. He would paint it for me and make it mine. It was practically a full apartment. Oh, the joy I felt that day! God had answered my prayers. I believed it had to be God because it felt so right at the time. The lonely praying girl's prayers had been answered. Looking back on it all now, I believe the Lord gives us the desires of our hearts even when it's not what He desires for us. And I wanted it bad.

G.P. and I had a whirlwind courtship and married five months later. I became pregnant immediately. At that moment, all was wonderful in the world. However, once that ring got on my finger, G.P. became a different person – more controlling and demanding. It seemed like almost overnight, I woke up in a crazed world. I never knew what was going to set him off. It could be a dirty cup left in the sink or his clothes not folded to his liking. Either would result in me getting slapped across the face, although he inflicted most of the abuse on areas of my body where he knew no one would see like my arms, the back of my head, and my back. To this day, I still have a raised scar on my back from when he dragged me across the patio floor while trying to prevent me from leaving the house with our son. A nail dug into my skin from a loose plank board.

During those days, I overate, trying to use food to numb my pain and forget. I gained weight, of course, and that's when the name-calling began. Mumpy was his nickname for me. (In Jamaica, mumpy means fat). Needless to say, my self-esteem plummeted.

G.P. wanted me to drop out of college and be a stay-at-home mom. He wanted lots of babies. I think he thought that would be his way of controlling me. I thank God for giving me the strength to put my feet down on that one. I let him know that he met me while I was attending college, and I was going to finish.

Years later, that college education was my leverage and strength to know that I could take care of myself. It was a struggle. I had to work a full-time job so I could have my own cash, go to school full-time at night, and take three buses home. Sounds familiar, right? Same situation as before, only I was now married and broken. But, God!

I went every Sunday to church, thinking if God brought me to this relationship, He would surely turn it around for me. I just had to remain faithful and believe. G.P. was smart, though. He used the scriptures to control me. One of his favorites was 1 Peter 3:1-6: *"Likewise, wives, be subject to your own husbands, so that even if some do not obey the word, they may be won without a word by the conduct of their wives, when they see your respectful and pure conduct. Do not let your adorning be external—the braiding of hair and the putting on of gold jewelry, or the clothing you wear— but let your adorning be the hidden person of the heart with the imperishable beauty of a gentle and quiet spirit, which in God's sight is very precious. For this is how the holy women who hoped in God used to adorn themselves, by submitting to their own husbands."* Another of his favorites was Colossians 3:18: *"Wives, submit to your husbands, as is fitting in the Lord.* The devil knows the scriptures really well and can quote them just as quickly as you and I. We sometimes forget he is a fallen angel.

I anguished in this living situation for five years. I now weighed about 250 pounds and was afraid to leave, thinking I could not support two sons alone. Then, one day, our four-year-old son tried to slap me. And I tell you, I was shaken to my core. My son, whom I gave birth to and adored to the heavens and back, was doing what he saw his father do to me. I couldn't believe it! I thought I had done such a great job hiding all those episodes from him. I even wore long-sleeved clothing to cover up my bruises. I never thought at his age that he knew what was going on. I promise you that woke me up. I was never going to allow my son to grow up treating me – or any women in his life – that way.

I soul searched and prayed hard for an answer from God. Long nights were spent crying, thinking I was a disobedient daughter for not having faith in Christ and for considering leaving my husband. I wanted the Lord to know I believed in His Word. I wanted Him to know I trusted Him. That I had the faith of a mustard seed and then some. Then, in my studies, I read: *"God is faithful. He will do everything necessary to fulfill his word. (Psalm 37:4)* He gives us this promise: "Delight yourself in the Lord, and he shall and will give you the desires of your heart."

Instantly, it was like a light bulb turned on. God did not want this for me; I did. I had desired this person who I thought was God sent. So, then I studied some more and came across 1 Corinthians 14:33: *"For God is not a God of confusion but of peace."* And my spirit rested. There could not be anything more confusing than this relationship. There was no peace in it, so there was no God. Our souls were unequally yoked. I had to file for divorce. The minute I filed the papers I thought would set me free, I found out I was pregnant with my daughter. I almost hesitated and stayed with G.P. because I didn't know how I would manage with three children. I now weighed 260 pounds and felt no other man would want my baggage.

But, I stuck to my guns. I moved to Florida from New Jersey, and having hit 300 pounds, I started a weight loss program. After a year, I managed to get down to a size 10. By this time, I had already graduated from college. Amen! I found an accounting job with a CPA firm making pretty decent money and a new church home at the same time. I started singing in the choir again and worked many ministries, including working in the church's finance office.

There are many testimonies I can give on other situations that the Lord brought me through. On this day, I am stronger than I know. I have my Lord's favor. I dance for His glory in my church praise and worship ministry, and I share my story with women who need strength. The Lord I now know took me through that lesson because I needed to learn to wait on His time. I had to learn how to be patient. Some lessons are harder than others, but I am getting there. I am stronger; I am wiser. My children are doing well, and we have survived together. I have since remarried. I have reconciled with my God, and I have peace in my heart that no man can take away.

Along this path of sharing my testimony with you, the devil tried to take me out and silence me. I was involved in a serious car accident. My car was totaled, a complete write off on a three-year-old vehicle. But, I walked away unharmed except for the seatbelt mark across my chest. No other car was involved, just me and a solid concrete median. But, God said, "She still has work to do." And so, I receive it! I press forward and do my Father's work. I present myself a living sacrifice to his glory and say, "Yes, Lord!" Sometimes tired, exhausted, and sleepless, from the bottom of my heart to the depths of my soul, I still say, "Yes, Lord!"

· ·

RECONCILIATION
Kimberly Ann Hobbs

All of us have been through rough situations where we have disagreed with another person, can't resolve our differences in a relationship, or our views collide with a friend, which puts us in opposition with them and results in a broken relationship. Most times, we try to go on with making the best of it.

The words "restoration" and "compatible" make up part of the definition of the word reconciliation. However, the root word is conciliation, which means the action of stopping someone from being angry.

God's Word teaches us that we need to make it a priority to reconcile for our spiritual help and wellness as well as others.

> *"If you hold anger in your heart, you're subject to judgement."*
> *(Matthew 5:21-25)*

> *"And in one body to reconcile both of them to God through the cross, by which he put to death their hostility." (Ephesians 2:16, NIV)*

We shouldn't live in an angry state of emotion. It's not healthy. Please don't carry anger in your hearts. Your health is affected as well as the future of your life.

So how do we get beyond anger? Ask God to help you with true forgiveness. The thing about God's POWER is it's in asking Him for it. If we only wait on Him, He will dispense it to us at His will. He wants us to take our problems to Him and seek Him for what we need. Our souls find rest in Him and peace in the midst of our storm. Then, when our anger is subdued, God can work.

We can pray for others at this point. We can ask God to make His presence known in the lives of others. We can ask Him to open their hearts so they can hear from Him. It doesn't mean there will always be an immediate response. Sometimes, it can take days, weeks, months, or even years. Yes, you need to be patient.

Everything that needs to happen in our lives – and in the lives of others involving reconciliation – cannot happen without the POWER and presence of God. This is absolute truth. Prayer invites and ignites both.

When you want true reconciliation with a person, trust God. Go to Him, and ask Him for not only your heart to change but the heart of the other person, as well. It's not just the other person; it's us. Please remember this. If this is important in your heart, then you won't give up!

If you feel the loss of a person in your life and the happiness their relationship brought into your life, I encourage you to take it to God with fervent prayer, which means praying with passion and intensity. We serve a God of triumph! Our God knocks down barriers, our God forgives anger, our God heals hurts, and our God mends brokenness. Our God loves you. Our God wants reconciliation. Please go to Him with your needs.

* *

 **Ping Wang Rawson** is a Chief Financial Officer of a Nasdaq listed company. She has over 18 years of financial, accounting and consulting experience and has served in a variety of leadership and management positions in several publicly traded companies. She is a frequent speaker at business and industry conferences.

Ping holds a Master's in Business Administration, and a Master's in Accounting from the State University of New York at Buffalo. She is a Certified Public Accountant.

Ping loves traveling and outdoor sports. She spends far too much time at her computer. She was born in Beijing, China, and she speaks Mandarin and Cantonese.

Ping is married and resides in South Florida with her husband, where they live on a small parcel of land with their two dogs and a cat: Aslan, Ginger and Cali, as well as their farm animals: sheep, ducks, and chickens. Together they love serving the Lord in volunteer leadership roles in their local church, inspiring people to pursue their relationships with Jesus, and spending time with family and friends.

Surrender –
Scars For Your Glory

Ping Wang Rawson

Leaning against my kitchen counter, Helen was in tears while telling her story to me. She had just broken up with her boyfriend and moved out. My heart was crying for her. I told Helen that she was more than welcome to stay in our spare bedroom since her family was not nearby, and she had no place to stay that night. Looking at this young lady, I could not help but think of my situation fifteen years ago...

It was summer in Buffalo, New York –the best season of the year. However, that summer was an exception for me. It was my last year of graduate school. I was in my first marriage, and we were living at my then parents-in-law's house. Our countless arguments and quarrels eventually led to a big fight that night. My mother-in-law was concerned that he would hurt me if we stayed together in the same room, so I had to move out of the house. In tears, I grabbed some clothes, got in my car, and left. I drove around Buffalo without any destination because I had nowhere to go.

Born and raised in China, I came to the United States to pursue my master's degree in Buffalo, where I met my husband. He was in the same graduate program as me. He was also from China, and he had immigrated with his parents to the U.S. a couple of years before we met. With our similar backgrounds, I believed we would live happily ever after, just like all newlyweds' hope. However, our marriage struggled from the very beginning. I tried everything that I could think of to sustain our marriage; however, fights and arguments were our daily routine. It was bad enough that our neighbor wrote several letters to us, complaining that our loud voices and the sound of us throwing stuff on the floor disturbed their peaceful lives. One time, the police came to inquire about our situation because my husband had kicked me on the school campus. I had never felt so emotionally exhausted and helpless in my life.

I was raised in a family full of my parents' love and believed hard work was the key to a good life. I lived that out in many ways. I always gave one hundred percent in school and at work. Even though I had experienced the loss of my mother due to cancer while I was in college, I was still optimistic about my life. However, my marriage was falling apart, and no matter what I did, nothing worked. My family lived far away in China, and I didn't have any close friends. I felt like life had made a big joke out of me. Once I had a beautiful American Dream, but now, I was homeless in an unfamiliar country.

I finally got hold of a friend who was moving back home for summer break and had only two days left on her apartment lease. She told me there was nothing in the apartment, not even furniture, but I could stay there for a couple of days. I had no other choice since I did not have enough money to stay in a hotel. So, I bought a sleeping bag from Walmart and slept on the floor in the apartment. In the middle of the night, I woke up and could not go back to sleep. While looking around the empty room, darkness overwhelmed me, and I could not breathe. Full of tears, I went outside, running crazily and screaming in downtown Buffalo. I was angry as I asked why was this happening to me. Two years had passed, and I had not yet graduated. Alone in a foreign country, I had no family, no friends, no money, and no job. I had nothing but a broken heart. I had never felt so desperate.

Regardless of how I felt, life continued. I needed to finish school and look for a place to stay. I found an ad where a student was subleasing her furnished bedroom for the summer break. That was perfect for me since I had no furniture, not even any luggage except for a small bag of my clothes. Most of her items were stored away in the closet, except for one book left on the bookshelf – the Holy Bible. I had heard of this book while I was in China. Once, I even borrowed one and read a few chapters, but I gave up as it read like fiction. I'm not sure how, but somehow, I got the idea that the Bible is an encyclopedia of life. Whatever your questions are, you can find the answers in the Bible. This time, I had many questions about my life and was also looking for the key to a successful marriage. How could I have a good marriage? What did I do wrong?

As I started to scan the book, the only answer I found in the Bible was, "Husband, love your wife; and wife, respect your husband." Later, I discovered that it was from *Ephesians 5,* where the Apostle Paul provided instructions for Christian marriage. However, I was not very satisfied with such a simple answer. What did that mean? I think we loved each other, and I did respect my husband. So, how come my marriage didn't work?"

One of my roommates, Charlene, was a Christian. (I now think of her as the little angel that God sent to me.) She saw my struggles and started to make friends with me. She took me to Bible study and student fellowship on Fridays, and also to church service on Sunday. On the very first Sunday after service, she introduced me to the pastor. I didn't remember anything the pastor talked about, except for him asking me if I would like to pray with him. My face was full of tears as I answered yes. I repeated what the pastor said sentence by sentence. Then he asked me, "Where is Jesus?" and I replied, "In my heart." Later, I was told that it was a salvation prayer.

I thanked the girl who subleased her bedroom to me for letting me use her Bible. To my surprise, she was not yet a believer and did not even remember she had left a Bible in her room. Hallelujah! That must have been a gift from God! That is truly a book from Heaven! In my desperation, I found God, the lifter of my head. In my weakness, hope was given by His Spirit. In my darkness, I got to know Jesus, who became my light and savior!

That summer became the turning point of my life. Other than my summer internship, my days were filled with Bible study, fellowship nights, and Sunday worship. My roommate, Charlene, became my best friend. We had long conversations almost every night. I asked her many questions about the Bible and shared my marriage struggles to such an extent that I thought she was probably tired of listening. However, Charlene was always kind and patient with me, no matter how many questions I asked or how late I wanted her company. She always heard me (not just listened to me) and prayed with me. She also recommended a book titled *The Purpose Driven Life* by Rick Warren, which made me start to wonder what God's purpose was for my life. After I finished the book, I still did not know what exactly the plan was that God had for me. However, I felt hope for my life again.

Three months later, I received a job offer from one of the Big Four (world's biggest) public accounting firms. It was one of those dream jobs that every accounting student wanted. Plus, it was in Manhattan, the banking and financial center where I always wanted to be! For a foreign student with no work experience in the United States and who still spoke with an accent, this great job offer was indeed a blessing! It made many of my classmates jealous.

Even though God showed His great mercy to us, my marriage didn't last long. We separated, but God continued to bless me in my transition from school to the workplace, from Buffalo to New York City. In so many ways, I experienced God's love, guidance, and provision. He was my company when I was lonely, my comforter when I was depressed, and my Shepherd when I lost my direction. I was ready to start my new life in a new city. However, deep down in my heart, I still felt shame because of my divorce.

I was raised in a traditional Chinese culture, where divorce was not common and not a good thing. I did not want to talk about my failed marriage to anyone, not even to any church friends. I could not forgive myself for the mistake I made, and I kept asking myself why I was so stupid. I regretted my decision and wished my marriage never happened. At the same time, I still wanted to have a husband, but I was afraid it would not work again. As I tried to figure things out, God started to correct many of my misconceptions and changed my wrong ways of thinking about marriage and relationships:

Me: If we don't try it out and live together first, how can we know if our relationship will work?

God: Be Holy because I am Holy! Obey My commands, because it's all about My blessings for your marriage.

As a new believer, I did not understand why God put so many rules, laws, and commands in the Bible. Plus, many things were the opposite of the trend of our culture, such as keeping pure before marriage. I felt like there were restrictions everywhere. I was so frustrated when I could not live up to His standards and do what He said to do. It reminded me of what my mother always said when she was disciplining me as a little girl. *"You will understand and thank me for my discipline once you are a grownup."* God is like our parents. Only when we grow up and become mature in His Spirit will we start to understand His heart and His love for us. What seemed like a restriction to me was actually a protection for me, because He wanted to protect me from dangerous situations and keep me from being hurt. So many times, I got involved too early physically in a relationship, holding unrealistic hope that this time would be true love and things would work.

A pastor's testimony about his no-sex-before-marriage experience was an "Aha moment" for me. I finally got it! Obedience wasn't about what we should do or shouldn't do, but rather, it was all about His blessings that He wanted to give to us. Many times, when I was struggling with temptation, I heard His voice loud and clear: *"Be holy because I am holy."* How could I turn away from His blessings? I was determined to obey God's teaching and do it His way this time because I wanted His blessings over my marriage. I knew that was the only key to a successful marriage.

Me: Once I have a good husband and marriage, I will be happy.

God: If you are not happy when you are single, you will never be happy in a marriage.

During the next several years as a single woman, God began doing a work within me and shaping my character. He dealt with my pride, my shame, and my enjoyment of life. I kept my life very busy with my job and career – working long hours, traveling for work, and studying for my CPA exams. It was partly to advance my career, but I knew the other reason was to hide the loneliness and emptiness in my personal life. At that time, I was living in a small studio apartment by Times Square in Manhattan. People would not usually associate loneliness with overwhelming crowds and neon lights. However, even when I was looking at those flashing screens and watching numerous people walking by in my neighborhood, I still felt tremendous loneliness. I started questioning God why I was living on this earth, because even living in the center of the city with a great job, I was still not happy. I felt I would be happy if I was in a good marriage and had a family. But, God said, "Rejoice in Me!" But how? How can I be happy?

I started to understand that being happy is a command from God. Staying happy is an "ability" that I needed to learn and practice, just like learning a new skill. Happiness is not dependent on one's outward situation, but their inner emotion and belief. It was not easy for me to pursue my happiness alone, but I had a helper, my friend, who is my Lord and Savior. I started to find my purpose in Him. He gave me strength while I was lonely and showed me how to enjoy my life. He also brought me new friends, and these new friendships gave me opportunities to try new things and experience adventures that life had to offer me as a single person. I made many good friends and had many memorable travel experiences during this season of my life. Now, I always tell my single friends, "Enjoy your time and freedom of being single, because you will be married for the rest of your life."

Me: I cannot see where I can find a Christian husband. Maybe Your plan is for me to marry an unbeliever and then convert him to be a follower of Christ?

God: No, trust my plan, *"for my yoke is easy and my burden is light."*

At that time, I was attending and serving in a small local Chinese church in Jersey City. Looking back, I did not have enough faith to believe God would give me a husband who also loved the Lord. In my mind, I had been entertaining myself with thousands of different scenarios, such as, "Maybe God will use me to convert my future husband." But, God's plan was determined. No matter what I thought and how I argued with God, His answer was still the same. In the end, I gave up and prayed, "God, I am not good at picking the right guy for me, but I know You are, and You've already had a plan in place. Lord, I surrender my future marriage into Your hands. I am tired of the dating game and only want the one that You picked for me. Will You give me a godly man I love who also loves me?"

I put my prayer on the wall, then my waiting period started and lasted longer than my patience could stand. I began to wonder if God would ever give me a husband. What if that was not part of His plan? I continued wrestling with God until I was exhausted. Giving up again, I prayed, "Lord, I am not going to be happy if Your plan is for me to be single for the rest of my life, but I will accept it." An unexplainable peace came into my heart once I prayed this, and I knew it was from God. God could not do His work in me until I fully surrendered myself to Him.

Step by step, God started revealing His plan to me. I began to feel that New York City was not the place I wanted to live long term, but I did not know where else to go. Then I met a man on e-Harmony who lived in Florida. While we were dating, we read the book *When God Writes Your Love Story* by Eric and Leslie Ludy. We shared the same beliefs: we both wanted to have God in the center of our marriage, and we vowed to have no sex before marriage. God answered my prayer, and I did not doubt that He handpicked this man for me. God's plan is always better, and His ways are always higher.

During our time of dating, God opened the door for me to transfer my job internally to our Florida office so we could spend more time together and get to know each other better. God moved both of us to better jobs, and we relocated a couple of times. We bought a house together and had a wedding on our beautiful property in Jupiter, Florida. Everything worked out smoothly over just a couple of years. We knew for sure it was all God's blessings because of our obedience. Currently, we both serve at church and have a wonderful church family and friends. God is so faithful, and we can't even count His blessings! It does not mean we haven't had marriage struggles, but God is always in the middle, leading us to overcome our issues.

Now I see the blessings of marrying a Christian man, as God's yoke is easy and His burden is light. What God put together, nobody can separate. Everything I have today is from God, who rescued me from where I was – the darkest moment of my life – and bought me to where I am today. *"I once was blind, but now I see."* I was dead, but God gave me a new life so I can live a life full of grace, mercy, and love.

I was not ready to write my story. However, when I saw Helen's face and her eyes, I knew hope was what she needed. I felt God tapping on my shoulder and saying, "This is my story, Ping! You can't keep my story to yourself, as it belongs to my people and me." I couldn't help my tears, but this time, they were joyful tears. Now I can see His beautiful purposes in my scars, and failure is not a shame anymore. I am thankful for my scars because they are for His glory, His people, and His kingdom!

"Waking up to a new sunrise, looking back from the other side, I can see now with open eyes. Darkest water and deepest pain, I wouldn't trade it for anything. 'Cause my brokenness brought me to you, and these wounds are a story you'll use. So, I'm thankful for the scars. 'Cause, without them, I wouldn't know your heart. And I know they'll always tell of who you are. So, forever, I am thankful for the scars." – "Scars" by I AM THEY

This is my story. However, I am not the author of this story. It's God's story, and I happened to be chosen by Him, the Creator of the universe, the God Almighty, and my Savior, to write it. God's not done with me, as He continues writing His story through His people. He is such a creative author, and I am looking forward to the next chapter of my life that He is about to write. What about you, my dear friend? I hope you have been encouraged by His stories. May our Lord hold the pen and write His wonderful story in your life, too. In Jesus' powerful name!

Surrender

Kimberly Ann Hobbs

Surrender to God. It may be a term we have heard others say, but what does it mean? When we hear the word surrender, it is not usually associated with positive actions. Examples of surrendering might be on the battlefield, which means giving up victories, or surrendering to law enforcement, which most likely means someone is in trouble.

If we surrender to God, what are we giving up? First, we must understand that God doesn't force us to give up anything. There may be those who choose to view God in this way, but that is "false evidence appearing real" or fear. People are fearful of what they will lose. We fear we may lose the "earthly riches" or the "shallow, meaningless life" we are living devoid of God, but these are just different views.

Miriam-Webster's definition of surrender means to yield; to give one's self up to the power of another. When we surrender to God, we are acknowledging that what we own belongs to Him. He is the one who created us. *(Jeremiah 1:5)* We are a good thing because God said He saw all that He made, and it was very good. *(Genesis 1:31)* Everything God has given to us – our property, our belongings, our life – we were given to be responsible over.

By surrendering to God, we are admitting His ultimate control over everything, including our present circumstances. Surrender is such a powerful word because it is an action that can change the direction of our lives for the better. Sometimes we evade being captured by the God who created us because doing so would mean surrendering areas of our lives that we'd like to control.

Surrendering to God allows us to release whatever has been holding us back from God's best in our lives. The first step can be the hardest because it goes against the grain of our stubborn hearts. As for me, I had to admit my sin and that I needed a Savior. I no longer wanted to continue my path of wrong, painful choices. So, by faith, I needed to embrace the Savior and receive His eternal, loving grace, which enabled me to surrender in the first place.

It wasn't an easy surrender, as you may have read in my chapter, Exceedingly Abundantly Beyond, in this book. It took years of pain and misery to realize the greatest advocate *(1 John 2:1)* and friend that I will ever have will be in Jesus. *(John 15:15)*

It takes strength, wisdom, and trust to surrender control of our lives to the Lord, the Creator who is our complete source of strength and wisdom. I'm not saying it's easy, but could you deny yourself, take up your cross, and follow Jesus? Total surrender to God through faith in His Son is the most important decision any person can make, but it starts with surrender.

Doris Clarke is a Regional Vice President of her own Financial Services Business. She has a passion for educating women to take control of their finances and empowering them to be the best version of themselves. She loves children and volunteers at her church in the nursery. Before getting into business, she was a stay-at-home mom who enjoyed volunteering at her children's schools and activities. She also took pleasure in hosting various parties in her home for many different occasions.

Doris was born and raised in Northern Virginia. She later moved to South Florida and still resides there. She loves to travel to see new places and she has an avid love of reading books that inspire her to improve herself.

Doris is one of the leaders of Women World Leaders ministry. It was the catalyst for her opening her own doors to revealing her own purpose. Writing is a new endeavor that has been unveiled.

Doris and her husband of 31 years have three grown daughters and three adorable grandchildren. Her biggest passion now is being able to spend time with her growing family that now lives all over the country.

The Glory Of God
Doris Clarke

I wake up with a new sense of excitement now. I feel like a child that is immensely happy because I have a Father who loves me so much. My relationship with our Lord and Savior has been strengthened at the perfect time.

> *"For as the waters fill the sea, the earth will be filled with an awareness of the glory of the Lord." (Habakkuk 2:14)*

God created us to encounter His glory. We exist so we can bring Him glory and dwell in it. God is omnipresent. When you let God reside in your heart, and you trust in His promises for your life, you can serve others more effectively because you are pouring from a heart that is overflowing with God's love and mercy. When you stop allowing your problems to consume your every thought and replace them with God's truth, you will be able to see God's purpose for your life. Everything we go through is for a reason. God wants to refine us so we can be a vessel for Him to use for His glory.

I didn't always feel this way. Most of my life, I have struggled with anger and depression. I was the fourth child of parents that immigrated to the United States. My siblings are much older than me, and I was spoiled. I learned very quickly how to get my way. By throwing tantrums, I would get what I wanted. My parents would give in, and I realized that I had complete control over them. I had no idea this was how I was going to live a good portion of my adult life.

I married my high school sweetheart, and we had our first daughter at a very young age. That anger, control, and manipulation were weaved into my new family. Quick-tempered, I would blow up at my husband when things did not go my way. My anger was out of control, and my husband was the target of my wrath. Everyone outside of my immediate family had no idea. To the outside world, I was the sweetest person with a beautiful smile that hid the dark, ugly side of my heart. After losing my temper toward my family, I would be sorry, but I didn't know how to stop my outbursts.

One night during one of my rages, I tried to hit my husband with my fist. In self-defense, he blocked his head with his arm, and our arms collided. I broke my arm and had to go to the emergency room. It was an awful experience. Because of the nature of the arm break, they kept questioning how I broke it. I lied, telling them that I tripped and fell as I was walking up the stairs while holding my six-month-old daughter. I was protecting my daughter's head, and therefore, all my weight came down on my arm. My husband went along with that lie. I think the medical staff was wondering if there was some abuse happening that we were covering up. They were right. The only thing was, I was the abuser. When I look back now at how I used to be, I realize the enemy was in control of my heart. God wasn't my priority; He existed in my life on occasional Sundays. I was so sweet to everyone except my family, who saw all of my horrible behavior.

After the birth of our third daughter, I suffered from postpartum depression. I had a seven-year-old, a two-year-old, and a colicky infant. Some days, I couldn't even find the time to take a shower. I was so sleep deprived that sometimes I didn't know how I got through the day. It got so bad that I had to take antidepressants. I was seeing both a psychiatrist and a therapist because of my suicidal thoughts. I was having a hard time being a young mother with no family around to help me. My husband worked long hours and would come home to a messy house, me at my wit's end, and of course, my out-of-control anger. This was a period of my life where God was non-existent. I was going through life living in numbness, but I somehow kept going.

As the years went by, the anger and depression cycle continued. My husband began traveling for his business. That was back in the day before cell phones, and the only way to reach him was when he was back in his hotel room. Communication was scarce, which added another element to my problems. Now I was alone with three young children and sometimes for weeks at a time. This caused strain and resentment in our marriage, and the enemy attacked in many ways.

As I'm writing this, I now see how God was always there. I just didn't know how to connect with Him. My upbringing was in the Catholic Church, so I was raised to believe in and love God. I also followed the same path with my own family. After my youngest daughter received her Confirmation, we stopped attending church regularly. We became a CEO (Christmas and Easter Only) family. We would leave church, and I would get angry at my family because all they did was complain. At that time, something was missing in my life, but I didn't know it then. When I went to church, I didn't feel complete. All the other families seemed happier than mine, so I stopped going for a few years.

About eight years ago, a friend of mine invited me to a non-denominational church on Easter. My family attended with me along with our friend's family. It was different, and I felt weird because it was not what church was supposed to look like. People were passionately singing and praising God. The music was loud, but it touched my soul. At one point, I started crying and couldn't stop. I didn't know what was happening, so out of fear, I didn't go back. My family felt the same way.

A few months later, another friend invited me to a Bible study at the same church. Having never been to one, I agreed to go. That was the turning point. I began reading God's Word, and my thirst for wanting to learn more began. It was as if God was speaking directly to me. The scripture I was reading was so relevant to my current life. All the years of searching to fill the emptiness in me were being satisfied by the Word of God. I started going to that church regularly with my friends. I got baptized and felt complete. My family was supportive as long as they didn't have to attend with me. The Holy Spirit began working in me during that first visit to this church. I had no idea what was happening at the time, but I felt at home. If you feel at all this way, I encourage you to keep investing your time in God's Word. His Word will slowly make more sense the more you read and study it.

All through this period of spiritual growth, I struggled with controlling my anger and battling my depression. The next season was one of losing loved ones. I was caring for my elderly parents, who both passed away, along with losing my mother-in-law and brother-in-law. This season was very dark and depressing, but I held on to the Word of God to help me through this difficult time.

> *"But those who trust in the Lord will find new strength. They will soar high on wings like eagles. They will walk and not faint." (Isaiah 40:31)*

On January 9, 2014, we found out that my mother-in-law had lung cancer, and my father had to have heart bypass surgery. That day was also my 26th wedding anniversary. The following year was very difficult, seeing how our parents were suffering physically. They were both fighters. My father lived another year, but his health began declining in February 2015. It was a struggle caring for him while still trying to work. My husband and I did the best we could. My siblings also pitched in by coming to help from out of town. Eventually, hospice had to be called in at my parents' home, and we watched as my dad slipped into a restful sleep.

On March 6th, I felt like I needed to stay the night there. I slept on the couch and woke up drenched in sweat around 2:00 a.m. I went to check on my father in his room. The overnight hospice nurse said his breathing was getting shallower. She asked if she could use the restroom since I was with him. He looked so peaceful as he slept. I spoke to him and prayed over him. When the nurse came back, she checked his vitals, and he passed away right after I prayed for him. I believe I was awakened so I could be with him when he passed away. This was a tough time for all my family, especially my mother, who was very dependent on him during their sixty years of marriage.

In May, my family traveled to Orlando for my middle daughter's college graduation. My mother-in-law also traveled to see her granddaughter graduate. When she was first diagnosed with lung cancer, the doctors did not give her much time to live. God had other plans, though. She fought through and had many treatments. Her will to live was strong despite the pain and suffering she was enduring. She was on oxygen and could barely walk. We were all able to spend some time with her. What touched me was how she spoke about her love of God and how He was taking care of her during this challenging time in her life. Her strong faith kept her going.

She was looking forward to this family event that she was able to attend. Unfortunately, her health declined after the graduation, and she had to be rushed to the hospital. We said our last goodbye before they airlifted her back to her hometown. She passed away a few days later. That was another parent lost only two months later. My family was hurting. Losing loved ones is so hard. When I think about my mother-in-law, Deuteronomy 31:8 resonates with me: *"The Lord himself goes before you and will be with you; he will never leave you nor forsake you. Do not be afraid; do not be discouraged."* Our loved ones are no longer suffering; they are no longer in pain. They are with our Heavenly Father. Still, my family and I miss them dearly.

My most recent bout of depression was after the deaths of my brother-in-law and my mother, who died within three days of each other in February of 2018. My brother-in-law had an aortic aneurysm that caused an aortic dissection. He had heart surgery to repair the damage to his heart and artery. My mother also had to have emergency surgery. I was her primary caregiver, so I was with her at the hospital. My husband flew to North Carolina to be with his brother and family. Unfortunately, the damages to my brother-in-law were too great for him to recover, and he passed away.

The day I was to fly to North Carolina to meet my husband and his family for the funeral of his brother, I found my mother dead on the floor. She must have tripped and fallen in the middle of the night. It was such a shock to find her that way. She had just gotten out of the hospital two days before from having her emergency surgery. Needless to say, I could not leave to attend my brother-in-law's funeral. I felt so guilty for not being able to be there for my husband.

He and his brother were very close. Death is never easy, but when someone dies at the age of forty-two, it's another level of grief. Getting through this time was also compounded by the fact that after the funeral of my mother, everyone went home. My husband's business was currently doing work in Puerto Rico, so he left. My three daughters don't live in South Florida any longer, so they left. My siblings all live out of state, so they left. It was one of the loneliest times of my life.

After handling most of my mother's estate and selling her home, I quickly became uninterested in doing anything. There were days that I couldn't even get out of bed. The depression hit me harder than any other time in my life. I felt isolated and alone. My energy level was nonexistent. I did my best to fake it, but deep down inside, I was crushed. I cried a lot. Anything would trigger the deep sorrow that I felt. I was longing for my family to be with me, to comfort me. I cried out to God to bring my husband home. I felt the need to be with the ones I loved. I was in a season of my life where I didn't know what my purpose was anymore. I was always caring for someone…my kids, my husband, my parents. I was ALONE. There was nobody to take care of, and I felt lost.

I was looking at being alone as a bad thing, until I started getting confirmations that God's plan for me during this season was to be alone so I could work on strengthening my relationship with Him. It was a simple mindset shift that started opening doors in my life.

One day, while feeling unmotivated to do anything, I was lying around watching TV when I got a call from a friend. Nobody but God knew what I was struggling with, and He was lining things up. She invited me to the first meeting of Women World Leaders in September of 2018. I started crying on the phone when she told me about this new women's ministry to help women find their purpose.

I attended that first meeting, and I knew God had perfect timing for me. I felt like this ministry was God's answer to my prayers. The women relationships I have made are priceless to me. This ministry has catapulted my spiritual growth. After several meetings, I realized God was tugging at my heart to get more involved. He was already preparing me for leadership through my business in financial services. I stepped out of my comfort zone and went through a leadership interview process, and I was chosen to be part of the leadership team.

"Trust in the Lord with all your heart, do not depend on your own understanding. Seek His will in all you do and he will show you which path to take." (Proverbs 3:5-6)

I felt lost and didn't understand why I was going through everything. I now know that I have to put all my TRUST in God. He is in control. If you have ever felt this way, put your faith and trust in His timing for your life. It will save you from experiencing all the depression and heartache that I went through for six months.

I decided to follow the path God had laid out in front of me. Then the enemy started the attacks because I was lining up with God's purpose for my life. The enemy wants to distract and stop that at any cost. The enemy wants to steal, kill, and destroy. It's up to us to stay in the Word and rebuke all thoughts and distractions that the enemy uses to veer us off course.

> *"We know that God causes everything to work together for the good of those who love God and are called according to His purpose for them." (Romans 8:28)*

Our first response to conflict is to consume our thoughts with the problem instead of praying to God. As human beings, we are selfish by nature and often ask, "Why me?" Instead, we should trust and obey what God has called us to do. When we make everything about us, the conflict will continue to happen. This is a reminder for us to fight through adversities with the help of our Almighty God. Look to scripture for the truth, and get a community of believers to pray for you and your situation. As I look at my past, I now realize the work God has been doing in my life. I am His new creation and a work in progress.

> *"My old self has been crucified with Christ. It is no longer I who live, but Christ lives in me. So, I live in this earthly body by trusting in the Son of God, who loved me and gave himself for me." (Galatians 2:20)*

I'm excited about my future because I have God by my side. All the tears I have shed have led to triumph. Writing this chapter was not something I ever imagined myself doing. Writing has never been my favorite thing, but this has been a soul-cleansing, God-inspired work. He is working in all of us, and when we get to the point of releasing the pain of our past, we will be able to receive the blessings that He has in store for us. I will continue to serve others through women's ministry and my business, and I give all glory to God for helping me through my pain, shame, and grief. I replace that with joy because I have Jesus living in my heart, and He is with me every step of the way.

"So let's not get tired of doing good. At just the right time, we will reap a harvest of blessing if we don't give up." (Galatians 6:9)

TRUST

Kimberly Ann Hobbs

How do we trust? Trust is not a natural response to a situation or in a person, especially for those who are deeply wounded. Please don't listen to the "voices of accusation" if you're wounded in this area. They are not "love vibes" uplifting you in a melodious way. If your trust has been violated, allow the Spirit of God to take charge of your mind and sort out the tangles of inflicted deception.

God is truth. If God is living in you, be transformed by His truth that is alive within you, not the lies the enemy throws out at you. There is a song I often sing, which speaks about the voice of truth that tells me a different story. When I find it hard to trust in someone or something, I revert to the inner voice inside me – God's voice of truth. It most always turns my unfortunate obstacle around to something positive. The voice of truth is where you receive trust.

When no one else seems to understand you, draw closer to the One who understands you most, who loves you completely and perfectly – the One who created you. Confide in Him and read His Word to gain your ultimate trust in any situation you are facing. God wants us to place all our trust in Him in all circumstances. Try praying, asking, and then going to His Word. He will equip you to get through your situation victoriously.

We may still have doubts and fears, but we need to identify that those don't come from God. It's a daily battle to cast down those doubts and fears and hear the voice of truth. By trusting in God alone, you will find it will allow His channel of peace to flow through you. His greatest work happens when we have a grateful, trusting heart. It's not something that happens on its own; we must seek it with purpose!

Instead of planning and expecting, try trusting and thanking God continuously, even if you are uncomfortable doing it. Believe it with your heart, and it will produce a paradigm shift that will completely alter your life.

> *"Trust in the Lord with all your heart; do not depend on your own understanding. Seek his will in all you do; he will show you which path to take." (Proverbs 3:5-6, NLT)*

Our prayer is God will restore trust inside your life as you pray over this Word.

Janet Berrong is the co-founder and vice president of Two Sisters Compassion Project, Inc. She is on the Global Leadership Team of Women World Leaders, Inc., an organization which has grown to World Wide proportions in its first year; a Ministry that empowers women to embrace their purpose. She has maintained a health and wellness practice of therapeutic massage and colon hydrotherapy for the last 23 years.

Janet has been a featured speaker on Women Health and Wellness issues at the American Heart Association's "Straight From the Heart Business and Health Expo." She is an ambassador for safe beauty through Crunchi, a locally developed toxin-free cosmetic brand.

Janet never turns down an adventure and loves to travel the world and indulge in different cultures, sharing her passion for Christ with others, as well as her entrepreneurial experience in support of women.

Depending On God's Unfailing Love

Janet Berroug

Sometimes life knocks the wind out of your sails entirely, to the point where you don't know if you'll ever be able to inhale and exhale again. I had been through very traumatic struggles, but nothing compares to losing the love of my life with no warning whatsoever. God was going to have to work overtime to heal me and bring me back from that. I was born into generational broken-ness and endured many hardships as I grew into adulthood, which led me to distrust men and to doubt the possibility of having a permanent relationship. If it weren't for God in my life, I would have been hopeless, but nothing is impossible with Christ, and I knew that to be true.

God is our provider, our comforter, the lover of our souls. However, it's hard to remember that when many of us don't have earthly fathers who we can relate to on that level. Personally, my father was not emotionally or physically available. My parents divorced when I was ten years old. At age twelve, I had an alcoholic step-father for the next fifteen years of my life. He was verbally and sometimes physically abusive. This led to my feeling abandoned and unworthy, and the unspeakable trauma of being raped in my early 20's by a church friend who I trusted. I no longer trusted anyone, including my own judgment.

I learned to bottle my emotions up, looking like I had it all together. I was always the strong one, and I knew I was going to have to take care of myself. By age twenty-two, I was a licensed massage therapist, and by age twenty-three, I had opened my first massage practice. I found great pleasure in my work. I could help people feel better physically and emotionally, and it warmed my soul. I poured myself into my work and the people. God blessed me and my business in many ways. It began to grow in size and expand into new therapies, treatments, and modalities. This was my mission field. But, age thirty-eight, I found myself still unmarried with no children. I was driven to succeed and realized years later, that work was where I was finding purpose and worth in my life.

It was the summer of 2013. I was at the airport on my way to visit my mother in the Abaco Islands, Bahamas. The statement "A simple hello can change your life" was very true for me. As I was at the gate ready to board the plane, I met a man who I had been watching earlier. His kind spirit attracted my attention. He was helping another passenger fill out his immigration paperwork. As we lined up to board the plane, these two were right in front of me. After a few minutes of waiting, we started making small talk and then boarded the plane. I could see this man had an interest in me.

Since the flight was not full, we could sit anywhere we wanted. Low and behold, as we took our seats, he sat in the aisle across from me so we could talk. Smart man! He knew he had a captive audience for the next fifty minutes. We had a lot of common interests, and he had a house on the island next to my family's. We were off to a great start.

That beautiful man gave me his phone number. Three days had passed, and I had not called him. He tracked down my stepfather at work to ask him for the home number to call me so he could ask me to dinner, and he did just that.

We met up a few times while we were on the islands. One night was dinner with his friends. The other was a day out touring the islands. He picked me up by boat, took me to lunch, and then island hopping. He showed me where he lived and all around his island. He was enthusiastic, charming, and smart. His name was Greg, and he was a handsome man. A head full of beautiful graying hair, blue eyes, and a genuine smile with perfect teeth. His posture was one of confidence – shoulders back, chest out. He was loving, charismatic, and bold.

An unspoken connection had quickly grown between us. It was as if I had known him before. My family loved him. He was engaging, attentive, and very present. His deep, sincere heart could be felt by all. Over time, my wounds of abandonment, unworthiness, and disrespected boundaries all started to be healed with his steadfastness and unconditional love. My faith in men was being restored. He showed me how a woman was supposed to be treated. Just as David said in *Psalms 23:3, "He restores my soul, He leads me in the paths of righteousness for His namesake."*

The holidays were special. Our spending quality time together and with family was priceless. His three grown kids were smart, well-rounded, engaging, and fun-loving. The love they had for each other was beautiful. I will never forget the first time I talked to his daughter, Ashley, on the phone. One phone conversation is all it took for the whole family to know. The kids definitely had each other on speed dial. "Hey, Dad's got a girlfriend!" When I met his daughter in person, I was so drawn to want to hug her. Afterward, I told Greg, "I can't help it. I just wanted to keep hugging her." Greg replied, "Yes, I know. That's the effect she has on most everyone. People love her."

January rolled around, and it was a difficult time for my family. My 56-year-old aunt in Atlanta was in her last days of battling cancer. Greg did everything in his power to make sure I got to spend quality time with her before her passing. He was so supportive, making sure I could drop everything to go and see her. Knowing I had God and a loving, supportive man to walk through this journey with me was a blessing.

Family has always been very important to me. I have a very small family network. One of my greatest loves is my mother. She is my rock, my pure love, my unfailing support system, and my best friend. Greg loved my mother. Wanting to do something special for her and me for Valentine's Day, he arranged for us to fly over to surprise her. Planning this for my mother made us so happy we almost couldn't contain ourselves. When the day came, Mom was overjoyed to see us both. Over the next few days, I was truly in my happy place with my mother, my love, and our beautiful family. God's hope filled us with joy and peace in believing, so by the power of the Holy Spirit, we were abounding in hope. *(Romans 15:13)*

A few months later, I was still healing from the loss of a friend who had taken her life recently. However, we pressed forward and started planning my 40th birthday for May 16th. We had decided to invite a couple of my closest friends and family to the islands to celebrate. The fun of planning had now begun! In April, we took a weeklong trip to spruce up the place for our guests – washing, cleaning, and painting the place. At the end of our very busy day, my mother and stepdad came over for a visit. As they drifted away from our dock, I had a moment of pure joy, bliss, happiness. I had finally made it to my happy place. I had my mother on a beautiful island next to me. She was happy, healthy, and had an amazing, godly man who loved her to bits, and I had a man who I loved and felt loved by. Here we were. Wow! That moment was so powerful! My heart was full. All I could say was, "God, you are so good! Thank you."

Things can change quickly, and I didn't know this was the calm before the storm. We were a few days away from heading to the Abaco Islands, and I was at work when I had an overwhelming wave of emotion come from the pit of my gut. Like something terrible had happened to Greg. Tears filled my eyes, and spit flew out of my mouth from the thought. I looked at my phone and noticed I had a voicemail from Greg's daughter's boyfriend. What came next was something I never thought possible. I went cold as I listened to his message.

"Janet, something terrible happened. Greg tried to take his life. He's on life support. Come now if you want to see him."

My heart sunk. I can't describe what I felt other than complete shock and disbelief. How could this be? Somehow, God gave me the strength to get in my car and drive an hour to the hospital to say my final goodbye. On my drive there, all I could say was, "God, I love you. I love you, God. I don't understand it all, but I trust You. I love and trust You."

When I got to the hospital, it felt like I floated through every door. I went straight to ICU, where his three grown children greeted me. I saw the despair in their eyes. Their dad had always been the strong one that bounced back from everything. This time, he wasn't bouncing back. The reality was setting in; this was the end of his life.

After a long embrace and tears, it was my time to see Greg one last time. A dear friend of the family escorted me by the arm down the hallway into ICU. The walk seemed like an eternity. As we rounded the corner of his room, I could hear the noise of the machines that were keeping him alive – the beeping from the monitors and respirator for his breathing. His friend kindly stood at the foot of the bed while I touched Greg's lifeless body. With my hand resting on his chest over his heart, I watched every breath and felt every heartbeat. The words "I love you. I love you. You are beautiful. I love you," naturally and uncontrollably rolled off my tongue.

After my respected time, the young man came up to Greg's bedside and addressed him with the utmost respect. He told him how much he loved him, then kindly stepped outside the door and waited for me to say my last goodbyes. I stood at the foot of Greg's bed, and while holding his cold feet, I sang "Amazing Grace" ever so softly. "Goodbye, Baby Doodles. I love you," I told him for the last time. Then, I turned and walked out. A piece of me died that day. It's true you are never the same after losing a loved one. Though it does get a little easier with time, you are never the same. Through all this pain, God was still at work.

As the loneliness set in and deep hurt continued to magnify, God showed up in a mighty way. Signs seemed to be everywhere I went. People would show up right when I needed someone. I had peace knowing that God was with me. He gifted me with special people, and I would always have the love of my heavenly Father.

Shortly after Greg's passing, I met an older man at a networking event. A friend of mine came up and asked how my boyfriend was, and sadly, I had to say he passed away. To her shock, she gave me condolences and walked away.

The gentleman in front of me took me by the hand and said, "I know why I'm here tonight. I wasn't going to come." He then said, "God told me there was someone who I needed to be here for. That someone is you. I'm a retired pastor of fifty years, and the women at my church make prayer shawls for healing. They knit the prayer shawls and pray over them. And I want to make sure you get a prayer shawl."

I just stood there in awe and full of tears. God is so good.

The next week, my mother was in town. So, she went with me to meet my new friend, Larry. We sat, talked, and prayed as he gave me the prayer shawl. I took it home and put it on my bed; it matched perfectly with my comforter. Jesus physically put a covering over my hurting heart, body, and soul. God reminded me that He would never leave me or forsake me.

> *"Be strong and courageous. Do not be afraid or terrified of them, for the LORD your God goes with you; he will never leave you nor forsake you." (Deuteronomy 31:6)*

The weeks, months, and year ahead were not easy. Most days, I had a hard time getting out of bed and carrying on about my day. I had no energy, no passion. I did the basics for survival. I felt like all I did was cry. In reality, I think I was releasing all my pain I had bottled up for so many years.

God was right there with me holding me up and providing the right people, testimonies, and love in my heart that I couldn't explain. I had this overwhelming feeling of love as if it was oozing out of my pores. It was the joy of the Lord. I wanted to love on everyone. Strangers could even feel it, from 8 years old to 80 years old. I would go out, and they would be drawn to me. That simple hello made me smile.

Before this, I had prayed and cried out every night that God would bring me someone who I could love and be loved by. I prayed for a man who I could love, trust, and would have the qualities that I was looking for. He provided that man. It just didn't end the way I thought it would. God has plans for me, plans to prosper me and not to harm me, plans to give me hope and a future. *(Jeremiah 29:11)* So, I am hopeful, and I know my God didn't show me such love to give me second best. He has someone waiting for me, and I have faith, which is the substance of things hoped for, the evidence of things not yet seen. *(Hebrews 11:1)* No matter what challenges life throws your way, know that God's love never fails! *(Psalm 136:1)*

· ·

LOVE

Kimberly Ann Hobbs

There are dozens of words expressing a range of emotions in the Bible when it comes to the word love. There are sexual desires, intimate friendships, and acts of mercy, kindness, and more.

There are three Greek words from the Bible distinguishing the types of love: Eros, which is a romantic, passionate kind of love. Agape, which is a parental, self-sacrificing love that seeks only the welfare of others, and Phileo, the love of great friends and siblings.

Since all three of these words are represented in the Bible, all three are considered to be created and blessed by God. Would you agree? Love in the Bible is like love in our daily lives. It's important, it's complicated, and at times, it could be hard to understand. But, ultimately, it is too powerful and mysterious to be fully defined or grasped by any of us. The different kinds of love represent different parcels of our lives within this world that God created and blessed for our nurturing.

Beyond anything we could ever comprehend is God's love for each of us. It is much more than how we could feel about someone else. God's love for us doesn't cost us anything. Love lays down its life. Our natural reactions in our human bodies and demands, which are part of our human nature, expect something in return. God expects nothing.

"In this is love, not that we loved God, but that he loved us and sent His Son." (1 John 4:10)

God's love gives not only to those who are good to Him. He gives to us all; He loves everyone. It doesn't matter if His love is ever reciprocated; it endures all things. God's love for us does not change according to circumstances. His love is rooted and grounded. There are no exceptions to God's love for us despite how undeserving we are. His true love, the ultimate sign of how much He loves us, was Jesus, who laid down His life for us.

Sometimes, we can say we are lacking true Godly love. If you need it, ask Him for it. We need to be willing to give up our own self-will and think of others before ourselves. God tells us how important love truly is. *"And now abide faith, hope, love, these three; but the greatest of these is love." (1 Corinthians 13:13)* This shows how important love is. You can read the entire chapter of 1 Corinthians 13, which is called the Love chapter in the Bible.

Can we all agree we should try to show love? God shows us love is unending. Love is what draws people: goodness, kindness, meekness of heart, patience, and understanding. Please pray that God can show you how to gain more of His love and His will. After all, His love for you cannot be measured. There are no exceptions to God's love pouring out over you and for you, because God is love. *(1 John 4:8)*

. . . .

 **Kelly Jo Rabbitt**, originally from Cleveland, Ohio, has made South Florida her home for four decades. Kelly is a health and wellness professional, a former award-winning actress, starting from age 9, and has served God with worship dance, praise teams, and speaking. A former Rotary U.S. Goodwill Ambassador to Europe, Kelly has served as class president at an International Bible School, holds a Masters in Divinity and graduated with top honors from a National Fitness School. She has also served in the impoverished parts of Appalachia and in Haiti.

Kelly's victory over severe Complex Post Traumatic Stress Disorder has given her an openness with the Lord due to the dozens of personal divine encounters she has experienced.

Kelly currently serves as a worship dancer, and choir member. She has a passion for prayer and infusing hope and healing into broken souls.

Kelly loves dogs and visiting botanical gardens.

The Sincere Actress
Kelly Jo Rabbitt

Dedicated to all those seeking freedom from dissociative issues.

> *"The ruined city lies desolate; the entrance to the house is barred."*
> *(Isaiah 24:10)*

I could feel my brain burning. I stood in the hallway of the condo I had lived in since 1989. It didn't feel like home, but it's where my mother lived and where I slept since I was nineteen. My brain felt as if it were disintegrating with fire. I knew I needed to see a specialist, but there was no insurance, and money had left my life years before. Lightly, at that moment, I heard deep in my spirit, "Be still and know that I am God." That was the only "insurance" I had.

I had fought hard to survive with Complex Trauma Disorder for over ten years at this point, and it had affected every part of my life. In 1989, I started having breakdowns during my orientation at the American Academy of Dramatic Arts in New York City. It had been a dream of mine since I was age nine to attend acting school in Manhattan. I worked diligent and hard in my youth, winning Best Actress in state competitions in high school and various lead roles. But, in reality, I was a shy girl, and I lived in my head – a lot.

With my mind broken in parts, it had been years since my life was marked by accomplishments, such as fastest runner awards in soccer and softball, twelve 1st place beauty contest awards during my teens, and a sprinkling of academic and writing awards. I was Salutatorian of my senior class in high school, graduating in 1986. I moved forward with a keen business sense, was well-spoken, and had adapted well to my charm school training on Palm Beach Island, where my father had sent me in my mid-teens. Now, a decade later, while standing in the hallway, I had foggy memories of who I had been. I could only slightly hope that life would turn around for me, as my burning brain was more confirmation that I was utterly helpless. My once starlit and caring eyes had grown vacant, and my soul was shattered.

"Woe to me because I am broken, my wounds are grievous."
(Jeremiah 10:19)

I had attended church since I was born, and I believed the Catholic church when they told me God had a plan for me to do well in the world. I also believed in Jesus. However, my childhood faith could not stop the stuttering when I talked, or fix the faulty wiring in my brain, or mend my broken heart. No doubt, these things were symptoms from enduring eighteen moves in twelve years as a child, bombs of rage exploding daily in the home, going to a different school every year, a fractured identity, and soul damage due to being raped numerous times. Top all of that off with having an abortion at the age of fifteen because the child was a product of a rape. All were part of the sinister plan of the enemy to kill me, no doubt. I was a frozen shell of my former self. There I was, my brain burning like electricity. Alone. I have heard a sound of dread, of terror, and there is no peace. *(Jeremiah 30:5)*

At age twenty, God led me to Maranatha Bible Church in Palm Beach Gardens, Florida. I wasn't sure what it all meant, but I knew enough to be there. As a young girl, I had read the Bible at times in my room and had always loved God, learning about Him in my CCD classes at the Catholic church. It had become very lonely at the Catholic church, and my parents' twenty-two-year marriage had dissolved. My father always attended mass, but I was not close to him at that time. Looking back to that time, that's when God started to show me the hiding place He would become for me.

"He will conceal me under the cover of His tent." (Psalm 72:5)

At age twenty-four, I started getting professional help for an eating disorder by way of a scholarship. Back then, in 1993, there was no such thing, but God used the seven weeks I stayed at the highly-respected Renfrew Center in Boca Raton, Florida, to begin the healing process. I brought my Bible with me, and not everyone liked that. My eating issues quickly abated as I got the emotional support I needed to start sorting out years of trauma. Medication consisting of Prozac and an occasional sleep aid eased the terror of "begging for death". There is mental pain so great that death would be better, and what I would face the next seventeen years of my life was a mountain I never thought I would have to climb. What I didn't understand was that God was weaving His songs to hide me in as I was breaking down.

> *"He is my hiding place, He preserves me in trouble, He sur-rounds me with songs of deliverance." (Psalm 32:7)*

The Weaving Of Him Into Me

In the early years of my healing, it was one good hour and seven bad days. I was afflicted with demonic dreams nightly and tortured in my mind in the daytime. Sleep and food were distant relatives. My days fused with no routine, no structure. I was a far cry from being the energetic, bright-smiled, "do the right thing" child I had been. My whole life was unfamiliar and a far cry from the stylish upbringing I had as a young lady. While others were getting married, having children, or pursuing education, I was marking silent victories of an hour with no mind torment or getting through a medication appointment at the county mental health center in West Palm Beach. It was during one of those appointments that I heard the most beautiful rendition of "Amazing Grace", and time stood still. A tall black man in the doorway of the clinic bellowed the words that flowed like silk from his vocal cords. As I was mesmerized, I knew God was speaking to my soul. *"I am here, Kelly. I know what is happening to you. I know it does not make any sense. But, hear me, child. You are mine, and this world is far more than you understand. I will guide you, Kelly."* The cobwebs in my mind did not unravel quickly. My suffering stayed. However, His power seemed to build up in me over the next fifteen years beyond anything I could have imagined.

Outwardly, I had learned to resign everything. Every. Thing. No plans, no expectations. I had been lonely since childhood, and now again, there was not a person to look into my eyes or say hello to me. God was to help me, or inevitably, I would perish.

> *"And He is before all things, and in Him all things hold together." (Colossians 1:17)*

As my spiritual gifts strengthened, my desire for this world lessened. At age thirty-two, I had my first dream that was not a nightmare since I was a teen. Soon after, I began having dreams and visions from the Lord, and these dreams and visions would come true. At times, I would feel a strong presence of the Lord, and lights would show around my hands while I prayed in the night. And pray, I did.

For many years, I prayed for the world. I prayed for the lost, the abused, the hungry, the angry, the forgotten, and especially for the men who harmed me in my youth and for my family members who suffered from traumatic home life. I grew up with three older brothers and my parents. I prayed and prayed. Finally, my prayers started to gain traction. I started feeling a purpose amid my anguish. I felt my "death" was bringing life somewhere. I could sense it from the Lord's spirit. My life had become minuscule, but God was creating an inner life in me that I never knew could exist.

In my daily life, every small victory was continually met with gratitude if it eased even a tiny amount of my suffering. I would praise Him endlessly without reservation for days. My healing was never a straight line, but my encounters with Him and deliverances from Him over time compelled me to hope.

One year while in Sarasota, Florida, while praying with a new-ly-found charismatic Catholic group, I heard myself say, "Why not, me?" instead of "Why me?" My heart was coming more to accept my situation. Then I continued to hope against hope that God would fully set me free one day.

> *"Seek me with all your heart." (Jeremiah 29:13)*

I wandered through life for years, seeking every drop of Him I could find. Praising Him and accepting any tokens of hope and light that crossed my path, I had become something and someone very different. During those years, I would attend prayer groups, conferences, and church as much as three times a week. Anything that had to do with inner healing or being set free was my com-mitment. When not doing the work, I would enjoy a rainbow, a walk in the rain, and let the world pass me by. I hadn't been part of it for so long, my routines and new traditions started to take shape, with the presence of the Lord with me. I was very quiet to the outside world about what I was living through, as trust was a major issue. I had made many friends over my lifetime but would control how much time I spent with others. That way, I didn't have to explain that my brain was broken.

I knew God's hand was upon me, but still, there was much heal-ing needed. The reality I would have to come to terms with again and again was that the severe Complex Trauma Disorder I had was from childhood trauma, and my personality had never fully formed. Memories of trauma were locked away in "parts" of me.

"My comfort in my suffering is this: Your promise preserves my life." (Psalm 119:50)

"Little by little lest the beast consume you." (Exodus 23:29)

After seventeen years, I was slowly coming out of the woods in my healing. Gone were the days of demonic night terrors and floating out of my body to dissociate. Fading were the fears of unstoppable mind oppression. I would have a string of good days but still kept websites handy of group homes for people with disabilities, as I was forever unknown about what would happen to my life. The gutter? Homeless? Dead? Mental trauma can rob one of every natural gift, but God chose to continue to increase my spiritual abilities. That's what kept me holding on to life – sacred, precious, holy life. I pursued the use of these spiritual gifts at every turn. Prayers, encouragement, faith, and the Word spilled out of me to anyone in need. Homeless people, addicts, the well-to-do, the scared, the lost, the humble, and the arrogant. Anyone anywhere was fair play. Often, I could see inside them and see their heart. Soon, a light talk with them would end in their tears across my small frame.

Having continued hope, I took off up the east coast of the U.S. to volunteer. With only fifty bucks in my pocket and my mother's phone number, I had to go. I needed to reach out to others. The time would never be right if I waited for a career or impressive finances. I was terrified but chose to ignore my fear. A month trip would last two years. I was alone. I met God there. Miracles happened. I met people. They were healed. I grew.

> *"Now to each one the manifestation of the Spirit is given for the common good." (1 Corinthians 12:7)*

In my late 30's, God began presenting me with opportunities. In 2007, I was chosen as a U.S. Goodwill Ambassador and represented America in Europe for Rotary International. I learned then that I had speaking and presentation skills. I saw God move in the people who I met, and I had divine appointments with some who restored their faith in God. I was in awe.

In 2009, I was led to apply on a scholarship to a small Bible school. I wanted to get more healing and thought this would be a productive way. I was voted class president, which posed many problems as I had come for healing. I learned some wonderful things there but also learned a dark side of ministry, leadership, and the reality of spiritual warfare even in Bible school. Though still alone, I grew.

In 2012, I was given a grant to attend a national fitness school in Fort Lauderdale, Florida. I decided to try and expect nothing but the experience. I ended up graduating top of my small class and setting a record in Anatomy class. I cried all the way home from graduation. I didn't understand this reality, and after many years of torment, doing well was never even a thought of mine any longer. God was healing my outside world, too.

During my time at national fitness school, I was asked to be on the game show *Wheel of Fortune*. Two weeks prior, I had a dream about letters and had set the Anatomy record due to "spelling". In my dream, letters were popping out of the walls. Big, block, English-style, proper letters—something I had loved in my youth.

I was confused about the game show as I had to leave acting years before. Now, God had pointed to this audition through a dream and a very strong inner prompting. God told me I was going to be on the show, and I argued for two weeks with Him. Didn't I lose everything I ever loved while growing up?! I wasn't very happy, and I let God know it. Still, I chose to surrender. After five more auditions in the process of elimination, there I was off to L.A.

> *"Before I formed you in the womb, I knew you, before you were born, I set you apart." (Jeremiah 1:5)*

> *"A man's heart plans his way, but the God orders His steps." (Proverbs 16:9)*

Seeing More of His Promises

By the time I turned forty-three, I had an awareness that my feelings of wondering if I would survive might be over. Though I had seen His mighty hand in many ways, I still did not know how to live life on my own. Also, my healing was not complete. He had provided my needs for all the places he sent me. He kept me fed and alive. But, I still had no place I felt I belonged. So, one day, my frustrations mounted, and I spilled out with anger at Him for unanswered prayers.

"I have honored you so much! I have obeyed you! I have sought you out. I accepted nothing as my life – no family, no dog, no children, no career, nothing! Do something with my life or take me home!"

I was serious. I was wrestling with God because I was still very…
confused. I knew the world; I prayed for years. I gave up and offered
up again and again. Still, I knew something was not right. I truly
felt rejected by God, as if He was a distant spiritual guru but didn't
come into my life personally to answer prayers that I desperately
needed to see answered. Where was my home? My family? My
puppy? My anything? I was still confused, and though respected
in my Christian circles, I was sad deep inside.

When I was a girl, the only thing I wrote in my book about what
I wanted to be when I grew up was "a mommy". I thought I knew
God, but did He know me? After years of supernatural manifes-
tations, divine intervention, watching His gifts of healing and
deliverance pour through myself and others, and thriving in missions across the country and overseas, why did I feel like God had
forgotten me?

> "'O God my rock,' I cry, 'Why have you forgotten me? Why must
> I wander around in grief, oppressed by my enemies?' Their
> taunts break my bones. They scoff, 'Where is this God of yours?'"
> (Psalm 42:9-11)

Puzzle Pieces

In 2011, through a series of promptings from the Holy Spirit, I
found myself staring at the website of a Dr. Roger Boehm, D.C.C.,
Ph.D., a Christian, spirit-filled therapist who specializes in dissociative disorders. I was then led to the testimonies of people who
had overcome dissociative disorders, including dissociative identity

disorder (D.I.D.). It's a brilliant gift actually, but the reason for it is, sadly, severe trauma most often before age seven, when the personality hasn't fully formed yet.

Gracefully, God led me to the testimony of Herschel Walker, the football legend from the '70s. I had admired him when I was a tomboy around age nine and was amazed he was one of the first testimonies I saw. I felt a piece of my life "fit" in place when Herschel spoke about his football career and how it wasn't him playing, but another part created subconsciously to survive a traumatically difficult childhood. It was time to face parts of me that were hiding.

> *"In God's mercy, He directed His light into my soul. He will return evil to my enemies; destroy them in your faithfulness." (Psalm 54:5)*

The Master Detective

When I met with Dr. Boehm via Skype, it was evident that I was in good hands. He specialized in D.I.D. and used an abundance of prayer. He wasted no time in getting to the root of issues and was used to being sensitive to clients and the leading of the Holy Spirit. As I shared with Dr. Boehm, the long-hidden parts of me started to surface. Some carried deep terror, and some could not verbalize anything but were frozen. Where I was holding pain, denial, gifts, or talents, these parts started to heal and integrate. Trust was the key factor.

With the realization of D.I.D., there came a decision I had to make. Was I going to deny in shame these hidden parts of me that were created to help me survive, or would I let God reach each one and complete my healing? I chose to take authority over the enemy's spirit of despondency and believe that God would heal me fully! God's anointing paved the way. It was painful at times as if I was going back to square one where I had started thirty years before. But, God is the Master at everything.

Two years after the start of my D.I.D. healing, I was asked to go to Haiti to assist with feeding a tiny village in a remote area where I had never been. With more healing than ever, I had a different experience than on trips God sent me in the past. Due to some mix-ups in our group, my flight was detoured back to the U.S.A. in two days.

As I was waiting in the airport during a four-hour layover, a man approached me. I will admit I was a bit afraid. I had never been there before. He was very well dressed and showed his I.D. to me. He was a diplomat for Haiti. I was dressed in tennis clothes for comfort. Somehow, he was led to me, told me that I was V.I.P., and to come with him. I was escorted to a luxurious diplomat's building. Strangely enough, members of the United Nations were there waiting for their chief to fly in. They approached me while I was seated on the red velvet couch and started telling me of their life stories. The officers were from different countries and in full gear, with sashes, hats, guns, and polished uniforms down to the tips of their shoes! We chatted, one by one, and the Lord spoke: *"Kelly, you have favor with the diplomat. Ask for an office here, and pray for those who want prayer."* I realized this was my assignment.

I led officers of the United Nations to a quiet office, where I laid hands on each one and prayed whatever the Holy Spirit brought to my heart. Soon after, the smiling diplomat was waving me to the transport cart to carry me back to the terminal. He stopped suddenly and said, "Look, look!" All the U.N. officers were lined up on the pavement, saluting their chief as he disembarked. At that moment, on a botched trip by myself in Haiti, God spoke to me deeply. He said, *"Kelly, I am your God. You are mine. And you honor Me like they are honoring their chief. I have much more for you, Kelly."*

I was soon escorted to the front door of the plane. "Kelly, come back to Haiti," my friend said, with a kind tenderness in his eyes as he gave me a gentle hug. I, a woman who lost so much in life, was now feeling so honored by her God. He was telling me to go past the boundaries of what I could see and trust Him to not only set me free, but to also give me a life far beyond what I could ask or imagine! (Ephesians 3:20)

The Songs Keep Getting Sweeter

For the first time in my life, in 2017, I started waking up in the mornings with un-fragmented thoughts. This is integration. Skills and talents that were walled away were now lighting up my days like fireflies. I know things about myself that I never knew before. The un-realness I used to feel because of D.I.D. started to fade. Today, I like to sing in the choir, and I am a worship dancer. I love learning new things, too, such as the different types of trees in a forest. I still struggle at times with daily living, but life is grand compared to what it was! A walkway at a quiet park, with the squirrels and birds, and the gentle sounds of the inter-coastal beckon me regularly until the next adventure the Lord sends!

"Thy Word is a lamp unto my feet and a light unto my path."
(Psalm 119:105)

It is surreal to see things take shape in my life. I wouldn't trade some of those moments of darkness because of how He met me there in them. I never asked for those times, but He did something in such ways I would have never experienced him otherwise. I found the vestibule of Heaven when all was lost and I was abandoned. His light seemed brightest then. As I connect with these memories forever infused into my soul, I know that no one can take them away from me. It was hard-won but pure, even though I am imperfect. I am more than grateful. These memories are my trophies of grace. I received them, but they are all His.

. . . .

HIDING PLACE

Kimberly Ann Hobbs

"He alone is my safe place; his wrap-around presence always protects me. For he is my champion defender; there is no risk of failure with God." (Psalm 6:22, TPT)

As believers, God is our immovable hiding place. When life seems to smother us, we can always run to Him and hide in His presence. This world has its way of bringing us troubles and problems, and sometimes, we are afraid of what we are facing or enduring while living life on this planet. You don't need to fear. The Lord is always with you. He is our "special fortress" when life overwhelms us.

Hide yourself in God's comfort and encouragement. Seek Him through prayer and keep your mind focused on Him because His presence is near and you are protected.

"You're my place of quiet retreat, and your wrap-around presence becomes my shield as I wrap myself in your world!" (Psalm 119:114, TPT)

"For you are my hiding place; you protect me from trouble, you surround me with songs of victory." (Psalm 32:7)

As we cry out to God in the place of our sorrows, He will hear your cry and bring relief. Keep your heart humble and pray to the Lord.

"Yet when holy lovers of God cry out to him with all their hearts, the Lord will hear them and come to rescue them from all their troubles." (Psalm 34:17, TPT)

Your comfort is in knowing as you pray in the midst of your pain and hide yourself in His place, God will defeat the enemy and bring good out of it that you can't even fathom. As you are snuggled deep within your hiding place, you will find goodness, clarity, and peace that the light of the Lord will bring, and God's presence of His glory will be revealed in you! Amen.

Lisa M. Jones is a transformational leader, skillful coach, strategic educator, influential philanthropist, successful business woman, and world renown inspirational speaker. She is the Chief Executive Officer of Jones Jewels & Associates, where she has leveraged over 25 years of business knowledge to educate others in the area of personal development, business strategy development and financial literacy. As a result of Lisa's innovative leadership, business, and financial coaching: individuals, teams, and organizations are inspired to maximize their fullest potential, reach their financial goals, and execute their dreams.

Lisa M. Jones, is dedicated to affecting and infecting people in a way in which their lives transform from vision to reality. Lisa is an impactful change agent, whose experiences ranges from facilitating professional learning for government agencies including, but not limited to: VOA, GSA, EPA, and FDA, and being the keynote speaker at over 150 leadership schools nationwide. An intellectual and virtuous woman of extraordinary faith, vision, talents, presence, and accomplishments, has allowed her to obtain a plethora of recognitions and awards.

Lisa M. Jones journey to greatness exemplifies that success is a "journey and not a destination." Through this journey, Lisa desires to inspire others with her walk, encourage them with her talk, and to elevate with her giving.

Three Generations Of Conquerors

Lisa M. Jones

Hello, my name is Lisa M. Jones, and I was diagnosed with Stage 4 Cervical Cancer.

Hello, my name is Shanina L. Jones, and I was diagnosed with Severe Lyme's Disease.

Hello, my name is Skylar L. Jones, and I was a preemie born three months early and weighed 1.15 pounds.

> *"For I know the plans I have for you,"* declares the LORD, *"plans to prosper you and not to harm you, plans to give you hope and a future." (Jeremiah 29:11)*

Life was great! My business was growing, my days were full of potential, and I was having fun with my family and friends. I didn't see it coming. I went to the doctor for a checkup because I was enduring some discomfort during my monthly cycle. Concerned about the discolored tissues, the doctor decided to do a biopsy.

Two days later, I received a call no human being wants to get. The nurse called to schedule me for a doctor's consultation, and while scheduling me, she said the doctor wanted me to be his last patient on the day of my appointment. I immediately called my mentor to share my concerns. When I went to my appointment, I wasn't ready for the diagnosis.

"Lisa, you have cancer, cervical cancer."

I looked at the doctor. Although confused by what he was saying, I remained calm. *What is this man talking about?* I was shocked. After apologizing profusely, he suggested that I see one of the top specialists in Maryland. Once I left that doctor's office, I called my mentor. That's when the tears started to flow.

My emotions were all over the place. *Cancer? I have things to do and places to go.* Instantly, I entered mental warfare with myself. I thought about my daughter, who was living in Atlanta, Georgia, at the time. I thought about my parents, who I committed to providing for years ago, and I thought about my business that needed my presence in order to keep thriving to the level that I wanted it to go. *God, you told me that I would go to another level this year. You never said it would be in the form of cancer.* I was angry.

I went to the specialist, and the diagnosis was confirmed. I will never forget what the doctor said to me that day. "Lisa, you do have cancer, and we have to do surgery," he told me. "But, God will perform the surgery. He's just going to use my hands."

Immediately following my surgery, I underwent several weeks of radiation treatment. At this point, I was supposed to be getting better. Instead, I was getting worse. My vision was impaired, I could barely walk, and I moaned all night due to the excruciating pain. My body was hemorrhaging. I couldn't go downstairs because I was too weak. Therefore, I stayed in my bedroom all day. Aside from fruit, I couldn't hold anything on my stomach. I was in total disbelief. I kept asking myself, *what did I do to deserve this?* I was sinking into a deep depression.

My journey through the process was the most painful experience I'd ever had. I cried many tears and isolated myself from most. I didn't want anyone to see me at my lowest point. I stopped wanting to live and accepted that death would be my outcome.

The Awakening...

In 2009, I started writing my first book called *The Extreme Makeover: The Five Areas of Prosperity – Spiritual, Mental, Physical, Relationship, and Financial,* but I could never finish that book because I was busy building a business. I wanted to impact lives by teaching balance. It never dawned on me that I wasn't living the balanced life I wanted to teach others. It took cancer to shut me down and cause me to do an internal inventory. It was then that I realized I had lost myself while trying to help everyone else.

I never thought about me or what I needed. I was so busy taking care of everybody else that I neglected to take care of Lisa. I was flying all over the country speaking for other organizations, always assisting my teammates, and showing my daughter support while she pursued her culinary arts degree. Although being there for others wasn't the worst thing in the world, I forgot about me. Things had to change.

In the word of God, we are told to love our neighbors as we love ourselves. God was very adamant about this because he made it one of the greatest commandments. I never paid attention to the part that said, "AS WE LOVE OURSELVES." I would venture to say most people miss that part. I remember asking God, "What exactly do you mean by, *as we love ourselves?*" That question was the inspiration needed to finish writing *The Extreme Makeover* finally. God was giving me a warning by inspiring me to write the book two years before my diagnosis, but I didn't catch it. I felt like I had a Job experience. God told Satan, "You can try Job, but you can't take his life." Satan must have asked God for permission to try me. I profess His name on every stage, and I give Him the honor for all that I've accomplished. Although I am far from perfect, I treat people fairly and operate on a high level of integrity.

I model my life after *1 Corinthians 13* – LOVE. I love hard, and I hate division. I hate poverty, I hate lack, and I hate low self-esteem. I hate these areas so much that I educate, empower, edify, and encourage people daily to strive for the opposite. I want to be an impact player, a change agent, a crusader, a vessel used by God to touch lives and set the captive free. I want to be a solutions provider. That's exactly what I was doing when I got the diagnosis, and like Job, I had to be tried to truly find Lisa.

The Shift...

Through all of this, I was fortunate to have the best support system one could ask for. My parents prayed over me every night, and my sister, Bridgett, and niece, Briana, waited on me hand and foot. There were many late nights that they took me to the emergency room because I was sick with fever and pain. When my daughter returned from Atlanta, she bathed me, cared for me, and even slept by my side in the hospital every night. My cousin, Andrea, visited me every day in the hospital and told me stories that would take my mind off of the pain and bring some laughter to my heart for a few moments. My mentor, Mike Evans, kept reminding me of the speeches I gave and the many stages I stood on worldwide. I had been on the operating table so many times and under anesthesia so often that I lost my short-term memory. The battle in my mind was real, but I was determined to win this war.

The only way to beat the negative thoughts in my mind was to replace them with positive ones. By using affirmations, I was determined to redirect my thinking. I also started listening to the word of God. I sang songs of praise and gave my ears to my mentors, who reminded me of who I am and where I am going. I praised God and started focusing on the prize, not the price.

It wasn't an easy journey. However, I pushed myself. Eventually, my mindset shifted, and my desire to live kicked in. My tears were many, my experience was horrific, but my victory was amazing. God healed my body, and he didn't restore what I had. He gave me more! My life is nothing short of amazing now. Mercy said, *No, I'm not going to let you go. I'm not going to let you slip away. You don't have to be afraid.* God knew what he was doing when he created me. The day I entered this world, there was an assignment for me to fulfill. I hadn't fulfilled that assignment yet, so I was healed and set free to move forward in His will. I am forever grateful, and the JOY of the Lord is my strength.

Overcomer #2

My daughter, Shanina, is a blessing to me. She has the most beautiful heart, and I am so proud of her. When Shanina was in Girl Scouts, she went camping and was bit by a tick. Shanina was a teenager at that time. It wasn't until Shanina turned twenty-nine that we learned she had Severe Lyme's Disease. The disease laid dormant in her body for over ten years. Unfortunately, we didn't learn of the diagnosis until after Shanina's trauma.

Last year, on three separate occasions, Shanina was on life support. One hospital diagnosed it as severe asthma, another stated she had vocal cord disorder, and the third said she was experiencing anxiety attacks. The doctors didn't know what was causing these coughing episodes that led to the swelling of her throat, cutting off her airway. It was a scary experience. I was like, *God, really? Are we doing this again?* I'd had my share of the hospital and didn't want to see it again.

Every night for weeks, I slept in a chair beside my daughter's bed, watching as the machine showed her heart rate dropping. I was exhausted, and once again, my faith was being tested. I could hear God clearly: *Do you trust me, Lisa? Will you serve Me even when things look bad?* I was determined the enemy wasn't going to get my mind this time. I said, "Father God, I trust you. My daughter will live and not die. You said by Your stripes we are healed, and I will stand on Your word." I prayed over my daughter every day and night. I claimed the victory and refused to lose this battle. I gave my daughter back to God the day she was born, and I had to remind Him of our agreement. I told Him to use her to glorify his kingdom. I meant it at her birth, and I meant/mean it now.

My daughter was miserable, but I needed to help control her thoughts. I kept telling her that she is healed by God, and although it didn't look promising, we must trust Him and know that He is the ultimate physician. I reminded her that God has the final say. Amid the pain, we must not give up. Together, we will fight. Together, we are the majority.

After three completely different diagnoses, I determined that we would never get an accurate diagnosis in Baltimore. So, I had my daughter flown to Scottsdale, Arizona, to be tested by the same facility that I attended for natural treatments for cancer. Envita Medical Center is amazing. They did extensive testing, and Shanina's bloodwork came back with a very high percentage of Lyme's Disease. A medical regiment was developed for Shanina, and she stayed in Arizona for treatment. Even though the process was painful, God turned our tears into triumph. Once again, we stood on the word of God, and once again, God did not disappoint. He healed my daughter, and she is living a productive life. Shanina is now a mother, and Skylar is bringing us much joy.

Conquerer #3

Skylar is what the medical field calls a Micro-Preemie. She is what we call our miracle. She weighed 1.15 pounds at birth, and she came at twenty-five weeks. How precious is life! Shanina and I witnessed a miracle right before our eyes. Every day, we visited Skylar in NICU and watched her progress day by day. I would hold her, sing songs of praise, hold her little hands, and pray over her. Her favorite song is My Redeemer Lives.

Again, I believed God would heal. So, I worked on her mind. I told Skylar how proud I was of her and how much Jesus loved her; I told her that she was healed and whole; I told her that every organ, lung, muscle, and joint of hers was strong and healthy; and I told her that she would touch lives worldwide and speak a word of deliverance on many stages. While I was praying, Skylar would lift her hands. I'm convinced she understood me and was praising God. When asked what I thought Skylar's first word would be, I said, "Hallelujah."

Skylar is now four months old and weighs nine pounds. After spending seventy-five days in NICU, she is home and healthy. Every day, I play a sermon, song, and speech for Skylar. I am feeding her mind and spirit now. How you do anything is how you do everything. She will beat the odds and be far greater than we imagine. I love this little miracle more than words can explain, and I thank God for once again showing us what love looks like.

As you have read, we have shed many tears. I doubt if our crying days are over, but I do know our faith in God is stronger than ever, and with the love, grace, and mercy of God, we will conquer whatever task is put before us. God said in his Word that no weapons formed against us shall prosper. He never said they wouldn't form; He just said they wouldn't prosper. I trust His Word, His love, and His direction. We are more than conquerors. We will walk forward, cry forward, heal forward, and pray forward. We aren't victims; we are victors. These episodes are not our story; they are just scenes in our stories, and we will not relive the same scenes over and over.

Our next level came in the form of Cancer, Severe Lyme's Disease, and a Micro-Preemie. Did we like the process? No. Was the victory life-changing? Yes. We will move forward and give God all the praise, honor, and glory day by day.

Eyes have not seen nor have ears heard the mighty things God is going to do with our lives. He's not finished with the three Jones Girls. He has great plans for our lives. World Changers, Change Agents, Impact Players, Healed and Honored, Healthy and Wealthy is our birthright, and we will walk in it. Our tears turned into triumph. To God Be All of the Glory!

. . . .

HONOR

Kimberly Ann Hobbs

"Those who have ears to hear let us hear this. The humble in spirit will retain honor. The Bible says that pride goes before fall and humility proceeds honor." (Proverbs 29:23)

Refining times are difficult. God uses them for our protection. When we honor the Lord in the refining process, He lifts us and blesses us before a watching world. Personal honor isn't the goal, but God honors us just the same.

Honor in the scriptures is far different from the type of honor that is sought after by this world. Those who thrive in this world's fleeting honor and stature are unmindful that "God opposes the proud but gives grace to the humble."

- 1 Peter 5:5
- Proverbs 16:5
- Isaiah 13:11

We live in a world that is corrupt because it does not give God the honor He deserves. Honor is found in God and His Son and in our being like Him. *(John 15:8, TPT)* When your lives bear abundant fruit, you demonstrate that you are mature disciples who glorified the Father!

As believers, we are to honor God and His Son, Jesus Christ, through our acknowledgment and confession that He is the one and only God. *(Exodus 20:3) (John 14:6) (Romans 10:9)*

We are to honor God and our recognition of eternal life that He gave us through the gift of salvation of our souls, and it comes from Jesus Christ, through humble adoration, and obedience to His will for our lives. *(John14:23-24) (John 2:6)* We need to seek God with all of our hearts to find out His will for our life. In doing so, we will find our purpose.

Through following through this, God says He will honor us when He seats us on His throne with Him in heaven. *(Revelations 3:21)* What a POWERFUL statement of honor He shares with us.

There's no greater place to be recognized as an overcomer and one who is victorious than to be placed by the Father into a seat next to Him on His throne in heaven. To be honored this way will be a triumphant celebration that I hope we can all partake in, and it can begin as we humble ourselves in Spirit.

• •

 **Traci Brown** has a passion to see broken and hurting people healed and renewed. Her heart is to use her life struggles to encourage others in their faith. She desires more of God, sharing His love wherever she goes.

Traci married her high school sweetheart, Grady Brown, in 1990. God blessed them with two children, Brittany Joy and Tannie. Brittany went to be with the Lord in 1999, but her story is a testimony of God's love.

Traci and Grady currently serve together at their church in Mathews, VA, where Grady is the Worship Pastor. Traci sings and plays drums alongside him on the Praise Team.

As founders of Brîtjoy Ministries, their goal is to spread the love of Christ through music and His Word.

Finding Britjoy
Traci Brown

Our daughter was to be born on August 17, 1996 – my mother's birthday. After being a week late, my doctor wanted to have me induced because he thought the baby was going to be too big. He was also concerned that he'd be on vacation when I went into labor. A week later, I went into labor without any help. When it was time to go to the hospital, our van would not start. So, I turned to my parents, and they immediately came to our rescue. We got to the hospital, and of course, my doctor was away on vacation. I reluctantly agreed to have the on-call doctor deliver my baby.

As labor progressed, the doctor tried to encourage me to get a C-section. They were concerned because the baby's heart rate had dropped a couple of times. The nonchalant doctor told us that we could go home with a brain-dead baby if we wanted to; he didn't seem to care since he had a golf tournament the next day. In fact, he waited in his office for most of the time while we were deciding what to do.

Being first-time parents, we were overwhelmed. Labor stretched to almost forty hours. Per my request, my parents stayed in the room with us. I knew my mother could be helpful since she had given birth to eight children. She would talk to the doctor and nurses on our behalf and help me stay calm. We even had worship music playing and scripture verses read over us. One time when the doctor came in, my mother talked to him about what to do. As he left, he said, "That woman is the closest thing to the devil I've ever seen." On the contrary, my mother is one of the most God-fearing women I know.

Finally, dilated to ten centimeters, it was time for me to push. Four hours passed without results. Our bundle of joy was too comfortable to leave the confines of my womb. After deliberations with my husband, it was decided that I would have a C-section.

Our baby's heart rate dropped again, making us frightened and unsure. I wanted to have a natural birth, but sometimes things don't always work out the way you plan them. Brittany Joy was born on my father-in-law's birthday – August 24, 1996. Weighing in at 6lb 13oz., she was beautiful! Clearly, she wasn't ten pounds as predicted, though.

Routine tests showed a hole in Brittany's heart, a heart murmur. The pediatrician suggested we take her to a cardiologist. Everyone told us it was normal and that many babies are born with a murmur. A fever kept me in the hospital longer than usual, but eventually, we went home now a family of three. Moments of feeling slighted plagued us. How could a baby be given such a fate?

Being normal was our new goal. However, worry and fear haunted us. Our daughter's future nagged our thoughts. Disagreements and stress frustrated us; we said and did things out of character. One day, my husband lifted the kitchen counter, breaking it in half and leaving a crack across the top – a constant reminder of our broken hearts.

The cardiologist identified Brittany's hole as Tetralogy of Fallot with A/V canal defect. He explained that one side of the heart was doing most of the work. He wanted to operate as soon as possible. We wanted to trust that God would heal her. We would pray, *"If this is Your will for us to proceed, help us know."*

We had to set up the surgery a couple of times, while still praying and asking God if it was His will. The first time her surgery was set up, she had a cold. Doctors never want to proceed with surgery if there is an infection. The second time, she had a clogged tear duct that had to be repaired beforehand. All the time we were waiting on God, we had times of worry. Once at a MOPS (Mothers of Preschoolers) meeting at church, I broke down and cried, expressing my fear of losing our daughter to a close friend. I remember thinking, *I asked for a child, and now, there's a chance she could be taken away from us.* I was so scared, but God always puts the right people in our path to help us through difficult situations.

One scripture that I leaned on was *2 Timothy 1:7 – "For God has not given us the spirit of fear, but of power and of love and of a sound mind."* We were at a place of uncertainty. We wanted God to heal her, and we believed He could. Feeling led to wait a little longer, we postponed the surgery again. This time, the cardiologist gave us an ultimatum. If we did not go through with the surgery, he would turn us in to social services. Of course, that made us worry even more. We know the doctor wanted the best for our daughter, but it was a big decision. Was surgery the answer? Sure, doctors are put here to help us, but they are not always right.

If you go through with the surgery, she will die, I heard. Was it fear talking? Or was it God? I believed it was a Word from the Lord.

"If God wanted me to hear this, He would have told me," Grady responded.

Unsure of what to do next, I asked God for guidance. I felt God telling me to let my husband make the decision. Whatever he decided, I would back him completely. Grady was the head of our home, and I trusted him. Maybe what I heard was doubt. God doesn't give us information to turn around and say the opposite. Giving the responsibility to my husband was what God wanted me to do. So, the decision was made, and Brittany's surgery was scheduled for April 13, 1999. It was the hardest decision we ever made. Whatever happened, we had to live with the outcome.

As we waited for her to go back for surgery, we prayed with her and tried to make her comfortable by playing games and being silly. We tried to let her know what was going to happen. I even explained to her at home beforehand. She had such an understanding of it all; it was like talking to an adult. She was the strongest little girl! I know God was with her the whole time.

Grady handed our precious daughter to the surgeon but felt like he had done something wrong. We watched them walk away and disappear into the operating room. Brittany had such trust in her eyes.

Grady is one of the strongest men I know, but giving his baby girl over to the hands of the surgeon took so much out of him. Grady accepted Christ in 1994 at an Easter production at our former church. He loves the Lord and his family. He desires to see everyone come to Christ.

But, when his grandma died in 1997 and then his dad in 1998, among other disappointments, he said more than once that he did much better living for himself because once he became a Christian, things started going wrong. Now, here he was doing one of the hardest things he had ever done. Brittany was his pride and joy! How could she ever trust him again?

As we waited for the results with family, I was determined to fast and pray. I knew God would hear my prayers and that she would be fine. Eight hours later, she came out of the surgery. Everything had gone well. Although she went in a two-year-old, she seemed to return a 22-year-old. She was a completely different person.

Once again, we were leaving the hospital. I looked forward to having a regular routine again. Looking back, I wished we stayed longer because soon after, something was wrong. Brittany wasn't eating. Food seemed to make her sick, and she had lost a lot of weight. The surgeon assured us this was normal and that she would be okay. Not sure if the surgeon was correct, I decided to take her to her pediatrician.

Her pediatrician knew the problem right away; Brittany wasn't getting enough oxygen. We were sent to Kings Daughter's across town. They tried their best to help her. Talks of another catheterization and possibly more surgery. We had always prayed that Brittany wouldn't have to go through surgeries her whole life. We wanted her to have a normal life. Then again, what is normal?

On July 2nd, I waited until one in the morning for my mother to come to stay with her so Grady and I could get some sleep. We were exhausted. Before I left, I told Brittany to call out to Jesus if she was scared. I had always said to her if she was ever scared, to call on Jesus, and He would help her. Before, she would always say Jesus right away. This time, she didn't want to say His name.

It was like she knew what would happen. When she did finally say Jesus, I immediately felt something change in her. I prayed over her once more and kissed her goodbye. Then we went to the Ronald McDonald House across the street to get some shuteye.

Once we got to our room, my mother called and said to come right away. Something was wrong. The doctors worked through the night to save her. After some time, they told us that she was brain dead. With friends and family with us, the doctor tried to help us understand what could be done to help Brittany. I didn't want to hear it anymore. My heart was breaking in two. I ran off and went to the chapel, where I cried out to God, "Don't take my baby!" I immediately heard God's voice say, "She wasn't yours to keep."

After many attempts to help her, she was pronounced dead at 5:00 a.m. My mother said that once I said goodbye and walked away, Brittany turned her head away and became lifeless. We visualized her taking Jesus' hand and walking into heaven that July 3rd. Grady would always say that Brittany received her independence, Freedom. She was so strong, even at the end. She always wanted to please us, so I imagined she wanted to stay for us. But, once she saw heaven, there was no coming back. I know the decision was hard for her, just like the one we had to make about her surgery.

The days that followed were excruciating. Life was different now. Things were quiet. Still. No little person in the home. Grady went back to work, and I tried to find a job so I wouldn't be alone with my thoughts. We both wanted to leave this earth. I even thought of lying on the road so a car could run me over. This was not the way things were supposed to happen. We both felt God had let us down. For the longest time, I even blamed myself for her death.

As time went on, we did our best to live without her. We had a lot of friends, but they couldn't make up for our loss. I read *The Power of a Praying Wife* by Stormie Omartian. This book changed my perspective on prayer. I would pray at the drop of a hat now. No matter what was happening, I prayed. More and more, God showed His love toward us. Grady had been given a guitar and wanted to get better at playing, but he lost interest after Brittany died. Brittany would come into the room where he practiced, and they would sing while he played. Sometimes she would drop pics in the soundhole, and he'd have to fish them out.

About a year after Brittany passed, I met someone at a paint store that was turned into a music studio. The gentleman had heard our story and wanted to meet Grady. They started guitar lessons right away, and friendship immediately grew. Six months into the lessons, he told us that God wanted him to stop receiving money, and they would work on music as friends. I believe this man was sent to us by God because healing was taking place in Grady. This wonderful man is still a friend to us today!

As a wife and/or mother, we always try to be there for others, but we forget about ourselves. I would do my best to care for Brittany, and then when she passed, I wanted to pray and help my husband as much as I could. But, I had not grieved for my daughter. I tried so hard to be strong for everyone else that I forgot about me. My mother even stated that she hardly saw me cry. How could I? I didn't have time to grieve. More so, I cried for my husband. I wanted him to be well. I couldn't stand by and watch him get knocked down and not help him back up. Prayer was the biggest part of our healing, but I forgot about myself.

In 2002, God blessed us with another child – a son named Tannie. Laughter filled our home again, but we still grieved. It takes a long time to process the loss of a child. No one knows how to act; it's not the usual order of things. Some marriages end in divorce. Some people turn to addiction. In our case, we spent money to fill the void, accumulating major debt. Debt that almost cost us our home. Because I didn't fully grieve when I needed to, I would get frustrated and not know how to deal with my emotions.

I recall one time when our son was three. I was getting him ready to leave the house, and something made me so angry that I screamed at him. It wasn't a typical scream; it came from the deep depths of my soul. I felt like the worst mother in the world! How could I yell at him like that? My mother helped me realize that it was all my grief that I'd held in for so long. I knew I had to focus more prayer time on getting well. I never wanted to react like that again, especially to my son.

As years passed, we began living for God as best we could. Volunteering at our church and ministering outside of the church – wherever God wanted us to go, we went. We would use our voices, and Grady would play his guitar. Lots of opportunities to minister were there for us. Through music, God had been healing us. Brittany always loved to sing, especially with her dad. I'd like to think she's in heaven singing her heart out in the most magnificent choir we've yet to hear.

We went through the MIP (Ministerial Internship Program) classes together in the Church of God, and Grady is now an Ordained Minister. He is the Worship Pastor at our church, and I lead alongside him. Our son, Tannie, also loves music. He has a great voice and plays the drums and banjo.

I told Brittany that I would use her story to lead others to Christ. One day in heaven, they'll meet Jesus…and her. Even at her funeral, we sang her favorite songs, "You Are My Sunshine" being her #1 favorite. We know many turned their lives over to Christ through her testimony.

I'm amazed at how God took two crushed people and turned them into walking miracles. If it weren't for prayer, we'd be at a different place in our lives. But God! John 16:33 sticks out in my mind: *"These things I have spoken to you, that in me you might have peace. In the world you will have trials and tribulation: but be of good cheer; I have overcome the world."* In life, we all go through tough situations. Where we end up is really up to us. We can either choose to turn away from God or walk beside Him. It's not always an easy decision to make, but I can assure you that walking with Him is the better one.

We never thought we would lose our daughter, but God is still using us. My husband and I are no one special. We are clay in His hands, and He continues to work on us for His glory. I can't promise you it will be an easy road if you choose to walk in the Lord's path, but I can guarantee you that He will always be there for you! I would love to grow in God without having to go through something so difficult. But, in the greatness of eternity, we will see our Brittany again!

One day, we will have the answers as to why we go through such difficult situations. My husband always says, "Once we get to heaven, it won't matter anymore. So why ask?" Press on toward the path that is set before you. I pray you all will live for Christ, no matter your circumstances.

In 2017, we started a ministry called Britjoy (pronounced Bright-Joy) after our daughter. God gives us a bright future and hope even in difficult times. He restores our joy so we can live this life for Him. We believe that through our healing, God has restored our joy. That's how we found Britjoy. We want to be used by God in such a way that others will be healed and renewed. We want to reach the lost and broken of this world. Through music and God's word, we want to use Brittany Joy's testimony and our love for Jesus to help win the lost.

. . . .

JOY

Kimberly Ann Hobbs

How many of us can say we have true inner joy? Many people get joy confused with happiness. Joy isn't like happiness, which is based on happenings or whether things are going well or not. Joy remains even in the midst of suffering. Joy from God's Word is a gift. There are over 150 references to joy in God's Word.

The two main definitions of joy are in God's Word: 1) gladness in the Lord, such as happiness, contentment, and delight, and 2) rejoice, which describes the outward expression of our internal joy. Both of these are connected. Rejoicing flows out of gladness in the Lord, and our gladness in the Lord increases the more we rejoice. How wonderful is this?

We should all desire to have joy in our hearts. It's what God's Word tells us. I used to sing a song to my children when they were small, using hand motions that went with it. The song emphasized the importance of the word. *I have the joy, joy, joy, joy down in my heart. Where? Down in my heart. Where? Down in my heart. I have the joy, joy, joy, joy down in my heart. Where? Down in my heart to stay.* And it went on, emphasizing the importance of joy residing in the heart and staying there. Joy comes from God. More specifically, it comes from the Holy Spirit. *(1 Thess. 1:6)* Joy is a fruit of the Spirit.

When we have faith and are obedient to God, the Bible tells us our joy will be complete. *(John 15:11)* Our closeness to God results in loving Him. The closer we draw to Him, the closer He draws to us. This love and faith in God fills us with joy, as Peter talks about in *1 Peter 1:8*.

When we are experiencing sin in our life, it hinders us from experiencing the joy that God intends for us to have. Sin separates us from God, who is our source of joy. It's difficult to look through a dark cloud that blinds our vision. We need to examine what may be hindering us from experiencing the joy that blesses us. Ask God to reveal it to you. If you are feeling depressed and lacking true inner joy, something may be blocking that internal joy. God will do it; He will show you where the problem is if you ask Him. You may find that repentance over the exposed sin will bring you the freedom and joy that transcends the circumstances. The gladness in your heart comes from God alone. God can't be present in a sinful situation. Confess your sins. God is faithful and just to forgive those sins and cleanse you from all unrighteousness. *(1 John 1:9)*

True joy can enter where God is present because where God is present, there is joy. Joy is the result of a life that is lived for God.

* *

Alicia Lane was raised in a 6-sibling family in Scottsdale, Arizona. Drawn to books and poetry at an early age, she began to write in elementary school. She continued her passion with a language degree, followed by a marketing and PR career in writing, editing and advocacy. She is a wordsmith at heart, and enjoys influencing others through her written contributions.

Writing allows her to bring others together and to refocus lives on the positive. The end of her story isn't written yet, because God is not finished with His design, but by trusting him she will arrive at His blessed destination.

When not at work, Alicia is a band mom, scout mom, and UF Gator mom. She and her family reside in South Florida with three lazy cats and the cats' fish tanks.

No Perfect Legacy –
Climbing Toward Resilience

Alicia Lane

"You are the salt of the Earth." (Matthew 5:13)

I recently lost my saltiness – my ability to give to and influence others. A turn of life made me question who I was and stole my identity. I curled up, pulled away, and closed off part of my heart – dead to the world and saltless. My energies were focused on my problems, with nothing left for the world. This story shares how I got my mojo back.

I was born the middle kid in a Brady Bunch family of three girls and three boys but without the housekeeper. Grandma was the spiritual giant in my life. She would braid our hair, buy us Easter outfits, and kneel with us for bedtime prayers. God was her core and her foundation. Her Italian-English Bible was a symbol of her wisdom. Like Grandma, I wanted to leave a legacy and find a way to make the world a better place.

The Bible says, *"Train up a child in the way he should go, and when he is old, he will not depart from it." (Proverbs 22:6)* Our parents worked hard to give us faith-based values. We attended Camp Good News and youth groups. Summers meant backpack trips to the Colorado Rockies. Dad was an electronics engineer but also a mountaineer and alpine climber. He raised our family to be strong and independent. The beauty of God's untouched wilderness offset freeze-dried food, frozen toes, and hiking with a heavy pack.

In time, Dad became legally blind from hemorrhages in the retinas of his eyes. Laser surgery could not save his eyesight. He could still climb but not see to read, watch TV, or drive. Bike wrecks and climbing accidents became his norm. He learned avalanche survival and volcano trekking, countering his visual handicap by training his other senses. He involved us in rappelling, white-water rafting, spelunking, and solo survival hikes with no food. We gained strength, independence, courage, and resolve from this training. Also, during this time, my sister struggled with anorexia, starving herself down to thirty-eight pounds.

"Be strong and courageous, for the Lord, your God, will be with you wherever you go." (Joshua 1:9)

With all the family challenges, my resolve was to build my own identity. I transferred to a college in Chicago and visited Grandma on weekends and holidays. My spunky grandmother helped with laundry and always sent me back with extra food rations. I studied languages and took my first trips to South America and Europe. In Quito, I met the American wrestler who would one day become my spouse.

I finished college and grad school, then married and moved to Baltimore. Shortly after, while working in Washington, DC, I received a call from the State Department. My alpine dad had just been killed ice climbing in Switzerland when he fell 1,500 feet. He died in God's country with his boots on. My saddest regret was not mailing his Father's Day card in time to arrive before he left the country, because he never made it back. He didn't get to meet my kids, but he left a legacy of resilience for them. I penned a poem in his memory:

Legacy in the Sky – For Dad

A peak, a mountain standing tall,
Sending an undying call.
Dressed in pearly virgin snow,
Sleek and chiseled, she did grow.
A thousand facets grace her form,
A million years since she was born.
Her special home 'twixt earth and sky,
Gives pause to fragile human eyes.
A regal splendor, heaven-blessed view,
And yet, this is where I lost you.
She welcomed you with open arms,
And gave you peace among her charms.
She coaxed you up where eagles fly,
It was for this you had to die.
You saw and felt and knew her all,
And so, she cradled your great fall.
The mountain's secrets she will keep,
For none was there to guide your feet.
And all our sorrows answer why,
Now paint your legacy in the sky.

> *"There's a time for everything, and a season for every activity under the heavens." (Ecclesiastes 3:1)*

I had moved away and was intentional about avoiding family drama. My husband opened a successful physical therapy clinic, where we treated 4,000 local patients in fourteen years. I was proud of the community impact we contributed through faith, family, and career.

Years later, as a property manager, I was interviewed as a recipient of a Manager of Excellence Award. One of my interview responses would soon become my biggest bane, and I never saw it coming. The family drama I had so deftly avoided over the years would catch up to me, and I could no longer sit on the sidelines.

The question: What is your proudest personal achievement?

My response: Two happy, well-balanced kids! Kids are the legacy we leave to make the world a better place. There are no do-overs. It's one job we must get right the first time.

It started in the spring when my husband was working with our son in the garage. Following directions and achieving results both proved unattainable for our son. I was not home to mediate, and tempers started to flare. When my husband grabbed his shirt, our son called the police. Mistrust built between the two for the next year. Our son's cell phone was taken away from him for several weeks, including during a 3-week family vacation. He began seeing a Christian family therapist. My husband, not seeing the gravity of the situation, chose not to participate.

That winter, after Christmas, the dysfunction finally arrived. My beautiful boy and my steadfast husband could not get along, and life imploded.

"My God is my rock, in whom I take refuge." (2 Samuel 22:3)

Our son wouldn't get up for church, so I decided we would stay home and do chores. He was impossible to motivate that day. Around lunchtime, he brought me an unfinished suicide note. Determined, I chose to work around it until we could make progress on the chore list. I had experienced a suicidal sibling and knew that steady reactions are critical. Unaware of the note, my husband kept adding tasks to the list, and they began to disagree. Both became full of rage and hurt, each insulting the other, and my life's legacy was destroyed. Our son picked up a kitchen knife, and my husband, remembering the first time the police were called, immediately called them again, introducing a potential felony for our son.

"The righteous are as bold as a lion." (Proverbs 28:1)

Without my purse or shoes, I put my son in the car and drove around the block, but there was nowhere to run. I watched as officers placed my fifteen-year-old, almost-Eagle Scout son in handcuffs while his chin quivered and eyes watered.

"Mom," he whispered, "I can't miss a week of school."

While providing a background to the police, I showed his suicide note to them. They would Baker Act him as "a threat to himself or others" and place him in Children's Hospital for observation. They also initiated a "No Contact Order" between my son and my husband. I had no idea what would happen next, but our teen would have to report to juvenile lockup due to the knife threat. During all of this, I remained calm and logical in my grief and despair. I prayed to God for wisdom and grace as I walked back inside my home that was now missing one hurting soul. My husband said our son was not welcome to come back home. To me, that meant I no longer had a home either. No mother should be asked to abandon her child. God gave us children to steward and develop, but they all belong to Him. My job was not yet finished.

I dove into action, creating a support team of women who loved my son and could serve as an inner circle. They had to be tough, outspoken, and love him unconditionally. I would need them to help with legal battles and family resources. I called my "adopted" grandma, "adopted" aunt, and two-family friends. All were strong women and huge advocates for my son, but only two belonged to God. Little did I know how much God's relationship would matter.

I will save you from the hands of the wicked and redeem you from the grasp of the cruel. (Jeremiah 15:21)

At first, everything was fine. One friend had legal credentials and experience with child advocacy. She helped my teen get released after the Baker Act expired, and she kept him until we could show up under her guidance for court. She arranged a legal advocate for him and contacted Child Protective Services.

The next friend offered to take him the following week during the No Contact Order. But then, those two friends advised me to take all my money and my son and run – start a new life. When I chose not to do that, they began proceedings to challenge my parental authority, accusing me of not protecting him.

> *"He rescued me from my powerful enemy, from my foes, who were too strong for me." (2 Samuel 22:18)*

They began sowing mistrust with my son and told me to contact a battered women's shelter if I wanted help. I was floored! They had just offered to open their doors to us, allowing me to stay with my son. Now they were trying to separate us and control him! They were communicating privately via text messages with my fifteen-year-old teen without parental consent. They asked if he felt unsafe and offered to contact 9-1-1. By the time I came across the messages, it was too late to stop what they had already initiated.

> *"Trust in the Lord with all your heart and lean not on your own understanding." (Proverbs 3:5)*

Child Protective Services called me at work for a meeting. The betrayal felt wicked and cruel. These were family friends who turned their backs on me. His things were at their homes. How could I have misjudged them so completely? When I questioned them, they said, "It's not about you." As they ruined our parenting credibility with the courts, Family Services, and even our local high school, I struggled to find a place to live until the No Contact

Order could be lifted. How could I survive the shame and guilt of this public failure, when I had said there were no do-overs? I felt like a hypocrite, a loser, a pariah in the community, homeless, and mostly, I felt lonely with nobody left on whom I could lean aside from my adopted grandma and aunt. All the emotional support for our son fell on me alone.

> *"Under His wings you will find refuge; his faithfulness will be your shield." (Psalm 91:4)*

A Christian couple took us in with the plan to set parameters for my son and help with a semester of home-based classes while I continued working. We joined their family life for a few weeks – partaking in parties, puppies, and personal support.

When mistrust sowed by the inner circle took root, our teen's attorney contacted CPS, turning family and friends against each other. I stayed up all night composing a legal response with evidence to support my case against contacts who were controlling my son's emotions and causing more crisis. During this stress, I realized I had surrounded myself with friends to protect me from the system; however, those same people were calling on the system to protect me from "friends." Our teen had no idea who to trust or believe. On Super Bowl Sunday night, he overdosed on anti-depressants issued by Children's Hospital. I sat by his side in the ER, awake all night, then changed clothes and went to work. After this, he was Baker Acted to a different facility located more than an hour away. Again, all the visitation and driving fell on me.

He seemed better upon his release a couple of weeks later, having been prescribed a new medication for anxiety and depression. However, with the stress of playing catch-up from weeks of missed school, and having to answer awkward questions from students and staff, he was Baker Acted a third time. Our host family was eventually visited by CPS, which was hurtful and insulting for them on top of the suicide attempt. Out of respect for their reputation, I left our temporary housing. All my other contacts were afraid to house us; the potential impact was just too risky.

> *"One who has unreliable friends soon comes to ruin, but there is a friend who sticks closer than a brother." (Proverbs 18:24)*

I hit bottom with nowhere to go but home – right where the old "friends" said I would end up because I was "too weak to stand up for myself." Work colleagues wondered how I managed to keep functioning since I never missed a beat, but my years of physical, mental, and spiritual training gave me the stamina to keep going. I resolved to push on and be strong for our son. The only way to survive was to shut down and just keep handling everything.

My husband contacted authorities to have the No Contact order lifted, but I was fearful of a possible explosion between him and our son. I needed to ensure that communications wouldn't break down again. I found myself helicoptering between them, smoothing things over, and scheduling activities to keep them separated. I couldn't risk a repeat of the trip to the depths of despair. Life was emotionally exhausting for several months as I waited for signs of trust to re-develop between them.

"He lifted me out of the slimy pit, out of the mud and mire; He set my feet on a rock and gave me a firm place to stand." (Psalm 40:2)

From the bottom of this pit, God began to provide a ladder for me to climb, with individual rungs to restoration and resilience, and I found myself finally believing I could claim His legacy step-by-step:

- A colleague walked back into my life, woke me up from my survival trance, and reminded me that life was not over. I am strong and valued, and the dreams and plans in my heart can become seeds for a whole new future. I just had to climb up and grab that rung.

- A friend requested I hand-deliver a letter, and that journey took me to a group, Women World Leaders, where I found a purpose for my faith, my values, and my global vision. I found the opportunity to build a new ministry with other women across the globe. Another rung on the ladder.

- My son finished his court-mandated therapy and progressed with his online schoolwork, allowing him to take a month re-bonding with family in Arizona. He now has renewed relationships with cousins, aunts, and uncles as part of his circle of support. This step toward helping him get healthy was another climb out of the pit.

- My daughter had the chance to study abroad and requested that I join her afterward for a quick mental break. We planned a budget trip via Eurail and hostels to eight countries in two weeks, renewing Italian roots and visiting Swiss peaks to honor Grandpa. This trip filled me with memories, energy, faith, and strength as I encountered young adults with a global vision who will lead our world tomorrow; they need wisdom, guidance, and love today. *"I have opened a door for you that no one can close." (Revelation 3:8)*

- Our family therapist reminded me: "God is never late, but he isn't early either. We must listen, and everything he plans will happen right on time. We cannot rush Him." This was a reminder that I have to climb at His speed, not my own. I can't arrive any faster by taking matters into my own hands. *"For I know the plans I have for you, plans to prosper you and not to harm you, plans to give you hope and a future." (Jeremiah 29:11)*

- My husband began meeting with a counselor from church and reading books on restoring his relationship with our son. Part of his progress included walking away from a career that robbed the life and vitality from his soul. He had to hit bottom in his own way, with God denying achievements and resources in the process. His road back to stronger family dynamics is in God's control.

Ultimately for me, a legacy dependent on my strategies alone was not sustainable. Perfect legacies come from flawed humans working hand-in-hand with a flawless God. He designs the steps on all of our ladders, and we are only responsible for our own benchmarks. It is up to each of us to complete our climb towards God's resilience.

I can now be the salt of the earth again, building a new purpose in my soul. My dream is stewarding young adults who can build their legacies by using God's wisdom to help them climb their ladders. College campuses, youth hostels, crisis pregnancy centers, community organizations, job training centers, and today's political parties are all hosts to world leaders of tomorrow. We must equip and armor young ambassadors to withstand the challenges they will face. Thanks to Grandma's nurturing, Dad's tested strength, and my trip to the bottom, legacies for Christ can be born anew and influence the world.

"She is clothed with strength and dignity, and she laughs without fear of the future." (Proverbs 31:25)

RESOLVE

Kimberly Ann Hobbs

Sometimes when a new calendar year begins, people tend to make resolutions to do something that will change their life, or they commit themselves to do certain things for progress or achieving goals. Many times, though, they are hard-pressed to follow through with their commitments.

The biblical model for us is to focus on being like Jesus daily. We need to resolve to live as servants of Him at all times. As our New Year's resolutions may breakdown and willpower and perseverance fade, change can occur yet again, and it may not always be for the better.

How can we be resolved to make sure our growth leads to actual improvement? Our improvements need to be measured by specific scriptural admonitions and standards. If our hearts are not burdened over a failure to honor God by submitting to His Word, we may waver with our behavior. That's because our minds are not conformed to God and His Word.

When we resolve to God, we need to listen to the Spirit of God at work in our hearts. I found this was the only way I could resolve to change. I often pray the same prayer that David did in *Psalm 139:23-24 – "God, I invite your searching gaze into my heart. Examine me through and through; find out everything that may be hidden within me. Put me to the test and sift through all my anxious cares. See if there is any path of pain I'm walking on, and lead me back to your glorious, everlasting ways – the path that brings me back to you."*

Without asking God for help, how could any of us resolve to any commitment and make it lasting? I know that instead of trying harder to be a better person on my own, I – like David – am learning daily where I specifically fall short of God's standards. I want to know where my sin is so I can forsake it. I ask God to reveal it to me each day, thereby growing and changing daily in my life. My resolve is to walk in practical holiness as the Spirit of God leads me to the everlasting way of God versus the way of the world.

The actual resolve to change is not complicated. Change is as simple as confessing our sin, repenting of it, and by faith walking in the spirit of obedience. Our ability to be sustained in holiness and obedience is dependent on our faith in Christ's POWER, grace, and faithfulness. May God give you the grace to believe the truth and scripture, and strength to walk in it. Resolve daily to follow Jesus. He will lead you to true and lasting change.

 **Jill Murphy** is the author of, Hearts Unveiled, a manual/handbook used in leading support groups for women who've been sexually abused. She has helped women across the United States, to include, Minnesota, California, Texas, and Florida.

She and her friend, Mary Varughese, founded a Sexual Abuse Recovery Program for women called "Hearts Unveiled Ministries." Mary is a psychologist and counselor with 20 years of experience in teaching and counseling in India. Through "Radiant Faces" (the international division of their program), she has conducted two group therapies and counseled many adult survivors in India, Australia, Dubai, and Kenya.

Jill is currently pursuing her PhD, and her dissertation is in the area of counseling Adult Women Survivors of Childhood Sexual Abuse.

For more information about having Jill or Mary provide one-on-one or group counseling, training members of your church or organization to lead a support group, or speaking at an event, please feel free to contact them via HeartsUnveiledMinistries. com, Hearts Unveiled Ministries Facebook page, or via Women World Leaders.

Surrender Your Past

Jill Murphy

"Hope deferred makes the heart sick; but when desire is fulfilled, it is a tree of life." (Proverbs 13:12, AMP)

Are you in a situation that is causing you to feel hopeless? If you knew your healing would come at the end of what you're facing, would it be worth the pain you'd have to go through to get there? You may be a woman who's just beginning to go through the valley of darkness, or you may be in the deepest part of the valley. Maybe you've come through and are on the other side of the valley. Well, I'm a woman who knows what it's like to feel stranded, abandoned, and alone. However, I can honestly tell you there is hope waiting for you on the other side of that valley. It's hard to see God when you're in the midst of the trial, and that's why I felt it was important to tell my story.

As a woman who was sexually abused as a young girl, I've felt hopeless. I know what it's like to think that my identity will always be tied to the abuse and fear that the damaging effects will always be part of me. But, God showed me that Satan is an identity thief! Not only did he try to steal my identity in Christ and cause me to feel unworthy, but he also tried to defraud God and make me believe things about Him that weren't true! Just know there will be a purpose that comes from your pain! I don't believe I would be where I am today had it not been for the pain I've experienced in my life. God was able to take my experiences and make me into who I am today as a result of His redeeming work!

You see, I was like many of you – not wanting to relive painful events in my past and trying desperately to fix myself. I've been a faithful follower for over forty years, and I've read countless Christian self-help books on how to live the best Christian life, be a good wife, mother, and friend. I've read daily devotions and journaled often over the years. What I realized as a result of doing all those rituals was that no matter how hard I tried, I wasn't changing…at least not in the ways I hoped I would. All of those things were just tools in the hand of God. If they could fix me, then I wouldn't need God! What I needed was for God to come in and heal me, but I first needed to know in what ways I needed healing.

My story begins with my sexual abuse, but it doesn't end there! There were ways the sexual abuse affected me that wouldn't manifest themselves until many years later. In fact, there have been three significant experiences in my life that have produced the most spiritual growth and faith in me, and I want to share with you what I've learned along the way.

As I mentioned, I was a victim of sexual abuse. Shortly following that is when I learned the first of the powerful lessons God had in store for me and what it truly meant to forgive someone.

"*For if you forgive others their trespasses [their reckless and willful sins], your heavenly Father will also forgive you.*" (*Matthew 6:14, AMP*)

As an indirect result of my sexual abuse, I became pregnant at the age of fifteen. Unfortunately, back then, the only alternatives for teen moms were to get married (the law requires your parents' permission, which mine would not give), keep the baby (this would have necessitated help from my family and being able to continue to live in their home or dropping out of school), or give up the baby for adoption (which ultimately was the only choice offered to me by my parents). Since I was so young and emotionally unprepared for what this involved, I didn't fully grasp the toll it would take on me. I'll come back to this part of my story later, but the first moment of grace of that otherwise life-altering experience came when the man who sexually abused me accepted Jesus Christ as his Savior and asked for forgiveness from me. I was able to grant that request with no regrets, and it was in being confronted with the choice to forgive him that God used him as the instrument for saving me! You see, if I hadn't forgiven him, I more than likely wouldn't have had an open heart and mind to receive the message of salvation for myself. I didn't realize it then, but I do now. So much more took place as a result of the sexual abuse than I realized at the time. Unfortunately, I would find out many years later, and I'll get to that.

After many years of believing the sexual abuse was part of my history, its tentacles found their way into my life again. I eventually became divorced as a result of my husband not being supportive or even trying to understand why the effects of my abuse lingered for so many years. I realized then the effects of the damage of sexual abuse remain dormant regardless of what has taken place in our lives since. It doesn't get erased from our memory, or its impact lessened just because we've gone on to live our lives as though it never happened. Despite forgiving my abuser, the stark reality was I had been subjected to the same harmful effects as every other sexually-abused woman. I also required healing from the damage it caused to my heart, mind, and soul. Restoration needed to take place!

What I discovered was that God knew what was still affecting me deep inside, and He wanted to set me free. Up until I went through a program for sexual abuse victims, there was no one else I knew who this had happened to. Then, all of a sudden, it seemed I would hear other members in my family and friends share their experiences, some of whom had gone to counselors for years. A desire – a longing, really – to help other women who were victims of sexual abuse began to take root in my heart, and I began to pray for God to use me to help bring permanent healing to these women. When I would pray for God to use me, I specifically prayed that whatever program I used would be one that would bring permanent healing once and for all to these women.

At around that time, I worked about forty-five minutes from home and used to ride a commuter bus to work. Between the drive to the commuter lot and the bus ride, it would take 1-1/4 hours each way, and something started taking place in me that I can only attribute to the Holy Spirit! God stepped in and revealed to me what takes place during the healing process for women like me. Thoughts of how to help these women flooded my mind in the middle of the night, while showering, and during my commute back and forth to work. I developed wisdom that didn't come from any education or training; I gained a new understanding of what they needed with no reason or explanation for knowing these things.

By the time summer was over, I had the complete outline and skeleton for material to be used in a different program than the one I intended to use. This was unexpected, and I wasn't prepared for what God was going to do. I could never have planned or created this on my own, and it was more than I could have ever asked for or imagined. That fall, I held my first support group. One of the biggest blessings I received during that time was God connecting me with another woman who also felt a calling to help women with this issue. She has since become a dear friend and partner in this ministry.

As I worked with each group, I gained a new understanding of what they needed and was able to compile enough content to put it into a participant's handbook/leader's manual, which I called *Unveiled Hearts*. I'm proof that God uses ordinary people! I don't have a college degree, professional license, or counseling experience. Yet, God chose to make me into a vessel that would provide a healing salve for women's hearts and souls! I truly see the work of the Holy Spirit as I meet with women, and they genuinely heal and transform in front of my eyes. The women who complete the program, which takes place once a week for twenty-nine weeks, are not the same women who begin the program. I've been so blessed and privileged to be able to witness the work of God as it unfolds, and it brings life to my soul to see His handiwork unveiled.

> *"You (Satan) intended to harm me, but God intended it for good to accomplish what is now being done, the saving of many lives." (Genesis 50:20, NIV)*

Remember what I said about Satan being an identity thief? Satan wants to rob God of the honor and glory due in His name! Satan wanted to use my sexual abuse to keep me in bondage and angry, but God wanted to use it to redeem my life and give me a purpose. Satan wanted to use it to make me feel ashamed and unworthy, but God wanted to give me hope!

> *"But you, Lord, are a shield around me, my glory, the One who lifts my head high." (Psalm 3:3, NIV)*

The first major lesson in my life was about forgiveness in the form of Jesus Christ. The next lesson I learned was about humility, and this is when I was introduced to the Holy Spirit. After having a few blissful years of meeting and being reunited with the birth son I had given up for adoption, that time came to a screeching halt when he decided to abandon our relationship and cut ties with us. This period of my life brought the most heart-wrenching, agonizing, emotional pain I'd ever felt so far in my life, and I called this period my personal "Garden of Gethsemane." I thought I knew what crying tears of blood and a breaking heart felt like. I couldn't speak; it hurt so badly!

> *"In the same way, the Spirit [comes to us and] helps us in our weakness. We do not know what prayer to offer or how to offer it as we should, but the Spirit Himself [knows our need and at the right time] intercedes on our behalf with sighs and groanings too deep for words." (Romans 8:26, AMP)*

As if it wasn't bad enough to experience this level of emotional pain, I felt alone. Either everyone around me didn't understand what I was feeling, or they judged and condemned me for giving him up in the first place. Their words and actions felt to me as though they thought I deserved what was happening to me, and I carried the guilt of that initial decision to give him up all over again.

For the first time in my life, I had nobody to turn to and asked to receive the Holy Spirit. I didn't comprehend at the time just what that meant, but I would find out later what a difference this decision would make in my life. I had no one else to help me or provide solace, and I knew I needed someone to come to my aid. So, I would bring my agony to the altar and lay it at the Father's feet and ask Him to bring me comfort. Just as God showed up for Jesus when He resurrected Him, He used the song "Oceans" to let me know this excruciating experience would bring me closer to God as I clung to Him and relied on Him for strength in this trial.

> *"The LORD is close to the brokenhearted and saves those who are crushed in spirit." (Psalm 34:18)*

In addition, I had made a selfish decision to pursue that relationship and hurt others who I love in the process. For the first time, I was no longer the one on the giving end of forgiveness, but rather, I needed to acknowledge the hurt I brought on others and ask for their forgiveness. The restoration in those relationships has taken many years and is still not complete, but thankfully, God is mending their hearts.

> *"He heals the brokenhearted and binds up their wounds." (Psalm 147:3)*

This is the part of the story where humility was born in me. I think this was a crucial step in making what would follow possible. I realized that God's purpose in all of this was to bring me full circle so I could finally grieve the loss of giving up my birth son as a baby. He knew I had just gone through the motions and did what I felt – and was told – would be best for my baby. But, I had shut off the emotions necessary to fully process and deal with that event in my life. So, it took God walking me through that all over again and me having to let go and "give him up" as an adult. As difficult as it was, I was able to see what God was doing in making sure this was something from my past I could finally let go and that it would not continue to stir up guilt and shame in me. Little did I know this last event was not the worst of what I would experience. There was more to come! The last of the profound lessons in my life was about love and was going to show me that what I knew and believed about God paled in comparison to who He is!

> "Even though I walk through the darkest valley, I will fear no evil, for you are with me; your rod and your staff, they comfort me." (Psalm 23:4, NIV)

I had been dating a man named Patrick for several years. One day while working, I received a phone call from a hospital telling me that there had been an accident at his workplace, and I needed to come to the hospital immediately. From the tone of her voice, I knew it was bad. So, I asked her if he was still alive, and she said he was. Then, I asked if he was conscious, and she told me that he wasn't. Because I wasn't a direct family member, she couldn't give me any details about what happened or any specifics on his condition. However, I prayed in the car on the way to the hospital that

I could speak to him one last time and that he would know I was there with him. I was not prepared for what I would be told when I arrived at the hospital.

When I went into the emergency room, I was directed to a private room. One of his adult daughters was there, as well. So, I asked her if she knew what was going on, and she said she didn't. A short time later, several people entered the room and informed us that Patrick had shot himself in the head and had been declared brain dead. They were only keeping him on life support to retrieve his organs for donation. I can't tell you the utter shock and disbelief I felt! Nothing prepares you for news like this! I had just seen Patrick a few days earlier, and we had spent the day together, having a pleasant time together picnicking down by the river.

As details emerged, it was disclosed that Patrick had been laid off from work and, probably out of concern for not knowing how he would be able to provide for his three daughters (two of which were minors at the time), he acted out of desperation, taking his own life. While there's more that I could share about not only the compassion God gave me for others who've lost loved ones as a result of suicide but also the understanding of how someone who loved God could commit suicide, I only want to focus on how God used that in my life.

As I was going through Patrick's belongings after his death, I came across a book titled *The Shack* and remembered that he had recommended I read it. So, I took it home with me and waited for God to let me know when I was ready to read it. I think it was a few months later, and as I did, my eyes slowly opened to who God is and His true character. By the time I was done reading it, I could say with certainty that I believe God only wants our good!

> *"Those who sow weeping will go out with songs of joy." (Psalm 126:5)*

I finally knew deep down in my soul how much God loved me and cared about every aspect of my life, especially the pain! I could picture Him hurting along with me, not on the sidelines just watching everything take place.

That's when I realized God hadn't changed; He was the same God in the darkness that He had always been in the light. Through each of these situations in my life, God revealed a new aspect of His character to me. Of course, as we all do, I've had more important lessons I've needed to learn in my walk with God, but those three have formed the foundation on which I now firmly stand in faith and trust as I move forward in life. Once my view of God was no longer distorted by my emotions, human frailty, and immaturity, I was able to trust Him no matter what came my way. I also understood what happened to Patrick's faith that caused him to give in to the temptation to kill himself. God reminded me of the parable of the seeds in Matthew 13, and I realized that Patrick represented the seed that was sown beside the road. I knew he had heard the Word and responded to the Word. But, unfortunately, he didn't understand the extent of God's love for him, and it never penetrated and took hold of his heart. How he felt about himself was more powerful than how God saw him.

Our perception of our situation sometimes clouds our ability to see Him and fully understand His love for us. Do we really believe he's our stronghold and defender? If so, then why are we afraid? You see, part of me believed that I didn't deserve to keep any relationship. I'd been divorced twice, had to give up my birth son twice, and lost someone I loved to suicide. In my mind, this was confirmation that God was punishing me for something I'd done. All that changed when I started believing what was TRUE about God!

> *"And we all, who with unveiled faces contemplate the Lord's glory, are being transformed into His image with ever-increasing glory, which comes from the Lord, who is the Spirit." (2 Corinthians 3:18, NIV)*

Now, I hold everything against the belief that God only wants my good, and I use that as the north point on my compass in life. These once seemingly traumatic events are now so far behind me, I no longer feel their sting in my life. No, they aren't hidden or suppressed or even ignored; they're healed! I now rest in the peace of knowing my God will never leave me or forsake me no matter what my circumstance. If you're not there yet, you will be someday. God is a God of hope, and he wants to use whatever circumstances you're in right now or going to encounter in the future to reveal Himself to you!

It's not the sexual abuse itself but rather what transpired as a result of that experience that became the focus of what God accomplished in my life, and it has had a significant impact on my life. You see, God has used my sexual abuse as the platform for His message to women. However, my story didn't end there, and neither will yours.

> *"For our momentary, light distress [this passing trouble] is producing for us an eternal weight of glory [a fullness] beyond all measure [surpassing all comparisons, a transcendent splendor, and an endless blessedness]."* (Corinthians 4:17, AMP)

You WILL be transformed, and your life will be so much better than it was before!

In my ministry, God taught me that, even though we're told in Genesis 19:17 not to look back to the past when we suffer trauma in our lives (especially as children), we MUST look back at the damage that was done in order to be healed and be able to put it behind us so we can move forward and accomplish ALL God intended for us BEFORE the trauma. I truly believe God gives an extra measure of mercy and patience to those who've experienced any abuse or trauma as children.

> *"Who is a God like You, who forgives wickedness and passes over the rebellious acts of the remnant of His possession? He does not retain His anger forever, because He [constantly] delights in mercy and lovingkindness."* (Micah 7:18, AMP)

Children can't fully comprehend the impact of sexual abuse. However, God knows, and I believe that's why God is so patient in restoring us. Unfortunately, it's not something that will go away or get better with time. There are no shortcuts, either. In fact, if not dealt with, our lives usually get more out of control. That was certainly the case with me. It was an important discovery because

it showed me that God knows what's deep inside that needs healing. God is patient and loving toward us until our faith is strong
enough, and we're ready to deal with it again.

I've encountered many women who acknowledge that they need
healing. However, they can't or aren't willing to yield and surrender
their pasts and do what it will take on their part. If they only knew
the healing that was waiting for them on the other side of their
pain. The Lord longs to be gracious to you. *(Isaiah 30:18, AMP)*
God is there waiting with the healing that you need, but He wants
your participation to make it possible. You see, it's His story to tell
through you, and God's not done writing it!

This life is about God fulfilling His desires and purposes through
you. When I discovered how great His love was for me, I began
to see the bigger plan. I learned that God was leading me back
to the Garden (of Eden) to His heart not only to show me who
He intended me to be but also to show me His desire for all of
us. Often, when we're faced with trials, much of our attitude and
responses stem from what we believe about God. Recently, my
pastor gave a sermon at my church on the parable of the talents.
In his message, he said Jesus praised two out of three servants for
their faithfulness, not the amount of their return that was different
for each servant. Their understanding of the Master caused them
to want to go out and do something with what they had been
given. They were willing to take a risk for the Master's sake. The
third servant, however, acted on a wrong understanding of who
the Master was, which caused him to operate in fear and not faith.
So, his belief about the Master kept him from stepping out or
committing to the Master. He only gave excuses and blamed the
Master. In the end, all three received what they believed about the
Master. The main point of my pastor's sermon was that everyone

has to evaluate what we believe about God because that will determine how we view our current circumstances.

A good example is a recent conversation I had with a woman who had said to me, "I don't want this (referring to sexual abuse) to be part of the story God uses in my life." How many of us can relate to that statement? She had used an alternative form of treatment as a means of healing from sexual abuse. I knew she had been undergoing this treatment and wanted to get an update on whether she noticed a difference or felt it was successful. She explained that she did feel it had helped her. She knows the sexual abuse had occurred, but she no longer remembers any of the details associated with it and, therefore, the feelings that come with it. She then went on to say that she used to think God would use her sexual abuse as part of her story, but now, she didn't feel it was necessary. I have to say this surprised me! I guess I didn't expect that coming from her —a devoted woman of God who served faithfully in her church.

So, I continued to mull over my gut reaction and took it to God. I asked Him why this was bothering me so much. In the days following, I heard someone on the radio make the statement that "Jesus didn't hide His scars." Upon hearing this, I immediately knew why what she had said continued to weigh on my mind and heart. If Jesus didn't hide His scars, then I didn't think we should hide ours either. He revealed to me that if we're truly healed, we aren't embarrassed, ashamed, or afraid to talk about what happened to us. Scars are evidence that healing has taken place. I began to feel sorry for this woman and prayed that God would help her see that He wants to heal her so He can use her story to bring glory to Himself and show others there's hope in their circumstance, too.

As a result of having this new revelation, I want to ask you, "Have you given God all that you are?" Many times, we think we've surrendered our lives over to God because we seek to devote ourselves to Him as wives, mothers, servants in our church, and maybe even missionaries elsewhere. However, is He the God of all your days, including those in your past? There's a song called "With Lifted Hands," and it's one of my favorite songs right now. In the song, Ryan Stevenson sings the words, "Lord, I surrender all that I have, the days yet to come, the days in the past. I'm giving You all that I am with lifted hands." You know you haven't given Him your whole heart if there's something you're holding back from Him, including unresolved pain from your past. When we withhold parts of our lives, they become idols or strongholds in the hands of Satan, and those are the strongholds that need to be shattered by the Almighty God. Darkness can't exist in the light; therefore, the darkness in your past must be brought out into the open and exposed to be removed permanently. You can't escape your past! It's part of your story, whether you like it or not, and whether you want it to be or not. After all, it's His story to write!

> *"And now, Israel, what does the LORD your God require from you but to fear [and worship] the LORD your God [with awe-filled reverence and profound respect], to walk [that is, to live each and every day] in all His ways and to love Him, and to serve the LORD your God with all your heart and with all your soul [your choices, your thoughts, your whole being]." (Deuteronomy 10:12, AMP)*

Our lives are not our own to live! Who are we to say that whatever we're going through right now isn't the very thing God will use to reach other people and be a living example of hope? When we let God write our story, it takes us places we would never have had the courage to go on our own! He can't change or redeem that which we're unwilling to lay down at His feet. Don't think for a minute that just because God didn't intervene, it meant He didn't care. He wants to use what happened to refine you. As I look back on my life, I know all of my painful experiences were part of the refining process to remove the dross from my life and make me into the precious woman He could use to accomplish His purposes here on earth. All along my life was not mine to live; God was writing His story through me. That's why it became a story of hope, and He wants to do the same in your life!

God wants to repair us in order to prepare us, but He can't change or redeem that which we're unwilling to lay down at His feet. God will do the healing, but He wants our participation in the process. It's a good thing we don't get to choose what's going to become part of our story because, if we did, our lives would look different, and we would miss out on so much of what God wants to do in our lives. He will stop at nothing to heal your broken soul. You may not be able to see this while you're going through the trial, but *"The Lord longs to be gracious to you." (Isaiah 30:18)*

God is using each situation in our lives to reveal Himself to us. He sees our potential, and He also knows what our faith is capable of. So, I believe He brings things into our lives that will require a certain amount of faith so we can see for ourselves what can be accomplished if we trust and believe in Him! God wants to reveal the woman He intended you to be!

> *"Your eyes saw my unformed body; all the days ordained for me were written in your book before one of them came to be."*
> *(Psalm 139:16, NIV)*

Before sexual abuse entered your life, God had a specific idea of who you were going to be and what you were going to do. Nothing that has happened to you in this life can change that unless you let it. As in all creation, God wants to display His glory, and our healing is the way His glory manifests itself in our lives. At this point in my life, I can finally say I'm thankful for what I had to go through and what's taken place in my life to bring me to where I am today. It wasn't pleasant, and I wouldn't want to repeat any of it. However, I'm extremely grateful for what has been accomplished in me and how God is using me.

I now understand why my story needed to unfold the way it did. So many women struggle with trying to cope and never really find complete healing. Well, I believe God made me an example of hope to show other women that lasting and permanent healing from this issue is possible. I want women to know that they don't merely have to survive; they can thrive!

As I've grown to understand God's heart, I can now tell you with certainty that He doesn't want to leave you in whatever difficult circumstances you're in at this moment. Herein lies the HOPE! God's great and wonderful plan didn't end with Jesus. God didn't leave me in the brokenness and shame of my sexual abuse; and God didn't leave me in the agony and loneliness of being rejected by my birth son; and God didn't leave me in the confusion and sorrow of losing someone I love to suicide.

"...And we rejoice in hope of the glory of God. Not only that, but we rejoice in our sufferings, knowing that suffering produces endurance, and endurance produces character, and character produces hope; and hope does not put us to shame, because God's love has been poured into our hearts through the Holy Spirit who has been given to us." (Romans 5:2-5, ESV)

He hasn't finished writing your story, and He won't stop until He's achieved the end that He intended for you. God knew who He designed you to be before you were born, and everything He does from that moment on is meant to redeem you and accomplish that. This life is about being transformed back into His image and glorifying Him. It's His honor that's at stake, and He will not let it be put to shame. Shame no longer holds my heart captive! Peace, love, and joy are what resides there now. The desire God put in my heart has been fulfilled and has produced a tree of life in me.

• •

HOPE

Kimberly Ann Hobbs

It is wonderful to know that in the wake of loss, believers can maintain a hope that rejoices despite the tribulations of this life.

Romans 12:12 says, "We should be joyful in hope, patient in affliction, and faithful in prayer."

As challenges come our way, we are weakened by the difficulties they bring. Hope provides strength for us as believers facing present difficulties. Sometimes our emotions can lie to us when we feel there is no hope in a situation. Be assured there is hope to be found in the midst of your pain.

The Lord's compassion never fails. He is good to those who hope in Him, who seek Him, and who quietly wait for Him. While some of us place our hope in someone or something else, it often is in vain and destined to fail.

Whatever your struggle, God is your object of hope. Cling to Him. The book of Psalms frequently promises blessings for each of us who put our hope in the Lord. Let these verses comfort you as you read them.

- Psalm 31:23-24
- Psalm 37:9

- Psalm 38:15
- Psalm 42:5

Hope comes to us as faithful believers who obey the Lord. We can be assured of the hope God gives us in the future and confident that faith will sustain us while we are in the present. Hope is certain to us, and we could testify of it because God is faithful and always keeps His promises!

(Deuteronomy 7:9) Hope, like faith, is based on the belief of the unseen promises of God.

In God's promises to us, we find love *(Romans 8:18),* and in His love, we grow in knowledge and relationships with God and others. In hope, we can endure some of the hardships that come our way, and as we hold on to hope, the Bible teaches us that hope leads to joy *(Romans 12:12),* boldness *(2 Corinthians 3:2),* faith and love *(Colossians.1:4-5).* Hope also leads to comfort as we encourage one another with the knowledge of the resurrection *(1 Thessalonians 4:18)* Hope also stimulates good works to take place. *(1 Corinthians 15:15)*

Jesus Christ is God's son who came to earth to save us from things like sin, sadness, loneliness, pain, and more. In God's Word, we can know how to overcome hard things with the help of Jesus.

In hope, we endure some of the hardships that come our way, but by keeping our eyes fixed on God, our Father, He gives us eternal comfort and Good Hope by grace and strengthens our hearts. *(2 Thessalonians 2:16-17)*

. . . .

Jan Leigh-Edmond is a retired Inpatient Obstetric Registered Nurse. She worked in Labor and Delivery delivering high risk babies for more than 27 years. She still has a current license. Before being a nurse, she had many employment opportunities. She had tremendous work ethic and drive to do well because she was raising two sons. She worked at the US Postal Service while attending nursing school and became a RN after graduating.

Jan was born in Brooklyn, NY and was raised in Queens and Long Island. After the birth of her third son, she moved to Florida to be closer to her parents.

She has been a member of the Negro Business Women Association. She now has licenses in financial services to help families become financially independent. She has a love for helping people. She is a member of Women World Leaders ministry.

Jan is a cancer survivor and has a very powerful testimony. She currently lives in South Florida and has three grown sons, four step-children, three daughter- in-laws, three grandchildren and eight step grandchildren whom she adores. She enjoys traveling to see her children and grandchildren who live out of state. Her firstborn son lives close by with his partner so she gets pleasure experiencing new things with them.

Strength

Jan Leigh-Edmond

"The Lord is my strength and my song; He has given me victory." (Psalm 118:14)

This has become a personal truth for me about God in my life. Understanding and believing God's words did not come easy for me in the beginning stages of my life. When I look back, it seemed that my parents, who worked around the clock, loved me with conditions attached. It certainly seemed that if I did what my mother wanted, she loved me, but if I didn't, I was the bad, difficult daughter. However, I can say that, in general, I was happy growing up, and I did get a private education at a Catholic school until my junior year of high school.

When it came to social activities during my teen years, I was active in baton twirling, choir, and cheerleading. Even though I was in a Catholic school, when it came to attending church, I was on my own, except for when my parents attended Christmas Mass. I'm not sure if they came because I was in the choir or because it was the most important holiday of the Catholic faith.

When I needed "mother and daughter" talks, I sought out a couple of women in the neighborhood and my best friend's mother.

I didn't feel comfortable talking with my mother; I felt she wasn't there for me in that way. I'm so grateful for those women who acted as surrogate mothers, as I looked at them as gifts from God. The Lord says, *"I will guide you along the best pathway for your life. I will also advise you to watch over you." (Psalm 32:8)*

There were four main men in my life over the years. Three of these men were the fathers of each of my three sons. I experienced many devastating hardships within all of those relationships. Domestic abuse, betrayal, extreme financial hardship, and abandonment were regular facets of my life during my years with them. These things broke my heart, all in different ways, and they took their toll on me, damaging the trust I might have had with the Lord.

If I were to compare what I had been affected by to the cries of some of the people in the Bible, my heart would cry out in this way: *Be merciful to me, Lord, for I am in distress, my eyes grow weak with sorrow, my soul and body with grief. (Psalm 31:9) My eyes are dim with grief. I call to you, Lord, every day; I spread out my hands to you. (Psalm 88:9) Why should we (I) die before Your very eyes? Just give us grain (help) so we (I) may live and not die, and so the land (my heart and my life) does not become empty and desolate. (Genesis 47:19)*

I struggled with wanting vengeance on these men due to the many sorrows I had experienced by their actions.

"Pour out your wrath on the nations that refuse to acknowledge you — on the people that do not call upon your name. For they have devoured your people Israel; they have devoured and consumed them, making the land a desolate wilderness." (Jeremiah 10:25)

I am grateful to God that I did not follow up on taking matters into my own hands, as the Word of the Lord tells me – *"Do not take revenge, my dear friends, but leave room for God's wrath, for it is written: 'It is mine to avenge; I will repay,' says the Lord." (Romans 12:19)*

Added Sorrow

My third husband, in particular, whom I did not have a child with, had a previous ex-girlfriend who showed up in our lives. She was filled with hate and anger, and she vowed numerous times that she wanted to destroy our lives. She even threatened my whole family. She employed other people to stalk me, harass us through phone calls and emails, and exhibited other dangerous behaviors towards my family and me. I had every reason to believe she would do physical harm to us. My husband and I didn't live together for years due to her nightmarish presence in our lives. I was sincerely terrified. Due to the stress and concerned for my safety, my husband prompted the end of our marriage, and for many years going forward, I carried fear inside me.

"Be not afraid of sudden fear, neither of the desolation of the wicked, when it cometh." (Proverbs 3:25)

I prayed every day to God for His mercy, blessings, and the blood of Jesus to protect all of us. The Lord gave me the strength to overcome these battles.

God continually taught me to pray and trust in Him that He would keep my family and myself safe from harm. Additionally, during the marriage to my third husband, I experienced horrible treatment from my *second* husband, such as threats to take my life, breaking and entering into my home, stealing my money, cutting up my clothes, and the keying and pouring of acid on my car. God provided me strength and His protection to feel safe and not be harmed. However, I was still stretched to the limit regarding my emotions.

> *"But now he hath made me weary: thou hast made desolate all my company." (Job 16:7)*

Even so, I could see the Lord working in my life, but I still had much healing to do. My life was being pulled from the darkness as I was transforming. My heart held on to His truths, such as: *Who is this King of glory? The Lord strong and mighty, the Lord mighty in battle. (Psalm 24:8) The Lord is my light and my salvation; Whom shall I fear? The Lord is the strength of my life; of whom shall I be afraid? (Psalm 27:1) I give thanks to Christ, Jesus our Lord, who has given me strength, considering me worthy. (1 Timothy 1:12)* Amazingly, I was able to raise my sons to be loving, caring, productive, and respectful men of whom I am very proud.

His Strength for the Next Mountain

Unexpectedly, during my last marriage, I faced the ultimate challenge of being diagnosed with a dreaded disease. In 2015, I was diagnosed with colorectal cancer. This came about after going from doctor to doctor looking for a diagnosis of why I was experiencing excessive abdominal discomfort, headaches, diarrhea, and weight gain, as well as severe gastritis. My body was breaking down.

> *"But thou, O Lord, art a shield for me; my glory and the lifter of my head." (Psalm 3:3)*

I finally went to a gastroenterologist, who ordered a colonoscopy. I was awakened with a new reality; I was now living with CANCER.

My prayers for strength increased in intensity. I was alone much of the time while at home. My oldest son helped me as much as he could. He was truly an earth angel to me. He traveled with me to Tampa for medical care, which I sought after being mistreated by a local physician who informed me erroneously that he had removed the tumor. I had five weeks of chemo and radiation that caused painful burns requiring medication. Pain and nausea were my companions during the treatments. I was able to get to the radiation treatment appointments because my girlfriend took time off from work to pick me up and drive me there. I'm sure God sent her to me, and to this day, I am still grateful.

> *"My help cometh from the Lord, which made heaven and earth." (Psalm 121:2)*

I underwent surgery to remove the large tumor in my rectum, along with the rectum. Fortunately, the doctors were able to get it all. Sadly, I had to have two ileostomy bags attached, as the first one applied was misplaced. God is my strength and ever-present help in time of trouble. The recovery from the surgery was painful, but I was in a better facility and care than the previous one. God had directed me to the medical team four hours away from home to render proper care.

I saw God support me still through the help of my son, who was patient and kind with my issues regarding the ileostomy bag and obtaining supplies. He also calmed me when I would freak out whenever the bag would dislodge, causing quite a mess. When I first got home from the hospital, I spent a short time with a family friend, who I considered my niece. Afraid of showing her and her family my challenges, I went home. However, I was grateful for all the support and care of her loving family. God was providing! I did not have to go home to an empty house straight from the hospital. At all times and indeed everywhere, I acknowledge, Dear Lord, these things with the deepest gratitude. *(Acts 24:1-8)*

Additionally, I had a visiting nurse to instruct me on post-op care. So, through many days and nights of pain and sleeplessness, I prayed, *"But be not far from me, O Lord: O my strength haste thee to help me." (Psalm 22:19)*

One night, I was in our business office, and a co-worker asked me how I was doing and if I would like to pray. We sat down in the conference room, and she led me in a prayer that comforted my sadness, my loneliness, and my fear that the cancer was not gone. Would I not be able to have anastomosis surgery to reverse the ileostomy? I also was afraid that I would leave my sons, grandchildren, and mother. Dementia, sadly, had introduced itself into my mother's life. So, I tried to spare her the knowledge of my illness.

I felt so alone, yet, I wasn't alone, for I prayed for God to send a guardian angel to be with both my mother and me. I was honored to sit by my mother's bedside when she took her last breath. My prayer was asking God to comfort me and give me strength and healing. God met me there and held me every step as I let go of my precious mother.

> *"The Lord is their strength, and He is the saving strength of His anointed." (Psalm 28:8)*

In Matthew 4:23-24, Jesus went about all of Galilee, teaching in their synagogues, preaching the gospel of the kingdom, and healing all manner of disease among the people. And his fame went throughout all Syria; and they brought unto him all sick people who were taken with diseases and torments, and those who were demon-possessed, epileptics, and paralytics; and He healed them.

As I meditated and learned scriptures like these, my faith grew for healing, and I started to see how much the Lord deeply cared for me and wanted to heal all of my life.

A Holy, Healing Visit

Beyond my understanding, I had a vision from our Lord. He appeared to me during prayer time. Tears were flowing down my face. I saw God way off in the distance. My eyes were closed, and there was our Lord clothed in a white robe and surrounded by bright white lights. The white lights shined a path to Him. I did not hear His voice, but I was made to hear Him assure me that He had cured me of the cancer disease, so therefore, I need not worry. God is our refuge and strength. Therefore, will not we fear. *(Psalm 46:1)*

God did it, and I was able to have the surgery. It was not time for me to go home to Him yet. All I could do was cry with gratitude and love for our Father, our Lord! In the day when I cried, thou answered me and strengthened me with strength in my soul. *(Psalm*

138:3) The Lord is my strength and my shield; my heart trusted in Him, and I am helped. Therefore, my heart greatly rejoiceth, and with my song, I praise Him.

I have been cancer-free for over three years! For He remembered His holy promise. *(Psalm 105:42)* I tell all who will listen about the gift I received from God!

I know I still have some health issues, but I face them with knowledge that God is with me. What a miracle He gave me. He has given me the opportunity to study His scriptures and look for His teachings. What a wonderful God we have! He is the Father of our Lord Jesus Christ, the source of every mercy, and the One who so wonderfully comforts and strengthens us in our hardships and trials. And why does He do this? So that when others are troubled and needing sympathy and encouragement, we can pass on to them this same help and comfort that God has given us. *(2 Corinthians 1:3-4)*

A Time For New Dreams

In later years, I was invited to a church and made that my new church home. I then became a fisherwoman, inviting others to my church and encouraging them to join Women World Leaders, a wonderful women's ministry that worships God and helps women around the world strengthen their faith. God even gave me a new profession so I can show others how to prepare themselves financially for their future.

I now have three beautiful grandchildren who I can visit in their home state to love, spoil, and teach. I was so worried about leaving my sons without their mother when I received the cancer diagnosis. We share such a close relationship, and I was not ready to leave a void in their life. I always told them that I would be there for them and love and support them. I am able to attend my youngest son's wedding in the next few weeks as of September 2019. The harmful men of my past are no longer around to hurt me. I believe God is protecting me from those types of men who are not pure in their hearts, but I do pray for them. I do dream about having a loving, Godly relationship with a devoted man, attending church, and praying together with him one day, though.

God has a plan for all of us. I feel I have been led on the path to the right time to tell my story, which will hopefully help another woman to pray for strength, stay strong, and fight the devil no matter how hard or useless their fight makes them feel. God guides us. He provides for us. Never think you can't ask Him for His help. Our help is in the name of the Lord, who made heaven and earth. *(Psalm 124:8)* God is always with us, and His plans are always good for us. *(Jeremiah 29:11)*

7 Messages of Redemption I Have Received from God:

You will prosper
You will smile again
Your storm is over
You will find peace
You are forgiven
You are safe with Me
You are loved

(Writing Mentor ~ Kelly Jo Rabbitt)

. . . .

STRENGTH

Kimberly Ann Hobbs

Sometimes we look at our situations and wonder how we are ever going to make it through. It could be a task that seems beyond reach, a sudden death of someone who we love, a divorce, a chronic illness, or a child raging out of control. Sometimes we feel it's beyond our ability to cope. No matter what darkest pit you must climb out of or the highest hurdle you may have to jump, God will wrap his love around you, covering and protecting you as you hit it head-on.

No matter how great the storms in your life are right now, God's love is so powerful that it can give you the strength and ability to overcome any situation. Remember, it's not *our* strength; the strength comes from God. But, please don't hesitate to ask Him for it.

> *"It is God who arms me with strength." (2 Samuel 22:33)*

> *"God is our refuge and strength." (Psalm 46:1, ESV)*

Don't hit the pause button when you're out of strength and weary. This is when we need to go to God. You and I need Him most at those moments. We hear this from Him continuously in His words to us.

"The Lord is my strength and my song." (Exodus 15:2, NKJV)

If you need strength, consistently pray for it. God will deliver it to you. All you need to do is ask Him for it. Be reminded not to face any difficult task on your own. God is your strength and the only One who holds all of it. Let Him be the power that gets you through your situation!

* *

Melissa Kessler is a woman who is living out her purpose on a daily basis. She is a wife and mom of two boys whom she loves beyond belief. She dedicates much of her life to raising the best family God created her to raise. After living many years struggling with not believing she was enough, she began an endless transformation and started building her relationship with Jesus. She now lives by faith in everything she does.

She is the owner of Melissa J Kessler, LLC, as a Certified Holistic Wellness & Lifestyle Coach. It is more often referred to as The Heart and Soul of Detoxing, where she serves women who are looking to make their chronic illness a thing of the past, empowering them physically, mentally, emotionally and most of all spiritually.

Melissa knew she had to share her story in this book as the experience of losing her mom has brought her closer to God than anything else ever has.

If you are looking for empowerment and support from someone who has been there and refuses to see sickness and disease take over more lives, you can find Melissa at melissajkessler.com or you can follow her on Facebook, Instagram and Pinterest @ theheartandsoulofdetoxing

Living In Faith, In Good Times And Bad

Melissa Kessler

> *"Truly, truly, I say to you, you will weep and lament, but the world will rejoice. You will be sorrowful, but your sorrow will turn into joy." (John 16:20)*

I remember the day my mother told me that she had cancer. There were many bad days in my life, but nothing could compare to the pain that news brought me. It had been a few weeks since she had biopsies done and still hadn't given me the news. I had hope and believed there was no bad news, or she would have told me, right? Being in the field of holistic wellness and helping women deal with health concerns, I knew a little about what was happening. When my mother first told me what was happening and that her hormone levels were off, I immediately knew what it was, but I refused to believe it. Could this really be happening to my mom, who was only fifty-eight years old and had grandchildren to watch grow up, graduate from school, get married, and have kids of their own? My mom who wanted to go on more vacations with her family? My mom who was creative and designed and planned all of the school artwork and made beautiful walls in the charter school where she worked? My mom, who my sisters and I would have many more questions for as we raised our children?

Even though this news brought many tears, I kept my faith that things would be okay. I did everything I possibly could, while still doing my work and raising my family. She didn't live around the corner, but a drive a little over an hour didn't stop me from getting to her a few times a week to take her all of the cancer-killing foods that I know of, along with essential oils and everything holistic I could get my hands on. She also chose to undergo chemo and radiation, which, even though it wouldn't have been my choice, I supported her. It was her life experience, and I had to do whatever made her happy. Not only did I do that, but I prayed like crazy. If it weren't for prayer, I'm not sure I would have made it through.

> *"The Lord is near to the brokenhearted." (Psalm 34:18)*

Chemo got hard and harmed her entire body. She had no more strength and no motivation to keep trying. She wasn't hungry, so all the good food in the world wouldn't make a difference. It was hard for her to even get up on her own. That's when things started getting worse, very quickly. Infection after infection, spending three weeks in the hospital just a day after Thanksgiving. She was home for the holidays, but we could see her pain. We had lost her already, even though she somehow outlasted me on New Year's Eve after I had spent the day taking her for radiation. My family – two boys and my hubby – stayed home that night and passed out before the ball dropped. Sure enough, she called me at midnight to wish me a happy new year, and it was the last time I talked to her.

She didn't answer my calls the next day, and on January 2nd, my sister and aunt rushed her to the hospital. By the time I got there, she had already been intubated, and it went downhill from there. A few days in the hospital went by, which seemed to be the longest yet quickest days ever. Only five months from starting her treatments, we lost her. But, God was with me through it all. In those last few hours of her life, we played worship music in her hospital room and prayed for peace and no more suffering – for my mother and for all of us who would have to live here without her. The peace that came over the room when that music played was like no other. It's even mentioned in her hospital records, so I believe God did something for the nurses and doctors who were walking by her room, also.

Now it was time that I faced the truth. Life would go on. I would have to keep raising my children, and I would have to become the best sister to my two younger ones. I had to be strong; I had to make sure they all knew we could do this with my mother watching over us and God having our backs. There was more to our lives, and our stories are still being written. This happened in January of 2019. Yet, God has given me so much strength to be the woman who He created me to be, with an enormous purpose in this life experience.

"I can do all things through Christ who strengthens me."
(Philippians 4:13)

As time has moved forward, I'm able to wake up with motivation and a purpose, rather than wanting to hide in a closet and never come out. Below are some new things I learned and that were reconfirmed to me during those five months of watching my mother suffer. They have given me fuel to live the life I was meant to live.

- I have a God-given purpose. *"For I know the plans I have for you," declares the LORD, "plans to prosper you and not to harm you, plans to give you hope and a future." (Jeremiah 29:11)*

- God will always be with me, even when fear sneaks in. *"Be strong and courageous. Do not fear or be in dread of them, for it is the Lord your God who goes with you. He will not leave you or forsake you." (Deuteronomy 31:6)*

- Live in the present every day. *"The thief comes only in order to steal and kill and destroy. I came that they may have life, and that they may have it more abundantly." (John 10:10)*

- Forgive more. *"And when you stand praying, if you hold anything against anyone, forgive them, so that your Father in heaven may forgive you your sins." (Mark 11:25)*

- Allow myself to feel my emotions. *"A time to weep, and a time to laugh; a time to mourn, and a time to dance; a time to cast away stones, and a time to gather stones together; a time to embrace, and a time to refrain from embracing; a time to seek, and a time to lose; a time to keep, and a time to cast away." (Ecclesiastes 3:4-6)*

- Treat my body like a temple. *"Don't you know that you yourselves are God's temple and that God's Spirit dwells in your midst? If anyone destroys God's temple, God will destroy that person; for God's temple is sacred, and you together are that temple." (1 Corinthians 3:16-17)*

Cancer has become a fear for many people in the world. In the social media world, we see someone diagnosed with some form of cancer almost daily, ranging in age from children to the elderly. We all wonder why. Why is this happening in our world and our lives? What is God trying to tell us? Is it that we need to make some serious changes in our lives, or is there a reason so many are being taken?

For me, it's taught me so much. My career focuses on health and wellness and learning more about ways to stop this from happening. I study about it day after day and insist on making changes for my family. If it means taking products out of our lives, we'll do it. If it means changing the way we eat, we'll do it. If it means spending more time with those we love instead of letting the chaos of life take over, we'll do it. More than that, I've paid attention to all God has told me through the experience of saying goodbye to my mother.

We all know that our day will come, and truthfully, until I lost my mother, death scared the ever-living daylights out of me. It doesn't seem so scary anymore because I know that not only is my mother waiting for me, but so is Christ. It will probably be the most beautiful place we could ever imagine. Thoughts about leaving my children, husband, sisters, nieces, family, and friends is still a tough one, but my faith is overflowing and reminds me daily that we will all be reunited in the end.

Thoughts of my demise and my mother passing on have opened my eyes more than ever before. There is only so much time we have in this human experience, so we must live to the absolute fullest. It has reminded me to live my life, and it's something you should consider doing, as well.

How to Truly Live Your Life

Your Purpose

It is so easy to forget our purpose when we are busy being women, mothers, business owners, and everything else God created us to be. As I was going through a tough week and starting to underestimate myself and my purpose, Epic Beauty Ministry held a Devoted Girls night, where we listened to Pastor Christina Gard speak. She spoke these words and told us to repeat them daily: "I was created on purpose for a purpose." Don't ever forget that.

Even though I was already the owner of a holistic wellness business prior to my mother being diagnosed with cancer, there were many times I questioned what I was doing. Who was I to be helping women walk away from disease? When my mother passed, I somehow was brought closer to God, and He assured me that He created me on purpose for a purpose. I will live according to that all the days of my life. I will NOT allow the enemy to get in the way of me and my purpose. God created me for this!

So, the question for you is, how can your loss fuel you to do more good in the world? How can your loss be reflected through your purpose? What can you do to make changes in the world? It doesn't have to be anything health-related. Just think, is there something the loss of your loved one brought out in you? Are you an artist who should be painting pictures for those who are grieving? Is there something people need to learn through their loss? How can you help others who may go through the same thing you have gone through? Ask Jesus, and He will tell you.

Know that God is Always with You

Start and end your days with him. I love devotionals that speak to me and what I am living through daily. There are devotional journals for mothers, business owners, and ones that focus on gratitude. I have several and pick the one to read that feels right at certain times of the day. Knowing that God gets me is the most amazing feeling in the world.

Get yourself a beautiful Bible. Find one that is pretty and speaks to you. Trust me; there are so many out there that you can find one that feeds your soul and personality. When you are having rough times – and amazing ones –turn to that Bible. Allow it to be the story of your life. Find scriptures that relate to exactly what you are experiencing. God wants you to live the life He created you for. Believe it, and stand true to it.

Live in the Present

As you probably know by now (not just through what I've written, but by seeing it in your own experiences), you don't know what time will bring. In the middle of writing this chapter, I lost my sweet seven-year-old niece to cancer, as well. It happened so quickly that it didn't seem real. Truthfully, it still doesn't. I've cried, thinking we won't ever see her grow up. We don't know the reason. Only God does. It has tested my faith a bit, but I have to believe that God has a plan.

Knowing that life can be short, it's that much more important to be present in EVERYTHING we do. Throughout my years in the wellness industry, I've gotten a lot better at this, but I'm still practicing as hard as I can because I'm not perfect, nor will I ever be perfect. However, I have changed the way I do things. I take my time with everything. I set boundaries, and if it's something that isn't necessary, I don't do it. I hug my kids more, kiss my husband more, and enjoy every minute we have together. We play more games. We go to the farmer's market and pick the most beautiful, organic, freshly-grown produce to nourish our bodies. If there are things I need that are not available at the farmer's market, I order them through a delivery service. I no longer tell everyone to stay home while I do it on my own, running around like a chicken without a head. I stop and take things slowly. I breathe more than ever. I take in the beauty of nature that God has created for us. I LIVE.

Is it possible for you to live more in the present and take in every moment of life? You just don't know how many more you will have.

Forgiveness

This one used to be hard for me. How could I forgive someone who has done me wrong? It's gotten easier as time goes on. It takes a lot of work, but I recommend you try it. I've learned that without forgiving, I'm hurting myself more than the other person. It feels so freeing to forgive others. It does not mean I forget, though. Forgiving and forgetting are two totally different things. You may not forget how someone hurt you, but you can forgive them. Most often, the people who hurt us are hurting themselves, and the best thing we can do is pray for them. Pray that they heal and stop hurting. For all of my country fans out there, as Luke Bryan would say, "I believe most people are good," and you should think so, too.

When we hold on to hurt, pain, anger, and resentment, it hurts us more than the person who hurt us. Forgiving others gives us the freedom to live in the present. It's easy to go down that rabbit hole as we keep reliving what others have done to us and continue living in the past. Worst of all, it takes away our chances to see the beauty happening in the moment. So, forgive and be present.

Feel the Emotions

Don't push it all so far down that you don't remember it anymore. Your subconscious doesn't forget. The further down those emotions are hidden, the more harm they do. These emotions may not be easy to deal with, but healing is a journey, and we need to take the steps. Allow yourself to grieve, to cry, to be mad and upset. Allow yourself to feel. You are human, and God created you to have emotions. It's okay!

When I think about my mother, I believe God took her to take away all of the pain. Not pain from cancer but the pain from her life. One of the biggest pains she had was my father cheating on her and leaving her with three daughters, the youngest just being born. She held on to all of the emotions to be strong for us. She tried to hide it, and it eventually caught up to her. I believe she was in so much pain deep down inside that God felt the best he could do was take her to his beautiful paradise.

Just a touch on forgiveness here, I'm still trying to forgive my father for all he did to us, especially my mother. As I mentioned, forgiveness is not easy, but it's so needed to move on so that you can enjoy life.

Treat Your Body Like a Temple

Our bodies are prized possessions that God has given us, and we must treat them that way. As women who have full schedules, it's easy to put ourselves last. This is NOT how He intended it to be. Of course, we should be taking care of our children and husbands and families, but that does not mean we shouldn't take care of ourselves.

I treat my body like a temple from the moment I wake in the morning to the moment I close my eyes at night.

Here are some of the things I do to treat my body like a temple:

- Only put the absolute best foods into it.
- Detox on a regular basis.
- Only use non-toxic products on my skin, to clean my home, and anywhere else products are used.
- Only use natural medicine.
- Surround myself with the people I want to be like and who have similar beliefs.
- Do not allow harmful words to get into my head.
- Avoid allowing Satan to make me double-think anything.
- Exercise on a normal basis.
- Give my body the rest it deserves; we only heal if we rest.
- Last, but most importantly, I PRAY! I pray in the morning, in the night, and every chance I get. I thank God for everything, even when it doesn't seem to be a good thing. I thank Him for the lessons He is teaching me to continue living out my purpose.

As difficult as it was to bring up each of the moments that happened when my mother was diagnosed with cancer, how things went throughout her treatment, and how I felt when she passed away, there is much gratitude in my heart that I was able to share my story to help you as you heal. Know that you'll get through it, too, if you are living through a similar experience.

The pain isn't gone, but I know God has me. He is always with us and shows up in times when we're not sure what may happen. As things were happening and days were coming to an end for my mother, I was in a difficult place. I was mad at God. How could He be taking my mom from me? I was only thirty-eight years old and needed her for so much longer. Who would I ask questions to or call when a great opportunity came up in my business, or for my children, or my husband? I was furious with God, but at the same time, I had this feeling in me that everything would be okay. He was assuring me of that. As I complete this chapter, it's been a little over seven months since my mother went to Heaven, and there are still days that I cry and wonder why. But, I am okay. Life is going on, and there is still so much MORE for me – and YOU if you are dealing with the loss of a loved one.

Remember, they are not gone. They just have a different address, as the priest said when we were saying goodbye to my mother for the final time.

"For we live by faith and not by sight." (2 Corinthians 5:7)

· ·

FAITHFUL

Kimberly Ann Hobbs

To be faithful is to be reliable, steadfast, and unwavering. Faithfulness is an attribute of God. When God says He will do something, He does it, even when it seems impossible. When He says something will happen, we can count on it happening. It's true from the past to the present and into the future. We must understand that if God were unfaithful, which He could never be, He would not be God!

Man has to work at being faithful. We fall short and many times hurt those around us who we love. God does not have to work at being faithful because He is faithful.

> *"So awesome are you, O Yahweh, Lord God of Angel Armies! Where could we find anyone as glorious as You? Your faithfulness shines all around You!" (Psalm 89:8)*

When we as people walk consistently with God, in humble service to Him, we can be called faithful. Being faithful affects every relationship we have. The Bible says faithfulness is a gift from God. When we receive Christ as Lord, the Holy Spirit indwells us and brings the blessings of love, joy, peace, and faithfulness.

But the fruit produced by the Holy Spirit within you is divine love in all its varied expressions:

Joy that overflows,
Peace that subdues,
Patience that endures,
Kindness in action,
A life full of virtue,
Faith that prevails,
Gentleness of heart and
Strength of Spirit.
Never set the law above these qualities, for they are meant to be limitless. (Galatians 5:22, TPT)

The Bible tells us in the Old Testament, *"The just will live by faith." (Habakkuk 2:4)* We obtain that faith and our faithfulness by the grace of God.

Our faithful allegiance to Almighty God is the only thing we can really count on; He is our hope in a fallen world. His provision of forgiveness and salvation through Jesus is the greatest benefit of all if we are faithful believers. One day, as we grow closer to seeing our savior face-to-face, we will want to hear His words as we read them from Matthew 25:23 – *"Well done, good and faithful servant!"*

* *

 **Kari Starling** was blessed with the two most amazing parents ever. Her childhood was the very best. She grew up in the country with a bunch of siblings and animals.

In her early 20's she moved from her childhood home in Glastonbury, Connecticut to Jupiter, Florida. She has lived here for over thirty years.

Kari is a single mom of four wonderful kids that are all almost gone from the nest.

Her passion is refurbishing old homes. She loves the old charm and character of a rugged old house with an up to date flare.

Kari is a regular volunteer for her church. She loves worship. Music has always spoken to her soul. It is in worship that God pulled her from darkness and lead her to Him once again. She believes with all of her heart that if we can help people to truly know not only the power of the Lord but his true love for every single one of us, this world would be a happier, healthier place to live in.

Miracle

Kari Starling

Having been raised by a Baptist preacher's daughter, my mother taught us to love the Lord early in life. Our mother is the definition of a sweet southern belle. She has a warmth and genuine kindness about her that's obvious to all. She has a firm hand and a huge heart. Mothering everyone came naturally to her, and she was good at it. Dad had a bustling business and was gone most of the time. He adored his family and took good care of us. We lived in a beautiful home, with my grandparents living on the same piece of land.

Our parents raised us in the Baptist church, as well. There wasn't a Sunday that we weren't there. I had three siblings growing up. Dan was the oldest, then Heidi. I was born a year after her, and Holly four years after that. We did everything together while growing up. We shared the same best friends and still have them as friends today. We live very near to one another and talk a few times per day.

What we didn't know was something was missing for our mother during her adult life. She never hinted to any of us that she was hurting or sad. When we were all in our early twenties, she sat us down and told us what had been on her heart all along.

When she was nineteen years old, she became pregnant out of wedlock by a man who was not our father. Keep in mind our mother was a preacher's daughter. That was fifty-plus years ago, and things were very different back then. When she told her parents the news, you can imagine it didn't go very well. A few days later, her aunt showed up with a suitcase and a one-way bus ticket for her. My mother was being shipped away to have her baby. She was sent to New Orleans – a place where no one knew her – to finish out her pregnancy at a Baptist home/hospital for unwed mothers.

What my mother didn't know was that after her baby was born, he would be given up for adoption. You see, she had every intention of keeping him. She took care of him for some time after he was born. We aren't sure for how long. Mom thinks it was a few months. It was long enough, though, for her to fall in love with him.

A few weeks later, she received a ticket to return to Florida with a note telling her the baby was not welcome to accompany her. Having no other option, she put him up for adoption and made the trip home without him. I can only imagine the ride home for her. After she returned to Florida, her parents never spoke one word to her about the baby. Not only that, they didn't even check to see if she was okay. Her parents barely spoke to her for the rest of her life.

For twenty-plus years, she didn't speak of it to anyone. Once she opened up to us, she was able to share how hard it was on her. I think my mother was relieved that she could finally be honest with us about what she went through and how she was feeling about it. She missed him terribly. She needed to know in her heart that he was okay and having a good life. She also needed to know she made the right choice by giving him up.

Mom didn't feel she had the right to look for him. She had no idea how he would react to her. I assured her that we would find him and put some rest on her tired soul. I set out on a mission to locate him. We had a blood brother who we all needed to not only know but to love.

Mom gave me everything I needed to find him through the adoption center/hospital. She had his hospital bracelet, records, and even a picture of the two of them before he had been adopted. I contacted the facility where she had him, but they wouldn't release any information. Everything had to come from the adopted child. Each of us tried contacting the hospital, but we all got the same answer. That was over thirty years ago – before the internet and before DNA kits became available for public use. We weren't sure how to proceed at that time. Life was busy for all of us. I had four small kids of my own, but in my mind, I often thought how I would feel knowing that I had a child out there and didn't have any idea where they were or if they were okay. Once I became a mother myself, I could understand her torment.

In 2005, Hurricane Katrina ripped through New Orleans and wiped out the hospital where my mother had my brother. All of the records were lost. At that point, we knew if ever we were going to find him, it would be a Divine Intervention. It was then that I started praying for a miracle because that's what it was going to take.

God is always placing people in our lives for a specific purpose. While in Tennessee a few years back, this man who I met told me a story about how he found a sister that he didn't know he had while looking for his genetic make-up through Ancestry.com. With tears rolling down my cheeks, I knew what I needed to do when I returned home. I bought a kit immediately. School was starting for my kids right after I returned. Fall sports began, life happened, and the kit didn't get opened.

All my siblings were very busy at this time, too. My brother Dan was moving into the neighborhood where my youngest sister, Holly, lived with her husband, Mark. Holly decided to move our mother in with them while they added an in-law suite to their property for her. Plans were done; they were just waiting for the builder to start. Mom had been in the same house for over thirty years. This was a big change for everyone. She was getting older, and it was time to make a change. Mom has an autoimmune disease that had kept her critical in the hospital for much of the prior year. It was time for her to be under a watchful eye and not have the responsibility of a house to handle on her own.

Three months after my mother moved to my sister's, Holly's husband died in a terrible accident. She was left with two small children to raise on her own and three businesses to run.

I thank God for my faith! Thank You, Jesus, for renewing my relationship with you as I was born again only a few months before this. God was going to use me to be the strength and hope that kept us going. It was during this time that my family leaned on me to support them through this transition. Had I not been fully planted in God, I'm not sure how anything that I had to do to keep my sister and her kids together could have happened.

"My grace is all you need. My power works best in weakness."
(2 Corinthians 12:9)

I knew God had a plan. I also knew it was God who gave us Mark. Mark was a loyal, loving, supportive, and wonderful example of a man. We were blessed to have him in our family for twenty years. God knew my sister was going to need hands-on help. I know this is why Mom was put in that house before Mark's death. It is also how my brother just so happened to buy a house not a mile from our sister right before Mark died. It was divine timing.

I have found some of my sweetest messages and prayer times are while I'm in the shower. It was March 20, 2018. I was standing in the shower, letting the water run over my head and thinking about the last sixteen months. I started crying. I thought about all of the ways God was there for us during our immense grief. We were going to be okay. The heaviness lifted from our hearts, and we were beginning to see the sunshine again. Our family appreciated each other more, and we were finding a new normal. God sent us people who loved us and counseled us during a terrible loss. I cried sloppy tears that day while thanking God for His grace, His love, and His devotion to each of us. I was truly grateful that we made it; we were still grieving, but we were all doing better. You see, I was humbly thanking God for easing our pain and seeing us through our darkest days. I wasn't asking Him for anything. I was going to Him in gratefulness and thankfulness for His mercies and His grace. I cleaned up my tears, then headed to work.

Mom was calling. *There must be an emergency; she knows I can't talk,* I thought to myself. When I answered, my mother blurted out, "My son is looking for me." I laughed, knowing my brother was on a plane headed to Lake Tahoe with his family. I reminded her of his vacation plans. "Kari, MY SON is looking for me," she said.

That's all she had to say for me to know what she was talking about. I almost dropped the phone. A deep sob came from my heart; my mind was racing. I honestly don't know if there are words to describe the overwhelming feelings I was having. Shock, disbelief, gratitude, awe, confusion and joy, incredible joy. How could this be? My prayer for a miracle was being answered right then and there.

Mom had ten brothers and sisters. We have about fifty first cousins on that side of the family alone. No one else in the family knew about our brother. It just never came up in conversation. Our cousin, Lisa, was interested in our family heritage and had done some DNA testing with 23&Me. She was matched as first cousins with our brother. Yet, she had no idea who he belonged to. Lisa sent my sister an email with a birth date, a place of birth, and a given name at birth (from our mother) that matched all information we had been given twenty years prior. His question in the email was, "Do you have any idea who he belongs to?" We were jumping up and down…and crying.

Within minutes, I was forwarded his LinkedIn profile and found him on Facebook. I messaged him immediately. I wasn't about to lose him again.

His name is Keith. He grew up in Texas, attending a Baptist church. He was raised with a brother that was six months younger than he. His parents were very successful people who provided a wonderful life, a bunch of love, and a great education for him. He is kind, full of integrity, and full of goodness. He's loyal, supportive, and exactly what we all needed. One of the best parts, he comes with an amazing wife, who he has been married to for thirty-four years, and has three beautiful adult daughters.

Last year, we spent the holidays together for the first time. It was a dream come true for each one of us. All our mother ever wanted was to know that he was happy. When he visits now, he makes special time for just the two of them. I catch her sitting outside with him holding hands. The love that she didn't have a chance to show him when he was young, she gets to share with him now. They love each other. Their relationship is very special. It fills my heart just being able to watch her finally love him. He looks after her, too. And he respects the choice she made for him all those years ago. Thursday nights for the last fifteen months are reserved for a life group. It has been during this time that I have had the opportunity to get to know their hearts. They are amazing people! Heaven sent for sure.

Through this entire experience, I have learned that in our lives, we will have hills and valleys. We will be faced with things that feel like we can't keep going. This is not our decision. When the good Lord calls us home, our work here will be complete. Until that day, we belong to Him. We are here to speak of His goodness, even when things look hopeless. Know that when there is a struggle, there will be a blessing. Push through the hard times and hold on to your faith. God will bless you. Even in times when you think He hasn't heard your prayers, He doesn't miss a one.

I have one last thing to share with you. As I wrote my story to share with each of you, there were times when I was at a loss for words. Keith called me several times, checking on my progress. As I shared my frustration with him, he told me that he was sending an email that I had written to him two weeks after he came for his first visit. Again, another blessing. My own words to my brother that he sent back to me.

April 5, 2018

I wanted you to know that because of you, Mom has peace within her now that she has never had. I went over and spent a few hours with her last night. She has a glow and a smile on her face that comes from the inside. You were the missing piece of the puzzle…her whole life. I'm so happy that her one wish that she had is coming true. Life can be very hard! Mom's had many beautiful years but so much turmoil, an inner struggle and torment because of giving you up. Her family shamed her, and they lost her heart by putting you up for adoption. Nearly two weeks ago now (feels like it's been a year), she received a message from you, bringing hope back into her life. She has spent her whole life loving and giving to others without expecting anything in return. Mom's wish for you was the same as my wish for her. So, from the bottom of my heart, thank you for giving Mom her heart back. It's been with you all along.

I let my mother read the letter before I sent it off for printing. She said, "I have chills reading this." I asked her if there was anything she wanted me to add. Always thinking of others, she replied, "I want you to tell them about his wonderful parents who raised him."

. . . .

MIRACLES

Kimberly Ann Hobbs

Miracles show us God's power and help us to believe in Him. Our eyes can behold all kinds of miracles if we are open to see them. Some miracles behold the supernatural acts of creation, and some went against the laws of nature, like when Jesus walked on water. Then some miracles involve healings, miracles of signs demonstrating divine power over death, and other miracles such as the miraculous power demonstrated over plant and animal life (as in Balaam's donkey). There are miracles in the past over material things (multiplying loaves and fishes) and so much more. We can read them from history in God's Word, or we can see many taking place today.

> *"There is nothing that is impossible with God." (Jeremiah 32:27)*

You may be asking God for a miracle today. When we can't see our way ahead, we must trust God. Our Lord can handle the vast mountains, oceans, and storms that appear to block our way. All over the Bible there are miraculous stories to acclaim what God has done. Those miracles are defined by the extraordinary measure that God reveals Himself to us. Miracles remind us that God doesn't depend on the elements of nature or man's abilities to do the impossible. God can do anything.

Many times, we are at a place in our lives where it seems everything we have is about to run out. What do we do? These are the times we must trust the Lord for everything we need. Draw closer to the One who loves you and understands you most.

There are ways in which we can begin to see the miraculous intervention we desire. It may not make sense to us, and it may require us to do things that aren't convenient for us. If we seek the Lord in wisdom and Godly counsel, we may start to see miraculous things begin to happen. *James 1:5, TPT* says, *"If anyone longs to be wise, ask God for wisdom. And he will give it!"* This is a truth from God's word – a promise that He won't hold back from you.

"No word from God will ever fail." (Luke 1:37, NIV)

God will give you Godly wisdom to make decisions and choices within your life if you ask for it. He promises that He won't hold it back from anyone who asks.

When you seek God's presence and request Him to intervene in your situation, you can see miracles happen. God has the ability and POWER over all creation to work a miracle for you. Pray. Believe by faith. Seek His wisdom as talked about in *James 1:5*. Wait on God. Miracles do happen.

Claire Ellen Portmann is wife to Brian, Mama to Kimberly, daughter to Janet and little sister to Larry. With a heart on fire for Jesus, she is running the race for the Glory of the Kingdom of God. Claire and Brian have worked for over a decade, breeding and raising English Cream Golden Retrievers for families all over the United States, but knew in their hearts they wanted to leave a legacy showcasing Gods faithfulness. With that in mind they took what God had blessed them with and trained their first therapy dog "Finn." Finn, and the rest of their growing team now go out to bring the Gospel of Jesus Christ to the lost and broken of this world.

Claire also focuses her time volunteering at her church, teaching Sunday school, and she also belongs to the outreach team of Women World Leaders. Claire, Brian, and their Ocean Golden Pups live in Jupiter, Florida.

The Call To Obey

Claire E Portmann

The phone rang at our home in South Florida; it was my brother, Larry. He had called our brother, Bobby, but he hadn't answered or called back. After several days had passed, he told me he finally called Bobby's wife, Faith, and my heart started to race. You see, my family isn't exactly the Cleavers. We love each other; we just do it from a distance. Then he said the words that would change everything: "Claire, he's in ICU at Mt. Sinai on life support."

It was a moment unlike any other in my life. I felt the pull, the call, the absolute compulsion to get to my brother as soon as I could. You see, I am the gatekeeper, the head of crisis management, and I've been so since around the age of seven when my parents separated. I immediately called Mama, but she didn't answer. Brian, who knew right away something was different, told me, "Honey, just go pack a bag, and I'll drive you up to DC." But, Mama finally called back, and before I knew it, I was in the air on the next flight out.

I also called Chris Kelsch, Bobby's best friend since kindergarten, and gave him the news. Chris met us at the door that led into ICU. "Ladies," he said, "he doesn't look good. So, you need to be prepared. He looks very different." Silently to me, his face said everything. When we got to Bobby's room, Mama gasped. Chris immediately grabbed her arm to steady her and held on.

I spoke with a nurse and was told that Bobby was no longer communicating by squeezing a hand or blinking his eyes like he had been able to do just twelve hours earlier. I was devastated. But then I thought, if Bobby had been able to speak, he might have told me that he didn't want to hear about Jesus and maybe have even kicked me out.

It was a long day, which didn't include any positive news. Chris was our rock in the storm. What I didn't find out about until later was the cost to him. Later that afternoon, he had convulsions while driving home (in the dark) that could have killed him; the seizures were due to complications from an accident years prior. But, for the grace of God, he wasn't hurt.

I was up most of the night on the phone with nurses but rushed to church, arriving after worship began. Walking down the aisle, a woman motioned for me to sit. I tried to sing, but the floodgates had been opened. I ugly cried for all it was worth. After the message, she and her husband led me to the altar and prayed over me. I felt God's presence not only in the room but in my heart, as well. I also felt the Holy Spirit telling me to get home to Mama.

I ran home to find her sobbing. I spent the day and that night quietly talking on the phone with the nurses while caring for her. It was a hard day as I wanted to be in Baltimore with my brother, but I knew Mama needed me, too. The following morning, she told me that she had to work. So, I walked her to the Library of Congress, picked up the car, and headed to Baltimore.

A song came on, and the words halted my heart because I knew God was speaking to me. *"Weak and wounded sinner, lost and left to die."* I didn't have much experience with the kind of information I had been taking in for the last few days, but I kept driving while thinking, "Jesus take the wheel and get me to Mt Sinai!" Let me be transparent for a moment. Basically, God had just told me that Bobby was dying, and I was driving on one of the busiest sections of road in the Mid Atlantic.

When I got to the hospital, I was met by a nurse in the elevator. "What floor?" she asked. I replied, "Four." Then, she asked, "Cardiac?" I told her, "No. ICU." After I relayed the situation, the doors opened. "I'm Robin. I work in CCU. Would it be alright if I came to visit?" she asked me. "Sure," I responded, then walked into ICU.

As I entered Bobby's room, it was clear to me that yes, he was dying as the Lord had told me in His own unique way. I stopped and asked the nurse outside his room, "Is my brother dying?" Looking at me with compassion, she said, "Yes, he is. I'm so very sorry."

There they were – words that hung in the air, heavy yet suspended, dropping like a thud in my heart. I kicked into what I would call "Claire Overdrive" praying. "What do I do now, Lord?" I asked, and He quickly answered, "Talk to him, Claire. Help Me bring My son home."

I had to let my mother know. I called, gently telling her the worst news a mother could hear, and then asked, "Can you come, Mama?" I barely heard the whispered words, "I'm sorry, Claire. I just can't." We ended the call with me telling her that I understood, but I was staying. He had been alone there for three weeks without a soul who knew him. Faith had stayed in Ohio, where they had moved. I believe he knew he was dying, moved her near her family, and had gone back to deal with the sale of the house in Baltimore.

In the pastoral care office, I met with Rabbi Sadler, as I needed a priest to give Bobby the last rites. But, shockingly to me, he said Bobby's paperwork indicated he wanted no religious affiliation, and therefore, the church would not send a priest. Shocked and upset, I called Chris, who suggested hospice. I called and left a message. The Rabbi walked me back to Bobby's room and then asked if it would be alright if he sang to Bobby. I nodded yes, and he sang something so very beautiful. I listened and wept while holding Bobby's hand. Afterward, he said it was the "Mi Sheberakh," a Jewish prayer for the sick. Then he sang a psalm, and I cried another ugly cry.

Hospice sent a woman named Leslie, who prayed over Bobby and then led me over to the window where we sat on the floor. She began reciting the "Lord's Prayer". The window was behind me, and I could feel the sun on my back. I remember being surprised that I could feel the heat when it was so cold outside. The warmth grew as I felt hands on my shoulders, and I sat there sobbing, looking at Leslie's hands right in front of me. I turned around to see who came in, but there was no one there. I knew what I was feeling were God's hands on my shoulders, comforting me. Leslie left, and I dozed off in the recliner.

Alarms going off woke me. Bobby's kidneys had shut down. His body was literally "weeping" with fluid from every pore, and the bedding was soaked. I asked the nurse if they had heard from Faith. She shook her head no and then said they hadn't since Friday. It was two o'clock on Tuesday morning. Where was she? Without

THE CALL TO OBEY - CLAIRE E PORTMANN

contact from Faith for this long, the nurse said the hospital was now legally responsible for his care. Because of this, the ethics committee was scheduled to meet later that afternoon.

Holding his hand, I whispered to him, "Sweetie, you're going to die, and it won't be heaven for me if you're not there, Bobby. You need to make your peace with God."

Norma Gaebelein, our childhood Sunday school teacher, knew my family well and how very much I needed to be loved. I grew up in a house filled with violence and turmoil, which my brother, Larry, and I suffered at Bobby's hands. We suffered physical and emotional abuse from Bobby. I also was a victim of sexual abuse at his hands from the time I was about seven years old. Growing up with Bobby was not easy, and I could have spent the rest of my life holding on to the anger and hurt. But, by forgiving him, I could be there for him in his last days and hours. The strength I needed to forgive him, I found through Jesus. When we were younger, Norma had assigned each of us a scripture verse to memorize to earn a Bible with our name in gold letters, and she thoughtfully chose the scripture *Jeremiah 31:3* for me.

"I have loved you with an everlasting love; Therefore, with loving kindness, I have drawn you and continued My faithfulness to you. (Jeremiah 31:3, AMP)

I thought of that verse that had held me up in some of my darkest moments, which prompted me to ask Bobby if he remembered his, but he didn't respond. I then played and sang "Come to Jesus", and he moved! He turned his head towards me; his face all scrunched up.

"I know you can hear me, Bobby. Jesus is knocking on the door of your heart. Open the door," I pleaded. "Please let Him in Bobby. He loves you so much and wants to take you home. This is your chance to see Sandy (his first wife who had died of cancer) again and finally meet your daughter, Cara (their daughter who they lost to a miscarriage)."

When it comes to my family, I have no pride and will "go there" if needed, without reservation.

That was the only time Bobby had reacted since I had arrived. I felt God's presence and purpose in what I was doing. I knew Bobby had heard me. So, as I always do, I pushed harder. I sang, prayed, and read "Jesus Calling", which stunned me.

> *"At the end of your life-path is an entrance to heaven. Only I know when you will reach that destination, but I am preparing you for it each step of the way. The absolute certainty of your heavenly home gives you Peace and Joy to help you along your journey. You know that you will reach your home in my perfect timing: not one moment too soon or too late. Let the hope of heaven encourage you as you walk along the path of Life with Me."*

Sobbing, I knew that day would be my brother's last day on this earth. I remember thinking, *I wish Mama was here,* and an instant later, she walked through the door. She said she realized that I needed her.

I got her a chair and told her, "Mama, say the things you need to say to him and the things he needs to hear."

She sat down next to his bedside and began to speak quietly to him. I heard stories about when he was little. It was easy and light. Yet, there was an underlying intensity about what she was saying to him, as if she needed him to understand where he came from, and possibly, what led him to where he was now. I got up and headed to the parking garage to talk to God and sneak a cigarette. Sadly, my crutch in a crisis. I got to the top and prayed, "Lord, I thank you for bringing me here and through the most difficult thing I have ever experienced. But, Lord, I need you to get Faith here or give me enough time to get Mama out of the room, and then please take him home, Lord!"

Walking into the waiting room, I had my license ready to show the security guard. He watched me as I opened the electronic security door. The look on his face said, "I'm sorry for what you are going through. I know who you are. It's okay. It's going to be alright." And then lastly, "I see you, and I got your back." I hesitated before realizing that those thoughts I equated with the look of the security guard were words from the Lord. *Claire, I see you. I'm right here with you. You are not alone. Do not be afraid.*

The electronic door opened, and there was Mama!

> *Isaiah 41:10 CSB – "Do not fear for I am with you; do not be afraid, for I am your God. I will strengthen you; I will help you; I will hold on to you with my righteous right hand."*

I must have looked shocked because she said, "It's okay. He's not dead, and Faith just got here. Where were you?"

I told her everything, and her pure "Mama" response was, "Wow! That was fast!"

I looked at her and said, "That's how Jesus works, Mama."

We waited and then walked back into Bobby's room. I hugged Faith, told her how very sorry I was, and thanked her for the time she allowed me to have with Bobby. Minutes later, a nurse came in and said the doctor wanted to speak to Faith.

While she and Mama were out of the room, I held Bobby's swollen hand in mine, whispering the last private words we would ever have. I told him that I loved him very much and forgave him for the horror I had suffered at his hands. That's when I saw the tear. One tiny tear rolled down his face, and it broke me.

I continued to whisper, crying to him, "God loves you, Bobby, and always has. He wants you to run to Jesus. Bobby, run into the arms of Jesus! He's going to take you home."

I quickly finished telling him that he would soon be meeting Jesus, and it all would be over – the pain, the suffering, the chaos. There would be peace, just peace, and I walked out.

When I walked back in, Faith was speaking to Mama about what the doctors had said. This was it. My brother was going to die, and it was going to be soon. Mama got up. I could see she was hanging on by a thread, so I held her and asked, "Mama, do you want to stay?" She sobbed, "I just can't." I called for Rabbi Sadler, and he was on his way. Out in the waiting room, I walked over to the security guard, explained to him what was going on, and asked him if he would keep an eye on my mother. He placed his bear-sized hand over mine, smiled at me, and said, "Of course, baby. What your mama is going through, no mother should ever have to face."

Robin, the nurse from the cardiac wing, walked into Bobby's room and asked how she could help. "My mother is in the waiting room," I responded. "Would you go sit with her until Rabbi Sadler arrives?" She simply nodded, and we walked out together. I introduced her to Mama. She sat down, reached out, and held both of my mother's hands. Mama began to sob. I panicked, but Robin held her hand up, wordlessly telling me, "Go, I got this." Women can say so much without words, can't they?

Weeks later, Mama would try to find her to send a thank-you note, but she didn't exist anywhere in the hospital's database, and no one in CCU had ever heard of her. God had sent an angel.

Hebrews 1:14 AMP – "Are not all angels ministering spirits sent out [by God] to serve (accompany, protect) those who will inherit salvation?" Of course, they are Bobby's nurse came in and asked if we would like a little more time. Faith quickly snapped, replying, "Yes, the lifetime we were supposed to have!" Then, she shook her head and said, "I'm sorry. No, it's okay. Bobby wouldn't want us dragging this out."

The nurse told us the last senses to go were hearing and smell, so for us to keep talking to him as she was sure Bobby could hear us. She administered a sedative and then left. When she came back in, she told us, "I'm going to administer the next syringe and then turn off the ventilator."

Faith looked up, and my heart broke for her.

I walked over to the right of Bobby's bed, his nurse following me, and Faith was on his left. I saw the nurse's left-hand reach for the line, the syringe in her right. It went in, and she pushed the plunger. I choked back a sob and let the tears fall. I held his hand while silently talking to him, telling him again that I loved him and would see him again, lastly saying the words to him again, *Run to Jesus, Bobby! Run to Jesus!* I watched the monitors and prayed for them to move as I was at my end, as well – no sleep, living on coffee, cigarettes, adrenalin, and very little food.

The number of breaths began to decrease, as did his heart rate. Then, there it was, a flat line, and his nurse came in. Quietly, I said, "Faith, he's gone." She looked up, and his heart started beating again. Of course, it was the last "Gotcha!" that I would get from my big brother. It was vintage Bobby.

The number of beats on the screen decreased. Then Bobby's heart beat one last time, and the line went flat. On April 14, 2015, at 5:15 p.m., my brother Bobby was pronounced dead.

I went out to the waiting room, where I found Mama and whispered to her, "It's over. It was very peaceful. He wasn't in any pain or distress. Mama, for the first time in his life, he is at peace." We sat there holding one another and crying.

I told Faith I needed to get Mama home, walked to the parking garage, and stood there letting the rain mix with my tears. "Lord, I know it doesn't work this way, but I sure would like to know if Bobby is with you." Chastising myself, I smoked a cigarette and descended those flights for the last time. It was then that I realized I wasn't really asking God if Bobby had made it. I was asking if I was good enough, but God only needed me to be obedient and to trust Him. I remembered He had called me and qualified me through my obedience and trust in Him. Because of that, I was able to help bring his son home. At least that was my hope. I clung to *Proverbs 3:5-6, TPT* – *"Trust in the Lord completely, and do not rely on your own opinions. With all your heart rely on Him to guide you, and he will lead you in every decision you make."*

I got to the 3rd floor and stopped. I felt a warmth and peace I had never experienced before in my life and heard these words: "Thank you, Claire. Thank you."

"Bobby?" I spoke.

Then, I heard the words, "Of course, it's me, Sara. Who else would it be?" Then there was silence.

God had answered me, honoring me with the gift of Bobby's words. You see, "Sara" was a nickname I hated growing up, and Bobby was the only one who used it. Thank you, Jesus.

. . . .

OBEDIENCE
Kimberly Ann Hobbs

Salvation comes by faith in Christ alone, and when Christ alone is Lord and King in our lives, we will desire to walk in obedience to God. Deep spiritual humility is obedience to God. *(James 4:6)*

The Holman Illustrated Bible Dictionary suggests that biblical obedience is to hear God's Word and act accordingly.

As believers and God's children, we're called to submit ourselves to a higher authority and do what God tells us. If we believe in Him, then we obey Him because He alone is God. From the very beginning, God made the issue of obedience clear to us. No compromises. No shady area! Our love for God should be all-consuming. The Bible says for us to love God with all of our hearts and with all of our souls and with all of our strength. *(Deuteronomy 6:5)*

This comes with a special promise of untold blessings. *"Now if you obey me fully and keep my covenant, then out of all nations you will be my treasured possession. Although the whole earth is mine, you will be for me a kingdom of priests and a holy nation." (Exodus 19:5-6)*

We find stories of following the Lord in obeying him throughout His Word. The opposite of obedience is disobedience, which is a sin. It disregards the standard set by God. Many places throughout God's Word, we can see examples of disobedience against God and the suffering and consequences endured as a result of sin and not obeying God. *(1 Samuel 15, 2 Samuel 11, and Genesis 19)*

Full obedience to God carries the instruction of total surrender to Him. The Bible affirms that our love for Jesus is the greatest motivator of our obedience to Him. What is so beautiful about this truth is that it carries with it numerous blessings from God.

> *"Blessed are all who fear the Lord, who walk in obedience to him." (Psalm 128:1, NIV)*

By being obedient to God, it will produce steadfastness, purity, freedom from scorn and slander understanding, strength, direction, preservation, and more. All these are found in Psalm 119:5-40.

Trust and obey God. Our faith in Jesus Christ is the active ingredient in trust. As we trust God, we obey him. Trust carries the weight of our belief. When we believe Him, He is able to do exceedingly abundantly more than we could ask or imagine. I get goosebumps just knowing what is to come from trusting God and being obedient. It's always more than I could imagine.

Obedience is evidence of our trust applied and carried out in our daily walk with God. Through obedience, we experience all the blessings of the Holy Spirit who lives within us. Anything less is sin in the eyes of God and cannot please Him. Obedience is key.

* *

Marquetta Curtis is a Mother, Grandmother, Bible Teacher, Singer, Songwriter, Life Skills Coach, and Entrepreneur. She has a passion for the less fortunate and has provided countless years of service in community involvement. She has serviced Local Food Banks and Summer Food Service Programs (SFSP) in various states, providing food to families who are at risk of hunger and helping children to maintain a nutritious diet during the summer months.

Marquetta has also served as a sponsor for the Toys for Tots program distributing toys to needy children in the Community as Christmas gifts. She is an advocate for people with intellectual disabilities.

Marquetta is a Member of Women World Leaders ministry. She resides in Port St. Lucie, Florida.

Hole In My Heart
Marquetta Curtis

> *"My flesh and my heart may fail, but God is the rock and strength of my heart and my portion forever." (Psalm 73:26, AMP)*

Surviving as a Child

Born in Michigan, 1963, the doctors discovered I had a hole in my heart. Severe asthma attacks caused by the hole in my heart landed me in and out of the hospital the first few years of my life. I was raised in a single-parent home with my mother, older sister, and brother. We often spent weekends with my grandparents and went to church.

> *"Dedicate your children to God and point them in the way that they should go, and the values they've learned from you will be with them for life." (Proverbs 22:6, TPT)*

My mother was an only child, very outspoken, and would constantly yell profane language at my grandmother. (Later, I found out that as a child, she went to boarding school, and the nuns were very cruel and strict, and she resented it.)

I always got along with my brother and looked up to him. He would take me for rides on his bike, teach me sports, and play with me until he reached puberty at age thirteen. One day, when I was six years old, I was home alone with him, and he called me to his room. He was masturbating, and taking advantage of the opportunity, he molested me. Then he told me not to let anybody else do that to me. It happened one time. But, that's all it took to damage me. A few years later, my brother started getting into trouble, and my mother enlisted him in the Army at seventeen years old.

My sister and I never got along. When no one was looking, she would hit me and pull my hair. She would yell how much she hated me and that I was Mama's precious little angel. In our home, there were steel support poles in the basement that she would throw me up against, while hitting and kicking me. One day, she was so mad at me that she put me in the clothes dryer and turned it on, causing me to have an asthma attack.

One summer night, when I was twelve, my mother had gone to work. While I was washing dishes, my sister told me to go to bed. I responded no because my mother said we could stay up late during the summer. She began to hit me in my back repeatedly like I was a punching bag. It hurt so bad. With tears rolling down my face, I didn't move. I kept my focus on washing dishes. Suddenly, while she was swinging at me, my body shifted to the left. Her fist hit the edge of the sink and busted both of her knuckles wide open. Her injury required stitches. God had his angels to move me out of the way of a brutal beating. God sends angels with special orders to protect you wherever you go, defending you from all harm. *(Psalm 91:11, TPT)*

During another occurrence, my sister started beating on me again, but that was the last time. While she was hitting me, I bent over. God gave me His strength beyond measure. I grabbed her ankles and flipped her over me. After that, she never touched me again. He gives strength to the weary and increases the power of the weak. *(Isaiah 40:29, NIV)*

Additionally, my sister and mother had much conflict. My sister ran away from home at age sixteen.

Seasons of Change

"The Lord is close to the brokenhearted; He rescues those whose spirits are crushed." (Psalm 34:18, NLT)

I was relieved when my sister left, but still very confused with my life. Mom was always angry and threatening. Still, I wasn't allowed to talk to my grandparents or even spend time with friends. I was so alone. I would write songs of my pain, and trying to fit in with the school crowd, I started drinking and using drugs. I had no dreams or goals, no example or role model. I didn't know what life was other than watching TV.

"Even if the mountains were to crumble and the hills disappear, my heart of steadfast, faithful love will never leave you, and my covenant of peace with you will never be shaken," says Yahweh, whose love and compassion will never give up on you." (Isaiah 54:10, TPT)

Mom eventually got married again to a very good man. Mom and I both calmed down. I stopped turning to substances and turned to God. Shortly after, we moved to North Carolina. I started going to church and joined youth group and choir.

> *"I will praise thee, O Lord, with my whole heart. I will be glad and rejoice in thee: I will sing praise to thy name, O thou most High." (Psalm 9:1-2, KJV)*

Mountains to Climb

Mom still had anger issues, but she was trying to do right and had become very active in the community. She assisted a family from the Bahamas who wanted their elementary school-age children to go to school in the U.S. She opened the doors to our home, providing a place for them to live. They had cousins who were college students in the area.

One day, Mom dropped us off at the campus to visit them. When we got to their dorm room, they had suitcases full of marijuana. They were drug dealers and using the kids to sell drugs for them at the elementary school. The dealers gave the kids little packets of marijuana, instructing them to hide it in the back of their radio. Soon after, their mother came over to the U.S. to visit them. While she was dusting their room, the back of the radio opened up, and the drugs fell out!

Quite naturally, being that I was sixteen and they were seven and eight years old, no one would believe the drugs were those children's. When my mother found out, not only did I get cursed out, but she beat me like a man. She sat on top of me and kept hitting me with her fist, blaming my boyfriend who didn't even use drugs. My stepfather was there looking at me. I begged him to help me. In his eyes, he looked as if he wanted to help, but he did nothing. I looked up to the mountains and hills, longing for God's help. But then, I realized that our true help and protection comes only from the Lord, our Creator who made the heavens and the earth. *(Psalm 121:1-2, TPT)* Due to all of this, Mom sent me to Drug Action and to a psychiatrist.

> *"In all this, Job did not sin by charging God with wrongdoing." (Job 1:22, NIV)*

All of these things happened when I was trying to get back to God. I was disheartened with all the yelling and being falsely accused of doing things. I'd had enough. I didn't care anymore. Day after day, the rage continued in our house. I hated to go home. I ran away, stealing my mother's car and going to my best friend's house. Her mother encouraged me to go home. When I got home, the beating began again. With so much anger fueling my mother, she threatened to kill me and my boyfriend, and then put me out.

> *"God is my keeper; he will never forget nor ignore me. Jehovah himself will watch over you; he's always at your side to shelter you safely in his presence. He's protecting you from all danger both day and night. He will keep you from every form of evil or calamity as he continually watches over you. You will be*

guarded by God himself. You will be safe when you leave your home and safely you will return. He will protect you now, and he'll protect you forevermore!" (Psalm 121)

I called those college "drug dealers" and told them what happened. They carefully arranged transportation to get me away. In the event we were being followed, we switched cars five times all the way to their aunt's house in New York. When I got there, I was so distraught and confused. Then I began to notice a large traffic flow of different men and women going in and out of the bedrooms. I realized she was a Madame! I told them that I wanted to go back to North Carolina. Thankfully, they put me on the bus, and my boyfriend picked me up from the bus station, then took me to his house. His mother talked to me and encouraged me. She welcomed me into her home because she didn't want me out on the streets. I got a job and helped out with food and bills.

"For I am the Lord, your God, who takes hold of your right hand and says to you, do not fear; I will help you." (Isaiah 41:13, NIV)

Tug of War

A few years later, I got pregnant, and we got married. Things were going good for a while, but later, we started having marital problems. After a year, we separated. But the Lord stood with me and strengthened me. *(2 Timothy 4:17, NKJV)*

Miraculously, my mother and I had reconciled, leaving a path for my daughter and I to move back in with my parents. I had a good job working 3rd shift. My daughter went to daycare during the day, and my mother watched her at night. My mother loved her very much. But, as for me, her verbal abuse was still intense. It seemed as if the verbal trauma would never end. In frustration, I started hanging out with my coworkers and getting high. My entire life was a giant question mark.

A Glimmer

One day while walking downtown, I met a guy who was extremely tall, very nice, and handsome. He was different. The way he stood, the way he talked. He was so pleasant. At that moment, he invited me to sit and talk with him. We chatted a little while, and somehow, my life challenges came up. Then he began to talk about God, and he told me that he was an angel. Then he told me, "God loves you. Do what you know to do. You know the way to go and the path to take. Do it." Next thing I know, I was walking down the street. I couldn't get what he said out of my mind. I knew it was God speaking to me.

"Hold on to instruction, do not let it go; guard it well, for it is your life." (Proverbs 4:13, NIV)

"Don't forget to be kind to strangers, for some who have done this have entertained angels without realizing it!" (Hebrews 13:2, TLB)

Unfortunately, I started hanging out with one of the employees at my daughter's daycare. While visiting some of her friends, I was introduced to crack cocaine. Sad to say, my little girl was with me when I took my first hit of crack. I thank God that they didn't touch her. My God sent his angel, and he shut the mouths of the lions. They have not hurt me, because I was found innocent in his sight. *(Daniel 6:22, NIV)*

I never took her in that environment again. One day, I heard a voice say, "Come." It was the crack calling me. I searched for it, and when I found it, I was raped by two men at the same time. I just laid there numb, wanting to die. I knew what was happening to me, but I was impaired. I couldn't move. I felt that same numbness many times before.

A few days later, I drove to an elementary school parking lot, where I parked and just sat there smoking, drinking, crying, and talking to God. Afterwards, I went to a Christian friend's house, and when she opened the door, I – in my drunken state – begged for scriptures. Then, I passed out. When I came to, I was in the shower fully clothed. My friend began to minister the Gospel of Jesus Christ to me and invited me to her church. She let me stay there a few days, and I told her that I would go to church with her one day.

Shortly after, I again heard crack calling me, so I met crack dealers at a motel. They offered to pay me fifteen thousand dollars in cash if I had sex with all of the men in the room. I refused. They started laughing at me and gave me a hit of "bad" crack. I started hyperventilating; my heart was pounding hard and fast. I was overdosing. Suddenly, my spirit left my body. I saw myself dying. I couldn't talk; I couldn't breathe. But, in my mind, I remembered the Lord's Prayer that my grandmother taught me. Instantly, I prayed it and told the Lord, "If you get me out of this mess, I will serve You. I will live for You!"

> *"And everyone who calls on the name of the Lord will be saved."* (Acts 2:21, NIV)

> *"For I am the Lord, your God, who takes hold of your right hand and says to you, 'Do not fear; I will help you.'"* (Isaiah 41:13, NIV)

Freedom!

Suddenly, they escorted me to the door. I jumped in my car, and while in no shape to drive, I raced over a narrow bridge on my way home. God's angels must have been driving my car that day because I could have easily crashed. When I arrived, no one was there. I went to my room and lay down. While looking up at the ceiling, I saw Jesus with his arms open wide! But when I looked down, I saw the horns of the enemy. I realized I was on the borderline of absolute destruction.

Compelled by deep concern for my soul, I contacted my friend and went to church a few days later. After the message, the minister offered a prayer for salvation, but I didn't go up at first. At the benediction, the minister again called me to come forth. He said, "God is calling you." This time, I surrendered. I walked to the altar and gave my life to Christ that day. But, oh, was the devil maaaad!

Before I could leave the church parking lot, a man walked up to me and said, "You weren't ready, were you?" I told him, "Yes, I'm ready." I knew I was ready. That day, the hole in my heart and soul was filled. Freedom was mine! I had been redeemed! I have been made whole!

> "Therefore, if any man be in Christ, he is a new creature: old things are passed away; behold, all things are become new." (2 Corinthians 5:17, KJV)

> "Then your light will break forth like the dawn, and your healing will quickly appear; then your righteousness will go before you, and the glory of the Lord will be your rear guard." (Isaiah 58:8, NIV)

Sometime after, I reconciled with my husband, and we had two more beautiful children. Many years later, my mother accepted Jesus as her Lord and Savior and went forth feeding, clothing, and providing shelter to many. My older brother also accepted Jesus as Lord. He and my older sister are now disabled. Without ceasing, I pray for them and do whatever I can to help them.

> "For he is our peace, who hath made both one, and hath broken down the middle wall of partition between us." (Ephesians 2:14, KJV)

"For God so loved the world that he gave his one and only Son, that whoever believes in him shall not perish but have eternal life." (John 3:16, NIV)

"In everything you do, be careful to treat others in the same way you'd want them to treat you." (Matthew 7:12, TPT)

Keep Going

Five years ago, my mother went home to be with the Lord peacefully in her sleep, and at the time, my stepfather was very sick with COPD and Pulmonary Hypertension. Years before, my parents had adopted a boy and a girl born with fetal alcohol syndrome (FAS). They were a younger brother and sister to me. I moved to Florida to help them both. Eighteen months later, my stepfather passed away. Due to his death, I had the honor of taking over guardianship of those two precious beings.

"Brethren, I count not myself to have apprehended: but this one thing I do, forgetting those things which are behind, and reaching forth unto those things which are before, I press toward the mark for the prize of the high calling of God in Christ Jesus." (Philippians 4:13-14)

My Beautiful Now

Today, my life is filled with everlasting joy and excitement. Accepting Jesus as my Lord and Savior is the best thing that ever happened to me. There are not enough words in this world to express the gratitude that I feel. His unfailing love has kept me and brought me through many valleys and mountains. I am such a grateful survivor. I have a beautiful family, and I no longer struggle with the asthma caused by the hole in my heart. It healed on its own by the loving touch of Jesus in my life.

My goal and purpose for life is to help others discover how valuable they are regardless of the color of their skin, their stature and shape, their imperfections or disabilities. I praise God for a new song for a new day rises up in me every time I think about how he breaks through for me! Ecstatic praise pours out of my mouth until everyone hears how God has set me free. Many will see his miracles; they'll stand in awe of God and fall in love with him! *(Psalm 40:3)*

You are valuable. Your life matters. You are important. You Matter to God!

"I praise you because I am fearfully and wonderfully made; your works are wonderful; I know that full well." (Psalm 139:14)

"For I know the plans I have for you," declares the Lord, "plans to prosper you and not to harm you, plans to give you hope and a future." (Jeremiah 29:11)

(Writing Mentor ~ Kelly Jo Rabbitt)

. . . .

FREEDOM
Kimberly Ann Hobbs

God created us and made us free to enjoy life and His creation for us as long as it's within the structure of how He designed us.

When we desire the biblical freedom God's Word tells us about, we need to begin at the inner freedom that comes from within ourselves, when we get "freed" from the bondage of sin. On a personal level, it's about redemption that applies to each of our lives. We are free when we are redeemed from sin.

> *"Creation itself will also be set free from its slavery to corruption into the glory of the children of God." (Romans 8:21)*

Freedom does not come by doing what you feel like doing without constraints. God's freedom comes by following Christ's commands because it allows you to be more of the person who God created you to be. The commands of Jesus give us guidelines so we can know how to live and love each other.

We are truly free from the bondage of greed, vanity, pride, pornography, addiction, abusive behavior, gluttony, selfishness, and other sins when we know the truth about ourselves and the world that we live in.

God says, *"If you abide in my word, you are truly my disciples. Then you will know the truth, and the truth will set you free. (John 8:31-32)* Knowing this allows us to discard the lies and deceptions that hold us to the bondage within. When we can cleanse our insides of these things, especially in our mind, it frees us to continue to serve one another on the outside.

> *"For you were called to freedom, brothers. Only do not use your freedom as an opportunity for the flesh, but through love serve one another." (Galatians 5:13)*

God's answer to our loss of freedom has always been Jesus. It starts with acknowledging our brokenness and admitting we are slaves to sin. It ends with choosing Jesus and following Him every day. Only Jesus can break the chains of bondage and lead us to true freedom.

• •

Wendy Wood has 27 years' experience working with preschoolers and school-age children. She has been everything from a certified Montessori/VPK teacher, to assistant director of a private preschool, the owner and operator of her own licensed home daycare, ASL teacher, a loving mother and, above all, a true child of God. The love and passion she has for children and families go hand and hand. She truly enjoys teaching and helping children learn and reach their greatest potential.

She was born and raised in Florida and was the youngest of eight in her family. She has been married for 21 years and is blessed with a talented son who longs to be a jazz musician. Her hobbies include photography, drawing and being a true prayer warrior to many.

Although Wendy always tries to smile and find the positive in everything and everyone, she also deals with hidden battles every day with her health. In 1979, on Halloween, she was diagnosed with Type 1 diabetes and was placed immediately on four insulin injections a day. She was only 8 years old. In 1983, Wendy became the poster child for the Juvenile Diabetes Foundation (JDF) and was crowned as the Butterfly Princess of a huge fundraiser ball.

That year they also sent her to a 2-week diabetic camp in Stark, FL, that completely changed her life. She no longer felt alone, scared or cursed. Instead she felt normal, alive and loved. She made long-lasting friendships that became part of her journey. She knew from that day on that nothing was impossible and as long as she kept her faith and continued to believe, then that word "impossible" only meant one thing...

"I'M POSSIBLE."

"God: Grant me the Serenity to Accept the Things I Cannot Change, Courage to Change the Things I Can and the Wisdom to Know the Difference." -- Reinhold Niebuhr

More Than Just My Imagination

Wendy Wood

Have you ever had the same dream or nightmare play over and over again? One that was so realistic, you felt you were living it right then and there, and it made your heart beat fast like you were having a panic attack? But then, you felt stillness, calmness, and totally at peace. The kind of peace where one minute you're lost, and then suddenly, you're safe and sound. Well, this happened to me back in 1988.

I was seventeen years old, and I dreamt I was at the hospital and something was wrong with me. I wasn't sure what had happened. All I knew is that it was serious. I dreamt that family and friends were around my hospital bed day and night, crying and praying – especially my mother. Everyone thought I was going to die, but I knew I wasn't. Yet, I couldn't communicate with them to tell them to stop crying because I was okay. My body just lay there lifeless.

I had this dream/nightmare several times. Each time, it kept getting stronger and more detailed to the point where it was time to let my mother know. So, I packed a small suitcase before telling my mother about my dream. Then I begged her to take me to the ER right then.

I remember my body was shaking. I was hysterical and could barely get the words out to her. She looked at me like I was crazy, then told me to test my blood sugar level while she grabbed some orange juice, thinking I was probably experiencing a low diabetic reaction. However, my sugar level was 133; perfect. I still wanted to go to the hospital, but she convinced me it was just my imagination.

> *"Even though I walk through the valley of the shadow of death, I will fear no evil, for you are with me; your rod and your staff, they comfort me." (Psalm 23:4)*

Two weeks on the dot, my imagination became a reality. I had gone into a diabetic coma. It was no ordinary diabetic coma, though. It was the most severe diabetic coma I have ever experienced, and there was no explanation of why it even occurred. It wasn't like I was eating a bunch of cupcakes, candy, or carbs, and I hadn't missed any of my insulin dosages. My blood sugars were then about 670, and my ketone levels were also increasing. My doctor placed me on an insulin drip and in ICU immediately. After a couple of hours, he brought in several other doctors to consult with, too, because no matter how much insulin they were pumping into me, my blood sugars kept rising. It rose to 800...900...1200, and then to 1400.

My doctor couldn't figure it out, and being a nonbeliever of God and miracles, he told my mother to have anyone who wanted to say their goodbyes to me to do so because he didn't think I would survive through the night. My mother had already called my sister in California to fly in. My other siblings were already there at the hospital, as well as my youth pastor and youth group friends. They all circled my bed, praying hard. It was exactly how I had described my dream to my mother. I could feel myself drifting in real life. I felt like I was having an out-of-body experience. I could see everyone in their pain and hurt. Then the machines started beeping... and I flatlined. My doctor pronounced me dead.

Why would God do this to me? Why would God do this to them, especially my mother? Why is God using my health against me?

Suddenly, I felt like I was floating through the clouds and right into this bright, safe place. Everywhere I looked, there were bright silhouettes. And the person I wanted to see was a brighter one. I knew who it was right away; it was my dad.

He grabbed my hand and said to me, "Wendy, it's not your time yet. Your mother needs you. But, now you know where you will be going when that time comes. And you know I will be here waiting for you. Keep your faith."

He then let go of the grip he had on me, and I suddenly felt my body falling backward through layers of thick, soft clouds.

> *"The Lord will protect you from all harm; he will protect your life. The Lord will guard your going out and your coming in from this time forth and forever." (Psalm 121:7-8)*

Meanwhile, my resting pulse had jumped to 121, and blood sugars were now 1,600. The doctor ordered everyone to leave the room except for my mother and the nurses. I suddenly came out of the coma, throwing my right arm straight up in the air while screaming for my dad.

"Don't go, Dad!"

My doctor looked at my mother and said, "Quick! Get her father in here!"

My mother just looked back at him with tears in her eyes and replied, "I can't. He's dead. He died seven years ago."

Ironically, it was me sitting by my father's bedside holding his hand – along with my mother on his other side – and hugging him, as we witnessed my father take his last breath after his battle with cancer and a brain aneurysm back in 1981.

Just then, my blood sugars started to drop. 1600...1500...920...780...548. They continued to drop throughout the night. They dropped down to 28, and my body went into grand mal seizures. I recall them giving me some sedatives to calm me down and a couple of glucose shots in my neck. My veins were very weak at this point. I felt as if I had been hit by a semi-truck, literally. But, I knew what I had warned my mother about two weeks prior was indeed more than just my imagination. Everything I had said to her, minus seeing my dad and his message to me, all came true.

The next day, my tongue was sore from biting it during the seizure, but I woke up to my hospital room decorated with toilet paper and balloons from my youth group and minister. Nurses had to duck under the streamers of toilet paper to take my vitals, but never once did I hear them complain. I even made the front page of our local newspaper, with my family sitting around my hospital bed joking and sharing the love we have for one another.

The best part was when my doctor came in to see my mother and me. He said that what he witnessed last night, with my blood sugars suddenly going down, and me coming out of the coma with no damage done, could only have been due to a miracle. If he hadn't seen it, he wouldn't have believed it. However, he did see it, and he said he was now a believer.

One of the reasons I felt God guiding me to relive and reveal this story at this time and for this book was because when this all happened to me, I was a Christian. However, I was also human. I admit I was angry at God. I argued with him afterward because every time my mother would see me, she would start crying. I didn't understand why God was allowing my illness to make others whom I love have sadness and overwhelming fear in watching me almost die. Who would put that kind of pain and heaviness on my mother, who had already lost her spouse and never did a cruel thing in her life? But then, I realized my mother was crying tears of joy. When things like this happen and we wonder why, we need to remember it isn't about ourselves. I was just an ingredient. God had bigger plans, and it was about the bigger picture.

So many praises I give to the Lord for that day. Several new believers came forth that week. I was reassured of where my dad is, and more so, where I will be when it is my time to be with the Lord. The experience has truly made me stronger in my faith. It also has made me believe that the power of prayer does work. I realize how important it is to pray for others, including your enemies, and not just for yourself in times of need.

> *"Therefore, confess your sins to one another and pray for one another so that you may be healed. The prayer of a righteous person has great power as it is working." (James 5:16)*

Now, don't get me wrong. Not all good came out of that day. I mean, there still is and always will be someone out there who thinks of me as a crazy Christian or a coo-coo bird. And that's okay, because I know God is behind me, in front of me, and always beside me. I lift my hands right now with praise and tears of gratitude that I survived – remembering that with every storm we go through, there is a lesson to be found.

> *"Rejoice always, pray without ceasing, give thanks in all circumstances; for this is the will of God in Christ Jesus for you." (1 Thessalonians 5:16-18)*

I am living one day at a time and enjoying one moment at a time. Accepting hardships as the pathway to peace, I am taking this sinful world as it is, just as Jesus did, and not as I would have it. Trusting that He will make all things right if I surrender to His will, I know that I may be reasonably happy in this life and supremely happy with Him forever in the next.

PRAISE

Kimberly Ann Hobbs

When it comes to praise, many scriptures instruct us to direct our praises to God. They remind us of how great our God is and who He is and that He is worthy of all of our praise.

The word "Hallah" is the most common word for praise inside God's Word. It means to boast, brag, or rave about God. If we go to sports games, we tend to shout, scream, and holler for our favorite team. Many times, it inspires other people to join in and participate. Often, we are considered a fanatic when we do this for God, but I can think of many reasons to praise God regardless if I'm deemed passionate or not. God rescues me from those who hurt me, and He has done incredible works within my life. Therefore, I will praise Him because He alone is worthy of my praise.

> *"But because God's love for us is better than life, my lips will glorify you as long as I live." (Psalm 63:3-4)*

> *"He is your God, and you have seen with your own eyes the great and astounding thing that he has done for you." (Deuteronomy 10:21)*

"Sing to the Lord! Praise the Lord! He rescues the oppressed from the power of evil people." (Jeremiah 20:13)

There are numerous ways we can praise God in our lives each day. We can praise God through song, prayer, giving, worship, and raising of our hands. "Raising hands" is one of the most explosive and meaningful expressions of praise we have. When we "pray", we can thank Him first for all He has done for us. (I experience inner joy when I get to thank my Creator for all He's done for me.) In "giving" to God out of a praise-filled heart, it reveals that God means more to us than our possessions. When we "raise our hands", it's an international sign of surrender. But in "worship as we praise", we are raising our hands in adoration and surrender to God.

Praising God is important and needs to become a daily exercise of expression to Him who is worthy of our praise. To a God who has given to us ALL that we have, let's PRAISE Him for everything he has done, with our hands lifted high to the heavens!

Thank you, Almighty Lord, for the abundant gifts You bestow upon us daily. We love You and praise You. To You, O God, be all the glory for everything You do and everything You've done! Forever, we will praise You! We praise you! WE PRAISE YOU, FATHER GOD. Amen!

· ·

 **Deanne Batterson** is an author and speaker from Northern Ohio. She serves on the board for Never Let Go Ministries, a non-profit organization that brings drug awareness to the community. She has been a guest speaker at various churches and organizations where she loves to share her testimony and encourage others.

Deanne loves gardening. When she is out working in her garden, she feels closer to God. It is in the garden where she loves to ponder on the scriptures she has read and talk to God. With her love of gardening, Deanne joined the Pulaski Garden Club where she now serves as Vice President.

Deanne is married to her wonderful husband, Jim. They enjoy spending time with their family and friends, especially their two beautiful grandchildren. Together they own and operate a prosperous Farming Business and are active members of their church.

A Mother's Love, A Child's Choices

Jeanne Batterson

> *"Submit yourselves therefore to God. Resist the devil, and he will flee from you." (James 4:7, KJV)*

This verse is so very true. There was a time in my life where I had to submit myself to God and resist the devil. It is a time I went through with my daughter and how my strength and faith in God helped me through it all.

The day my daughter was born was such an exciting day for me. After months of waiting for her to arrive, with much anticipation, she was finally here. Being a mother – her mother – was something I longed for, and I had dreams of what her life would be like here in this world. Each day watching her grow, learning, and enjoying life was such a pleasure. She was a beautiful daughter — caring, loving, and always doing the right thing. I always called her my Godsend; she was such a blessing. She was raised in the church and loved talking to me about God. We would spend hours reading and discussing scriptures and topics in the Bible. She was excellent in school and received good grades. She was in the gifted and talented program, involved in sports, and always had a job. She was helpful at home, too, and I knew I could always count on her. So, I had no reason to believe that at the age of nineteen, my beautiful daughter would turn to a life of drugs, but she did.

I started suspecting that my daughter may be doing drugs during her first year of college. But, I would tell myself, *I'm imagining things. Not my daughter. She wouldn't do drugs.* Well, I was wrong. Whenever I confronted her and asked her, she would tell me that she wasn't doing drugs, and I would believe her. (Because that's what I wanted to believe.) However, I could not deny it any longer. The change in my daughter's lifestyle was so significant that I had to be honest with myself. After numerous times of confronting her, she finally admitted she was indeed doing drugs.

This was the start of several times of her going in and out of rehab. Each time she was in rehab, I thought for sure she was going to stay clean and become the daughter and friend who I remembered her to be. However, the reality of it all was that she would only stay clean for about a week, then turn back to drugs. It broke my heart. I didn't know what to do at this point. I remember crying from the depth of my belly. It was that painful. My deepest thoughts at that time were of all the dreams I had for my daughter's life. What was going to happen to my daughter's soul if she were to die from her addiction? I had started planning her funeral in my head because I was sure that's how this would all end. I was angry, as well, at those who introduced the drugs to my daughter. (My daughter had told me how she got started using drugs and who gave her the drugs.) However, I realized that my daughter could have said no to drugs and was responsible for her addiction.

My daughter's third time in rehab was no different than the others, except this time she met a guy and ran off with him to another city. It was with him where she first started using heroin. Talk about a mother's nightmare; this was it. I did not know where she was living – if any place at all. I am sure there were times they slept under the stars. I would text her every day, hoping to hear from her to know she was alive. The only time I would hear from her was when she needed money. She would tell me anything I wanted to hear and create stories to convince me to give her money. She used my love for her and my heart as a monetary means to support her addiction. She knew I loved her and used it to her advantage.

As a drug addict, my daughter was not a very lovable person. However, no matter what she did, I never stopped loving her. I know she was unaware of the wounds she inflicted on her family and me. There were countless nights where I could not sleep or would cry myself to sleep. Every imaginable thing goes through your head of all the horrible things that could happen to your loved one. You don't know when the sheriff is going to knock on your door only to tell you that your child is dead.

I finally told myself this is enough. I prayed and then gave it to the Lord; I put my trust in the Lord to protect my daughter. It was by the grace of God that I was able to keep myself together. My prayer life became my lifeline. It was already a big part of my life, but now it was essential. It was at this point where I began to realize God already knew the depths of her addiction and where she was. So, I cried out to Him and laid it all before Him. And you know what? He cared. He really cared. He was just waiting for me to let go and really talk to Him. Once I did, my relationship with God grew, and I began to have peace. I could finally sleep peacefully at night. I knew I could trust my God with my daughter's life, no matter how bad everything looked.

1 Peter 5:7 states, *"Cast all your cares upon him; for he cares for you."* And Proverbs 3:5-6 states, *"Trust in the LORD with all thine heart; and lean not unto thine own understanding. In all thy ways acknowledge him, and he shall direct thy path."*

About two years after my daughter ran off, she told me that she was pregnant. The thought of becoming a grandma was exciting. However, thinking about the heroin my daughter was using while pregnant took away the joy I should have been feeling. I tried to encourage my daughter to get clean for the sake of the baby, and after a few months of pleading with her, she agreed to get help. I drove down to where she was and took her to a place that would detox a pregnant woman. She was there for a week, then returned home to live with me. It was a battle, but I had thought for sure this time she was going to make it. (She was six months pregnant at the time.) But, after about a month, she took off to return to her boyfriend, the father of her baby. She started using heroin again, and I thought this battle was surely lost for her and the baby. I was ready to wash my hands of her and give up hope.

John 10:10 calls the devil a thief because he steals, kills, and destroys; he is after all of the good stuff in us, our families, and our lives. I came to realize the devil was working hard at trying to rob me of my child – my blessing and my seed. He schemed to weaken me and destroy my family. Was I going to let him win?

I told myself, "NO! I am not going to let him win! I cannot give up on my daughter or her baby." John 4:7 (KJV) states, *"Submit yourselves therefore to God. Resist the devil, and he will flee from you."*

I prayed to God and gave it all to Him; I again put my trust in the Lord to protect my daughter. I was reminded again that God already knew the depths of her addiction. He knew where she was, and He knew how to reach her. So, I cried out to Him and laid it all before Him. And when I finished praying to my God, I resisted the devil. I yelled at the devil and said, "Devil, you can't have her! She is not yours! You take your hands off of my daughter!"

A few months later, on a cold and dark night, my daughter sat on the steps and thought about her future. She took a serious look at herself as grief and guilt overwhelmed her. She closed her eyes, feeling her heart clench as she prayed for the first time in a long time. She prayed, "God, please, I don't want this addiction anymore. God, please, I want to be a good mother. I promise I will never use again."

Two weeks before the baby was due, my daughter returned home to me. We took her to the hospital, where they helped her get clean and set her up with some counseling. On January 21, 2014, my daughter gave birth to a beautiful baby girl. My daughter has been clean now for over five years and is a wonderful mother, who just recently gave birth to her second child. My granddaughter is doing very well, too. She is smart and has a beautiful personality. You would never know she is the child of a heroin addict. Also, the baby's father changed his lifestyle and has been clean now for over five years. I had been praying for him, as well. We do serve a wonderful and awesome God!

Epilogue

The disease of addiction is not just physical and mental; it is also spiritual. The hold it has on an addict is far beyond anything that science and matter can contain in itself. The chains and cages an addict is locked into are greater than any physical abstraction (their family, friends, and loved ones). I truly believe that God is the only and essential ingredient to beat the powers addiction has on an addict. I have seen it with my own eyes. God cleansed my daughter's mind and body of the overwhelming desire to use drugs. Heroin is no calling on my daughter anymore! The only ones calling out to my daughter are her two beautiful children. I am very proud of my daughter and the wonderful woman she has become.

Do I ever wish that we did not have to live through those painful years when my daughter was an addict? Yes. I wish that almost every day. No one ever wants their child or loved one to endure the struggle of addiction. It is an awful disease, and I can't emphasize enough how much I hate drugs. I hate what they do to the individual who is living a life of hell because of them. I hate how they tear at the heart of the family. And I hate that not every addict survives their addiction. However, because of my daughter's addiction, I have two beautiful grandchildren who I wouldn't trade for anything.

I am also part of a ministry that ministers to families who are affected by addiction. My view of addicts has changed tremendously. I know now that they are somebody's child, somebody's parent, somebody's sibling, somebody's friend, a blue-collar worker, a white-collar worker, and a child of God. This disease affects all walks of life, and not one family is immune to it. We must not let our life's circumstances defeat us. We must continue to "pray without ceasing." *(1 Thessalonians 5:16)* Addiction can be beat! Matthew 19:26 states, *"With man this is impossible, but with God all things are possible."* And remember, God is no respecter of person. God shows no favoritism. *(Romans 2:11)* If God answers the prayers of a lowly servant (me), He will answer your prayers, too!

"The righteous cry, and the Lord heareth; he delivereth them out of all their troubles." (Psalm 34:17)

"Therefore, I tell you, whatever you ask for in prayer, believe that you have received it, and it will be yours." (Mark 11:24)

"And pray in the Spirit on all occasions with all kinds of prayers and requests. With this in mind, be alert and always keep on praying for all the Lord's people." (Ephesians 6:18)

COVERING

Kimberly Ann Hobbs

Who is your covering? There are different ways a person could have a covering over them. You may have heard the term "spiritual covering." This would be having a Christian authority, such as a pastor of a church or a mature Christian who is accountable to God, offer their support to a submitted believer in need. As Christians, we could receive tremendous benefits when it comes to counsel, guidance, and help with biblical precepts. If we accept their guidance, they can act as a "spiritual covering" in assisting us.

When reading God's Word, we find out each person is ultimately accountable only to God *(Romans 3:19 and Matthew 12:36)* and not to another person. We carefully need to use wisdom where we place our trust. Consulting with others for guidance can often prove extremely helpful, *(Proverbs 1:14)* and learning wisdom of others *(Proverbs 5:11-14)* is commendable. But, God says our approval comes from Him, not men! *(2 Timothy 2:15)*

Our "covering" comes when we submit ourselves to the will of God. His Son, Jesus Christ, is our "true covering". He gave His life to be the covering for our sins. When we accept this gift of eternal life through Jesus, by faith and by grace which you are saved, we choose to submit ourselves to God's will for our lives, and we do it through obedience.

By doing this, we will have respect for the authority that God places in our lives, and we will learn to cooperate with other believers as the Bible instructs us to do. By placing all of our trust in the Lord and not men, we won't be led down a crooked path or be hurt from someone who may have the potential to step into sin.

God uses spiritual authority in our lives. It's very important to submit to the wisdom of those God entrusts, but God is our ultimate covering. it's in Him who we should put our total trust. Allow others to guide, strengthen, and assist you in your path toward abundant living, but God reminds us to trust in Him through His Word.

> *"Trust in the Lord with all your heart and do not lean on your own understanding. In all your ways acknowledge Him, and He will make your paths straight." (Proverbs 3:5-6)*

As a believer in Jesus, we can be assured of a new life covered under God. God is your provider, your protector, and nothing can separate you from His love. Rest in Him. No matter what hardship you face or are facing, God is your covering.

· ·

Lois Daley has walked with Jesus over 50 yrs. She is a Bible teacher, speaker and prayer fanatic.

Being the daughter, and first born of two powerfully effective Bible Scholars and teachers, she was saturated in Bible knowledge from an early age. Besides her academic degrees, Lois graduated from Emmaus Bible School.

She has team led most ministries in the churches she has attended over her lifetime.

Lois has spent many years writing Bible study sessions for her church, creating materials for both children and adults. She has a unique gift of translating the Scriptures, so that others can understand the text.

Lois spends a lot of time on her knees in prayer and cherishes adding your name to her list for daily intersection. She strongly feels that talking to God about even the mundane is a must.

Music is one of her passions. Singing comes innately to her, hence she has sung solo, in choirs and even conducted. You may catch her weeding, fertilizing or fiddling around her many species of flowers. During the Fall, she becomes a different person. She is abnormally 'nuts' about football.

Lois is married with three adult children and a grand kitty. Her commitment to Christ and her family is demonstrated in her unconditional love of righteousness and an intentional, what-ev-er-it-takes attitude.

Her life verse, "For to me to live is Christ, and to die is gain," can be seen in her tender, unbashful conversations, prayer and/or sing-ing about God anywhere.

Living for God's Glory
Lois Daley

It was the beginning of another adventure. The last (and easiest) surgery should've only been about fifteen minutes long. I had packed up the house and scheduled the movers. After the emotional half-year of goodbyes, I was ready for the last hurrah. When this was over, I would relocate fifty plus miles away.

So far, my life had been an adventure with God, surgery after surgery, but alas the abnormalities were over. The lifetime schedule of operations were coming to an end. I would be well and functioning on top of the world.

I had recently gone to the doctor due to excruciating annoying pains in my right side. I hoped it was not my appendix giving me issues. Then, regret settled in. I should have had my appendix taken out when given the opportunity.

"I don't want to have another surgery. But, if it is what it is, I have to do it."

Having another surgery meant finding babysitters and making arrangements for my children to be picked up from gymnastics, ballet, baseball, basketball, Awana, and regular church activities.

My husband usually traveled, worked late, or didn't get the reason for the busyness of these three small offspring who I indulged in extracurricular activities to keep them well-rounded individuals. I would rather keep their minds and bodies busy with positive activities than have them attached to an electronic lit tubing.

Since I had to go under the knife again, I surmised that adventure is the mother of new knowledge. I asked my doctor if I could switch hospitals and have the surgery at one that I hadn't been to, so long as he had privileges there. We got the green light. It would be a greater distance from home, though. So, family visits would be limited, but the stay would only be a few days. I could live with that.

Well, the fifteen-minute surgery ended up lasting four and a half hours. Dah! Some other problem was either discovered, something went wrong, or there were unanticipated complications. Little did I know the uncomfortable feeling I had in my gut while they were prepping me for surgery was not just gas. But, I mentally shrugged it off as the usual pre-surgery rituals that I had become accustomed to not being performed at this hospital.

Alas, after seven post-op days, I was discharged. While getting into the car, I experienced a sharp pain on the right side of my body. Although it hurt even worse than before, I didn't say a word since when I had mentioned it in the hospital, they told me the area was just sore from the surgery. My pride whispered for me not to be a complainer.

More than that, leaving the hospital was an emotional reprieve. I was too excited to see my little folks who I treasured so much. I had missed them and longed to hear all that happened in the past week. They, too, were excited to see their mom back home. Oh, the joy! Absence does make the heart grow fonder.

Unfortunately, as the night passed, danger raised its ugly head, and the perils of the long surgery and excruciating right-side pain became evident, increasing with intensity. Tears streamed uncontrollably down my cheeks as I laid in bed. Desperate for some relief from the pain, I took two pain medications and attempted to sleep.

I had only gotten a couple hours of sleep when the peep of dawn glistened through my window blinds. I attempted to go to the bathroom, but my legs wouldn't move. Actually, one leg was swollen and wouldn't budge. My toes looked like five mini balloons. It couldn't be from weight gain because I hadn't eaten much while in the hospital. The food hadn't been very appealing. Plus, they only rationed out three small servings per day. Of course, the surgery prep had flushed all goodies from my insides.

I did not know whether to scream or cry, but the waterworks involuntarily burst from my eyes. Not wanting to alarm my family, I waited until I figured I could get a response from my doctor after telephoning his answering service. After I explained what was going on, my doctor told me that the area might be inflamed. He went on to explain that there had been a bit of a complication during the surgery – adhesions from prior operations were bleeding out and not behaving as they should. Hence, the surgery took much longer than expected.

Nonetheless, he advised that I come to his office so he could examine me. With no urgency, my husband got ready and lifted me into the car. By then, the leg had grown from that of a calf to a baby elephant. I was heavy and could hardly transport myself into the doctor's office.

The horrifying expressions on the faces of medical staff as they stared at me gave me a good reason to become even more scared. Then I heard my doctor scream at my husband, "ER NOW! Don't wait for an ambulance. It's only a couple blocks away!" I knew then something was terribly wrong. NASCAR drivers had nothing on my husband that day as he drove to the hospital in record speed, regretting that he couldn't fit the car through the door of the hospital's entrance. Once again, I saw that same horrifying expression on the faces of the hospital nurses and doctors. One man even covered his mouth in shock.

At this point, I figured I was in a critical state and might be dying. There was a somber hush as the doctors examined me and hooked me up to whatever tubes they could find. The swelling in my leg was not going down; it was getting larger. The medicine they administered to me through the IV helped subdue the pain, but all I was concerned about were my children left at home and the ugliness of my mammoth leg. The emotional pain had defeated the physical, and the tears were now wrapped around the heart.

I was dozing in and out when my ears perked up. The conversation outside the curtained room was faint, yet I heard the discouraging words. When my husband came in and announced that he was going to put the kids in bed, I informed him that I had heard the doctor telling him that I would not make it through the night and that they were keeping me as comfortable as possible. What nonsense! I grew very upset. I blamed myself for choosing this hospital to handle my surgery. Not only was it a little further than the one that I usually went to, but it was in a town that most of the people who I knew didn't want to drive in. I was so distraught. My husband couldn't stay and watch me slip away. So, I accepted that I would go through the transition alone until I met with my Jesus.

All night, I laid there wondering when the cold hands of death would arrive. The wait seemed to go by in bits of seconds. I was hungry, anxious, and bored. Therefore, I did the only three things I could do: pray, sing, and cry. At times, I did all three at the same time. Eventually, I dozed off only to awaken to a shadow standing nearby – my surgeon. I looked at my watch and realized it was five o'clock in the morning. When I shifted my body in the bed, I noticed I had been moved to a regular room. Wait a minute! I was still alive!

I squinted through the dark and asked my doctor what he thought he was doing sneaking up on me like that.

"You scared me, Doc!"

"One scare deserves another. I've been practicing for twenty-seven years and have never had a DVT patient before," he responded, then said goodbye and wished me luck.

Luck! I don't have any luck. I have Jesus! Big difference. Now alert in the darkness, I returned to praying, singing, and crying. Apparently, the medical staff felt there was a medical solution to my problem. Hence, I laid there hooked up to the tubes.

Well, things went haywire. Progress was slow, but Jesus was quick. After a couple of nights, I asked my husband to bring books for me to read. He brought my Bible and my *Power of a Praying Wife, Praying Parent, and Experiencing God* book. I asked my husband why he chose those books, and he said, "You walk with them." I didn't even know he noticed. But, it must have been a part of God's plan.

My girlfriend, who I depended on seeing from day one, gave me a flippant excuse and never came to the hospital. I was lonely and discouraged, but the Lord reminded me of His presence and His promise. Years later, I realized God used those moments to hug and love on me. He was going to be the nucleus of my thoughts for a while, as well as get some glory credits.

One night, the nurse on duty noticed the title of the books and asked me about my relationship with God. That question proposed to me is like giving a lollipop to a two-year-old child or an overdose of Geritol in a glass of Boost to an elderly person. As she stood there keenly listening to my testimony of God's greatness, His faithfulness, and His many promises to me, the nightly technician, who came to take my blood, shared her curiosity and chimed in with her questions, too. That was the initiation of Bedside Book and Bible Study. When their two o'clock a.m. break came around, the night nurses who were not busy joined in the soft and holy moments of God showing himself real at my bedside. This was church; this was God getting the honor and glory amidst my pain and discomfort. There were nights of tears, confession, and transformation. Some nights we would have to start later, depending on their schedule or my condition. But, this was what living was all about. One night, a nurse even commented on the fact that it was a mystery how I was still alive. That was such an opportunity to rejoice in the magnificence of God. The nightly Bible study became such a norm that sometimes I didn't mind being in the hospital.

After several weeks, I was sent home with a walker. The swelling had gone down somewhat, but being immobile for so long, I had to go through therapy and learn to walk again. Of course, this was not fun. The thrill of being at home overrode the physical misery, though. This time, the kids were timid as they approached my bed. I could see fear screaming out of the three pairs of eyes. They had experienced their mother in and out of the hospital so many times that sometimes I wondered if they felt abandoned. It was the longest time that I had been hospitalized.

A friend from church came over and assisted with the kids. She became a source of help to our family, along with many others who attempted to make life as normal as possible for my children. That first night, we sang and thanked God that I was back home. Little did I know the jubilation was premature.

That evening, my husband flew out to work in another country. He had been away from work for over two months, taking up the vacancy of my absence.

Sleep was difficult for me that night because I had a persistent cough. Early the next morning, I noticed a bluish substance in my phlegm as well as coming from my nose. I reached over to the bedside phone and called my regular physician. Hearing my story, he directed me to call 911 immediately! I hung up from talking with the physician and dialed emergency. Next, I called my FBC church family, the folks who were always there when I needed them to step in as my extended family since I had no blood relatives around. Those days, Florida Bible Church demonstrated the love of Jesus in many ways. Even now, although I left that city almost two decades ago, my closest friends are people from that congregation who embraced my family and cocooned us in their casings of love.

The paramedics came, and after doing their usual questioning and vitals check, they put me on their medical cart and commenced quickly to wheeling me out of the house. By then, one of my neighbors curiously came over. No one had arrived yet from my church. I didn't want to leave my kids behind, but the EMTs said they could not ride with us in the ambulance. Just as they were putting me in the ambulance, Debbie Hangendurf from FBC drove up. Tears streamed down my face at the pain of my thirteen, eleven, and nine-year-old having to watch their mom leave again, considering she just got back home the day before. The pain pierced through the veins of my soul. I was slightly comforted by the glimpse of Debbie's car. In times like these, God's tender provision is visible.

The ambulance drove off, and before long, I was unconscious. Shortly after ten o'clock that night, I woke up to Pastor Bob's amusing remarks.

"So, Lois, you've decided to come back to the land of the living!"

I half-smiled.

Bob was not alone. Pam from the church choir was there, too. Well settled in a chair, she had a thermos of coffee, Bibles, books, sweaters, and blankets.

The nurses came in and informed me that the doctors would come to see me soon.

Bob thanked the Lord for my return to consciousness and prayed for my recovery to health. Pam explained that she would be at my bedside for the night and offered a Bible to me. Apparently, she didn't realize my feeble condition. I dozed off a little and awoke to much chatter. I'm not sure how much time it took to rally the troop of four doctors, who asked Bob and Pam to step outside.

After their short inquisition about how I was feeling, the leader of the quartet of doctors asked me the location of my husband and children.

How should I know? I thought. *Even a dunce would understand, having been in the state of missing a whole day of my life, I wouldn't know where anyone is!*

Despite what I was thinking, I respectfully told them that I didn't know exactly where my family was but had a pretty good idea.

Then, Mr. Lead Doc asked how I would like him to talk to me. Such a question!

"I'm a big girl," I responded. "I've had enough medical dramas to keep a hospital afloat. I'm not afraid of any news."

With the other doctors keenly staring, he stepped closer to me and told me that I would need to find my family. My blood was virtually diluted out; high levels of thinner were in my circulatory system; and I had an unidentifiable object snaking within my body. There was absolutely nothing they could do for me. An attempted surgery would mean immediate death. Nevertheless, I had just a couple of hours left. I would not make it through the night.

Where have I heard that before? I thought. For the next few seconds, everything else they said sounded like Charlie Brown's mother was speaking. *Wha, wha, wha.*

The Spirit reminded me of God's promise. So, I had to share it with those medical geniuses. I informed them that God had told me that He would not be taking me home to heaven until my children could take care of themselves.

"My Jesus has plans," I told them. "Besides, my husband can't cook," I added with a grin.

No! No! No! This was not happening now. God always keeps his promises.

One of the doctors then leaned forward, and while looking over the shoulder of the lead doctor, he asked me if I understood what they had told me. So, I regurgitate the fact that my blood was basically nothing, a nasty UFO was squirming around in my abdomen, and they didn't have a solution.

We said our goodbyes, and I asked for Bob and Pam to return. After I explained the diagnosis to them, Bob went into "fix-it" mode. First, to find my husband. I knew the hotels where he would stay when out of town, so it was just a matter of calling around. Then, to find the children. To my surprise, they were home alone. A neighbor who had committed to staying with them reneged. Livid, I started to cry. Soon, I was comforted with the promise that someone would get to the house to be with the children. By now, it was after 11:00 p.m.

Pam read a few verses to me from Psalm. Then, I just wanted silence. I wanted to talk to Jesus, my comfort. Ten minutes later, one of the doctors who had visited my room to deliver the Doomsday news came in to speak with me. He had an idea.

"Would you agree to a blood transfusion?" he asked.

With nothing to lose, I replied, "Yes."

The transfusion was ordered, and what do you know? The nurse on duty was new and messed it up. The needle was in my muscle. What a nightmare! But, whenever things go wrong, I know the Lord is going to show up big time. And so, He did.

By 3:00 a.m., the problem was noted and the transfusion corrected. Within a couple of hours, I was being wheeled to the operation room. As my bed was going through the door, in a trice, my husband was stepping in. Someone from church found him and flew him back in time to kiss me and squeeze my hand. I could see the stressed expression on his face, but I assured him that I would be okay. Of course, no human physician made any promises.

Later that day, when the doctors came in to see me, I noticed the puzzled look on their faces as they explained the procedure and expected results. To their amazement, the contrary happened.

"This is amazing!" one doctor exclaimed.

"It's called Jesus at work," I stated softly. "Remember, I told you last night that God promised me life until my children can take care of themselves? And they definitely cannot!"

The two looked at me as if I was a strange phenomenon. One even smiled and muttered something about luck. A miracle is what it was all about! God's power showed up, and He alone gets all the praise and glory.

I spent two weeks in the hospital. While there, in between sleep, grogginess, and pain, I had the privilege of showing off my Lord. I even got reprimanded by a nurse when I unplugged myself from the machines and went next door to a screaming patient's room to tell her of Jesus. For no suffering for this present time can be compared to the glory that will be revealed.

To God be the Glory!

GLORY
Kimberly Ann Hobbs

God, our Creator, is in a class all by Himself. He has infinite perfections, infinite greatness, and infinite worth. Because of God's holiness, He is in a class all by Himself in His perfection, greatness, and worth.

The "glory of God" is the manifest beauty of His holiness as it is brought to our attention. The way He puts His holiness on display, and how people seem to understand or perceive Him, is a question. Do you recognize who He is? The glory of God is the holiness of God-made manifest.

God tells us in Leviticus 10:3, *"He will be shown to be Holy among those who are near Him and before all people, He will be glorified."*

"The heavens are telling of the glory of God." (Psalm 19:1)

How can we comprehend this? One way may be to look at God as if He were shouting at us. He shouts with luscious landscapes, He shouts with grandeur mountains; He shouts with breathtaking sunsets; He shouts with galaxies and stars uncountable. God is telling us He is glorious! He wants each of us to open our eyes and realize that if we know who He is, it will be so much more magnificent for us!

God's Word says, "Holy, holy, holy is the Lord of hosts; the whole Earth is full of his glory." (Isaiah 6:3)

If you could have eyes to see, you would see the Lord everywhere. We need to have those kinds of eyes. Each of us was made for this deep down in our hearts – to see God in His infinite perfections, to see all the glory He has waiting for us when our eyes are completely open to Him.

God, in His infinite glory, is immeasurably more than we could imagine. God wants us to see Him as He is.

 **Diana Daniels** is the wife of a retired pastor. She is also the mother of two children, Sheri and Troy, plus two step-daughters, Debbie and Becky, and the grandmother of 10. She and her husband Dave live in West Palm Beach, Florida, where they work together in her business as independent jewelry distributors.

Diana loves to travel, and has visited Austria, Germany, the Bahamas, Trinidad, Mexico, Uruguay, and now Alaska. Her passion is music. Before retirement she served as the director of the music program at her former church. She still enjoys the opportunity to sing solos at her current church. She loves to share her story and to bring hope and encouragement to ladies.

My Amazing Journey

Diana Daniels

I was thirteen years old when I first laid eyes on him. He was sixteen, tall, dark, and handsome. It was love at first sight, and I never changed my mind. When I was fourteen, he told me that I was the girl who he was going to marry, and I believed him. Shortly after I turned nineteen, Ray Dukes married me on June 14, 1968.

My life's dream was to get married, have children, and be a stay-at-home mom. My favorite verse was Psalm 37:4 – "Delight yourself in the Lord and he will give you the desires of your heart." We were both in Bible college when we married. I was delighting myself in the Lord, and He was giving me the desires of my heart. Much later, I would discover this verse had a different meaning.

Upon graduation in 1970, we moved from Florida to Paducah, Kentucky, where we worked with teens in a ministry called Youth Ranch. Two weeks after arriving, we learned I was pregnant. We had a little girl, and three years later, we had a little boy. The Lord was allowing me to be a stay-at-home mom, fulfilling my desires. Life was fun and exciting! We eventually moved back to Florida, where Ray became the pastor of a local church.

In 1982, Ray was involved in a head-on collision that ejected him from his vehicle and ruptured his spleen. At the hospital, he was given blood transfusions. Fourteen years later, we would find out that he also received Hepatitis C with those transfusions. It's called the "silent killer" because the disease has no symptoms. It was discovered from bloodwork. Thankfully, it was moving very slowly. Because of this diagnosis, the cost of our health insurance began to rise. Eventually, we had to cancel our insurance because we could no longer afford it.

In 1988, I was introduced to a jewelry business called Premier Designs. The extra income sounded good to this stay-at-home mother with teenagers. Ray was the breadwinner of the family, but it was nice to have some extra money for little niceties that we could not afford, such as eating out and vacations.

About ten years later, as I was having my quiet time with the Lord, He revealed to me something surprising. I was reading my life verse, Psalm 37:4. He gently showed me that the verse is saying that if I delight myself in Him, He will put His desires in my heart. Therefore, He will fulfill them because He put them there. Wow! Understanding the verse this way will play a huge role in accepting what is coming in my future.

Ray and I were enjoying the most exciting time of our lives! He was pastoring a church with wonderful, loving people, and I was playing the keyboard, singing, and leading the praise team. We had been married for forty years. Suddenly, out of nowhere, he began having some unusual symptoms that we could not explain.

One Sunday after leaving church, Ray got in the driver's seat but didn't close the car door or take the sun shield out of the window.

He just started driving. I was horrified! I took the shield down so he could see the road, and we managed to make it home. Once at home, I called my son and daughter to tell them something was terribly wrong.

With no insurance, we couldn't afford to go to the emergency room. So, we waited to see Ray's doctor the next day. After examining him, the doctor looked at us and said, "You either had a stroke or have a brain mass. I won't know until you have an MRI. Don't go home. Go straight to the hospital so I can save your life!"

Nothing more needed to be said. We went to the hospital for the MRI, and later that night, we got the results. He had a brain tumor the size of a plum. They admitted Ray, and I spent the night with him so that I would be there in the morning when the doctor arrived. He informed us that Ray had glioblastoma, the most aggressive form of brain cancer!

Everything began moving very quickly. They performed a full-body scan on Ray to see if there were any other tumors. Thankfully, there were not. Brain surgery was scheduled to remove the tumor. In only two and a half days, it had grown to the size of an orange! After surgery, the doctor reported to me that he got most of it but couldn't get it all. He told me that Ray had a 5% chance of survival. With radiation and chemo, he had 6 to 15 months to live!

Ray's surgery was on Friday. On Monday morning, while with him in ICU, I was told I had a call at the nurses' station. Who would be calling me? When I picked up the phone, it was Ray's doctor informing me that he was on the hospital board. He had spoken to the board, and we would not be charged! He said he didn't want me to be worrying about it. Ray stayed in ICU for ten days and in the hospital for five weeks. The bill came to $295,000. I never received any billing invoices from the hospital, the doctors, or for the treatments!

When he came home from the hospital, I became his caregiver. People all over the world were praying, but I knew in my heart that he was not going to be with me much longer. Fear began to creep in. How would I survive as a widow? I had married at nineteen and had no career. Who would hire a 60-year-old with no experience? Even if I did find a job, how would I make enough money to pay the mortgage and other bills? These types of questions haunted me.

One day while walking down the hall, I heard the Lord speak to me. It wasn't an audible voice, but I heard it loud and clear. He said, *"I have taken care of you for sixty years. Why are you worrying about next year?"*

I stopped and looked up at the ceiling. "Okay, Lord," I said. "I'm giving it all to you. I am not going to worry about it anymore!"

I honestly did give it over to Him right then, and I watched Him work in miraculous ways. Get-well cards containing checks started arriving. In the next three months, we had received $20,000! A woman was referred to me to join my Premier Designs jewelry business. While I was home taking care of my husband, she was out building her business, which ultimately built mine, too. I was in awe of God and how He was so lovingly taking care of me.

During the six months after Ray's brain surgery, I didn't question God. I knew He loved me and that He never makes mistakes. He would somehow bring glory to Himself through this, and I felt privileged that He felt we were worthy enough to choose us to go through it all. He trusted us to show Him off!

Ray passed away exactly six months after surgery. I have often said I would never choose the path He gave us, but I would never change it either. My relationship with my Lord grew, and Proverbs 3:5-6 became very personal. *"Trust in the Lord with all your heart, and do not lean on your own understanding. In all your ways acknowledge Him, and He will make your paths straight."*

Widowhood arrived for me at the age of sixty. My duties at church remained the same. My son, wife, and five grandchildren had me over to their house once a week for supper, and I spent time with my girlfriends. But, over time, I became lonely for companionship. After having such a good marriage, I wanted to do it again. This is where God reminded me about my favorite verse, Psalm 37:4. I believed He put the desire in my heart to be married again, and so He would fulfill that desire.

One day, I decided to join an online dating site, but I made a commitment to God at the same time. I told Him that I would not contact any men. I would create my profile and then wait for the Lord to bring me the right man. I asked God to bring him the way He brought Eve to Adam. I joined for one month. At the end of that month, my membership would automatically renew. I was not pleased with the men who had contacted me. I was looking for a Boaz, but all I kept coming across were Bozos! So, I decided to cancel my membership. On a Monday night, I got on the site to cancel. The night before, David Daniels had joined and found me! When I read his profile, it sounded too good to be true. He was my age, a pastor of a church near me, widowed (after forty-one years of marriage), and had two grown children. So many similarities! We wrote back and forth on the site for several days, and then he asked me for my phone number.

I had also committed to my son that I would not meet any man without going through him first. So, I called Troy and had him come over. At that point, I shared all our correspondence from the week. I said,

"Dave wants my phone number," I told my son. "So, what do I do now?"

"Have him call me," Troy replied, then said, "Mom, if this is of God, it will be quick. It won't be a two-year courtship."

Dave called Troy, and they set a lunch date to meet. Troy spent two hours asking him questions about every topic possible. When Troy gave Dave my phone number, he told him that if he would like to meet me, he should come to dinner on Friday night. So, he did. He met the family before he met me! When I arrived at Troy's home, Dave handed me a dozen long-stemmed red roses.

It wasn't love at first sight this time. I was cautious, not wanting to make any mistakes. We continued to see each other in different settings, with his church family and mine. Troy's prediction came true, though. In four weeks, Dave told me that he loved me, and a week later, he asked me to marry him.

God does answer prayers but not always in the way we want. Before I met Dave, I prayed and made a list of the things that I wanted in my next husband. Two things were negotiable. One was that he would be willing to move into my house so I wouldn't have to move; Dave was renting an apartment. The other concerned his height. I asked for someone that was a perfect huggable size. Ray had been over six feet tall, and I'm only 5 feet and 3 inches. So, I was always hugging his belly. God answered my prayer and gave me everything on my list with Dave!

I had been a widow for about four and a half years when Dave and I met in March. We were married four months later in July. God was obviously in this relationship. All of our family was in agreement, and all attended the wedding. My son, Troy, married us, and my daughter was my matron of honor. My son-in-law gave me away, and four of my granddaughters were flower girls. One hundred people attended the wedding. It was a beautiful ceremony, and everything went as planned.

Looking back, I will never understand this side of heaven why the Lord chose to take Ray at the age of sixty-three. I do know that many people were watching us to see how we would respond. Not only was our faith strengthened, but so was their faith. My love relationship with the Lord grew so much! I learned to depend on Him in a way that I had never experienced before.

Many have told me that my story gives them hope. The most exciting part is that I am now experiencing another great marriage with the one who God has chosen for me. I am blessed beyond measure!

And my God shall supply all your needs according to His riches in glory by Christ Jesus. (Philippians 4:19)

. . . .

ABUNDANCE
Kimberly Ann Hobbs

A life of abundance refers to abounding and joyful living. Strength of your mind, body, and soul and how to share your life with others is what matters.

We can think of abundant life as being mentally alive, grateful for what you have, and making the most out of every opportunity. When we look at abundance from a biblical perspective, we see that having a new life in Jesus Christ is abundant living. *(2 Corinthians 5:17)*

What does this new life look like? If you ask five followers of Jesus, you may end up with ten different answers. They all may be right in some way, but new life given to us through Jesus is more than just material blessings.

> *"A thief has only one thing in mind; he wants to steal, slaughter, and destroy. But I have come to give you everything in abundance, more than you expect – life in its fullness until you overflow!" (John 10:10, TPT)*

There are many people in the Bible who we can relate to who've had lives of struggle, suffering, and pain, but they seem to experience abundant life. How? We know some things can only come from God and nowhere else. For example, God gives us peace that passes all understanding. Another way is we see people who have been changed by the POWER of Christ. I know that because I am one of those people. Now I can walk in an abundant living lifestyle because of that change.

People prosper when the gospel of Jesus changes them. They become better in their jobs and better in giving – not only financially but by blessing other people, as well.

Abundant life and living within it are about what we receive as a gift from the Lord. Knowing we are stewards of the blessings of God gives us another perspective. How we share our lives with others is a factor to consider. Displaying mercy, peace, love, grace, and wisdom should be evident in our lives. As God blesses us, we bless others, and we'll genuinely have the making of a "life of abundance" that we can achieve.

* *

Afterword

We live in a world where everything in our lives can change in an instant, and we can't be sure what tomorrow will bring. We see it all too often. Many times, we may not know whether we are coming or going, let alone what our purpose and plan are for our future. However, there is one thing we can count on: God is certain. God never changes. He is the same yesterday, today, and forever. I want to remind you that despite your struggles and past circumstances, God has a great future for you. He says you have not seen or heard or imagined anything as great as what He has prepared for you. We may often wonder why certain things are happening or had to happen, but God tells us that *"the sufferings of these present times are not worthy to be compared with the glory which shall be revealed in us." (Romans 8:18)*

Despite what has happened in the past or currently, God promises a future full of hope and blessing. But, it doesn't happen on its own. You are responsible for some things, such as prayer and obedience. God will help you with both of these if you ask Him.

God has a plan for your future, but so does the devil, whose intentions are not good! The devil's plan cannot succeed if you're walking and talking with God, living in obedience, worshiping Him, and standing firm in His Word! Despite what's happening around you, the devil will be defeated, but he will try to wreak havoc until he is. Ask God for strength and endurance to continue in what you must do. Don't give up; don't ever give up. Remember, if you start getting consumed by the present tears in your life and feel as though you are getting nowhere, God has you! God is preparing you for what is next. Don't get overwhelmed.

> *"The Lord is near to all who call upon Him, to all who call upon Him in truth. He will fulfill the desire of those who fear Him; He will also hear their cry and save them." (Psalm 145:18-19)*

One day, you will be with God in heaven if you choose to. He will wipe away every tear from your eyes. He tells us, *"there will be no more pain, no sorrow, no crying." (Revelation 21:4)*

Your triumph over tears is coming. Hang in there, and remember, *God is able to do exceedingly abundantly above all that we ask or imagine, according to the power that's at work within us. (Ephesians 3:20)*

He has more for you than you can imagine. The triumphant joy that comes when you stay entirely focused on God is the key. Don't take your eyes off of Him. Look up to your Creator. He will keep you in perfect peace as He moves into the future with you.

> *"Don't remember the former things nor consider the things of old. Behold, I will do a new thing." (Isaiah 43:18)*

God wants to equip you to do a new thing, and as the doors of opportunity begin to swing open, keep doing what is right. When you least expect it, God will give you your assignment.

The creation of "you" has been conceived for a specific purpose. You are valuable and loved, and you belong to God. You are to bring glory to God. What a privilege to honor Him in this way, with your life as you completely surrender it to Him!

Our prayers continue over you as you discover and grasp God's "perfect peace" within your lifetime and the plan that He has to use you in mighty ways unimaginable.

Remember these stories of triumph, and may God use them to bring hope and encouragement in your present life.

Made in the USA
Lexington, KY
06 November 2019